LI-'AKUNA MA 'AL SADIQIN

To Be With the Truthful

Author

Muhammad al-Tijani al-Samawi

Translator:

Hasan M. Najafi

In The Name of Allah

The Beneficient, the Merciful

"O Ye who believe! Be careful of your duty to Allah, and be with the truthful"
(9:119)

CONTENTS

Preamble 5

Introduction 9

The Qur'ān in the Perspective of Ahl Al-Sunnah and the Shi'ah   11

The Prophetic Sunnah in the Perspective of Ahl Al-Sunnah and Shi'ah
.... 17

Doctrines in the Perspective of Shi'ah and Ahl Al-Sunnah 29

    BELIEVING IN ALLAH THE EXALTED BY BOTH SECTS 29

    BELIEF IN PROPHETHOOD BY THE TWO SECTS 33

Belief in Imāmate by Both Sects 41

    1. IMĀMATE IN THE HOLY QUR'ĀN 42

    2. IMĀMATE IN THE PROPHETIC SUNNAH 44

    AHL AL-SUNNAH'S OPINION ABOUT CALIPHATE AND ITS
    DISCUSSION 48

    'ALI'S GUARDIANSHIP IN THE HOLY QUR'ĀN 51

    A COMMENTARY 63

    VERSE OF RELIGION PERFECTION RELATES TO CALIPHATE TOO
    70

    DISCUSSING THE CLAIM THE VERSE WAS REVEALED ON 'ARAFĀT
    75

    THE SIGNIFICANT ELEMENT IN THE RESEARCH 92

    GRIEF AND SORROW 110

    OTHER EVIDENCES FOR 'ALI'S GUARDIANSHIP 117

    FIRST EVIDENCE 117

    SECOND EVIDENCE 119

A COMMENT ABOUT SHURĀ 122

Disagreement about Al-Thaqalayn 127

    ANOTHER SELF-CONTRADICTORY STORY BY ABU HURAYRAH . 137

    THE DISPUTE BETWEEN AISHAH AND IBN UMAR 138

    DISAGREEMENT AMONG SCHOOLS ABOUT THE PROPHETIC SUNNAH 138

    DIFFERENCE BETWEEN AHL AL-SUNNAH AND SHI'AH ABOUT THE PROPHETIC SUNNAH 140

Fate and Destiny 149

    IN THE VIEW OF AHL AL-SUNNAH 149

    SHI'AH'S BELIEF IN FATE AND DESTINY 158

    A COMMENTARY ON CALIPHATE WITHIN FATE AND DESTINY . 163

Al-Khums (One-Fifth) 167

Imitation (Taqlid) 173

Doctrines with which Ahl Al-Sunnah Revile the Shi'ah 179

    (BELIEF IN) INFALLIBILITY 184

    NUMBER OF IMĀMS (ITHNĀ 'ASHAR) 190

    THE IMĀMS' KNOWLEDGE 191

    PRINCIPLE OF AL-BADĀ' 194

    TAQIYYAH (DISSIMULATION) 201

    AL-MUT'AH (OR TEMPORARY MARRIAGE) 210

    CLAIM OF TAHRIF OF THE QUR'ĀN 218

    PERFORMING TWO PRAYERS TOGETHER 231

    PROSTRATION ON CLAY 238

    AL-RAJ'AH (RESTORATION TO LIFE) 242

EXTRAVAGANCE (*GHULUWW*) (IN LOVING THE IMĀMS) 246

AL-MAHDI, THE AWAITED 251

Bibliography-Exegesis Books 261

Hadith Books 263

History Books 264

Sirah (Biography) Books 265

Other References 266

PREAMBLE

In the Name of Allah, the Beneficent the Merciful

All praise belongs to the Lord of the worlds, Who bestowed upon us guidance, grace and power, and Who favoured His bondmen with all good in order to be righteous. He is enough for whoever relying upon Him, protecting him against the devils' stratagem, while those diverting from His straight path shall verily be among the frustrated and defeated.

Benediction and peace be upon the one delegated as a mercy for all the worlds, the supporter of the oppressed and those reckoned feeble, the beloved of the needy who believed in Allah, out of desire for the rewards that Allah the Glorified — has prepared for His truthful bondmen...And also upon his good and pure Household, whose status is elevated over all other creatures, so as to be a good example for the gnostic, a beacon of guidance, and ship of deliverance, of which whoever stays behind will be verily among the perished ones.

God's pleasure and assent be upon the Prophet's good Companions, who swore allegiance to and aided him against his enemies, never being among the covenant-breakers, and those who kept abide by the covenant, never altering or reversing, and being among the grateful... and also upon those who kindly followed their guide, from among the earlier and latter (people) till the Day of Resurrection.

My Lord! Dilate my bosom, ease my affair, and untie a knot of my tongue so that my words will be comprehended. My Lord! Make the truth, with which you guide Your faithful bondmen, be revealed for whoever reads my book, and open his insight.

In the beginning, my book, *"Then I was Guided"* was encountered with good approval among dear readers, who, furnished us with some significant remarks regarding miscellaneous subjects in the book, asking for more details concerning the issues that created controversy among a large number of Muslims — Sunnah and Shi'ah.So, for the sake of eliminating any ambiguity and obscurity about this matter, for those seeking to reach the truth and be acquainted with the minute details of the issue, I have compiled this book with the same style I followed in the former one, so that the equitable researcher can easily attain to truth through its nearest routes, as I have reached it through investigation and analogy. I have named the book — with Allah's blessing — *To be with Truthful* (Ma'a al-Sādiqin), deriving it from the saying of the Almighty:

"O ye who believe! Be careful of your duty to Allah, and be with the truthful." (9:119)

And is there anyone among Muslims ready to refuse or abstain from being with those truthful ones!

This was in fact my own belief, and the fact I am trying to elucidate for others, as possible as I can, without dictating my opinion upon the others, but with full respect for others' opinions. And Allah alone is the Guide, and He is to take the custody of the upright people.

Some people have opposed the title of my previous book *"Then I was Guided"*, due to its implying an abstruseness entailing contemplation and wondering, whether others are misguided, and what indication is got from that misguidance when that meaning being intended?

For this objection I give the following clarifying reply:

First: The word *dalālah* (strayal) is referred to in the Holy Qur'ān to mean forgetfulness, when the Almighty said:

"He said: The knowledge thereof is with my Lord in a book, my Lord errs not, nor does He forget" (20:52).

He, the Glorified the Exalted, also said:

"...so that if one of the two errs, the second of the two may remind the other..."(2:282)

Further the word *dalālah* is cited in the Holy Qur'ān to indicate the state of investigation, searching and questing, when Allah, the Almighty addressed His Holy Messenger by saying:

"Did He not find you astray, and guide you?" (93:7),

meaning that He found you looking for truth and He guided you toward it. From the biography of the Prophet (Allah's peace and benediction be upon him and his progeny), it is known that he, before the descent of the Revelation (*wahy*) over him, used to desert his folk at Makkah seeking seclusion in the Cave of Harra,' for many long nights looking for truth.

Out of this meaning too, the Prophet (s) is reported to have said: *"Wisdom is the lost property of a true believer; wherever he may come across it, he is the one who deserves it most."* And this the very meaning implied in the title of my first book.

Second: Supposedly the title implies the meaning of deviation that comes versus the guidance, which we intend to refer to intellectually, in order to obtain the right Islamic trend and plain course, that leads us toward the straightforward path, as commented by some readers, then let it be so. This is the abstract truth that some fear facing it with a constructive sport spirit, and creative objective breath... and whose conception goes in line with the Messenger's (s) saying:

"I am leaving behind among you two precious things (Thaqalayn): the Book of Allah and my Kindred ('Itrah) my Ahl al-Bayt. As long as you adhere to them you will never go astray after me."

This tradition (*hadith*), explicitly and expressly refers to the going astray of whoever not adhering to both the Book and the '*Itrah*.

Anyhow, I am certain that I have been, with Allah's favour and grace, guided to hold on to the Book of Allah and the Kindred of the Messenger (may Allah's benediction and peace be, upon him and his progeny) All praise be to Allah, who guided us toward this (path), and we would have never been guided (to it) had not Allah guided us... the messengers of our Lord have been delegated with truth.

The titles of my first and second books are derived from the Holy Qur'ān, which is the most truthful and best of speech. And all the information I compiled in both the books, if not being true, they be nearer to truth, as being among that upon which all Muslims Sunnah and Shi'ah — have concurred, and whose veracity was approved by the two sects. As a result, I produced — thanks to Allah — these two books — "...*Then I was Guided*," and "*To be with the Truthful*."

I implore Allah to guide the *Ummah* of Muhammad (s), so as to be the best *Ummah* and able to take the leadership of the whole world toward light and right path, under the standard of the awaited at-Imām al-Mahdi, with whom we were promised by his grandfather, to fill the earth with justice and equity after it was filled with oppression and tyranny, and so that Allah shall perfect His light, however much the disbelievers are averse.

INTRODUCTION

In the Name of Allah, the Most Compassionate and the Most Merciful, and benediction and peace be upon the noblest of messengers, our master and Mawlā Muhammad (s) and his good and pure Progeny.

And then, religion basically, depends upon the doctrines that constitute the principles and cornerstones in which the followers of every religion believe. Also their belief in them should be established on a decisive evidence, and explicit proof that emanates from the rational intuitions in which all people believe, so that it can convince people to believe in what it calls them to. Despite all this, there are several ideas whose explanation is uneasy for all scholars, as it is difficult for reason ('*Aql*) to believe in them at first blush. There are examples for this, one is the fire's being coolness and peace while science and intellect concur on its being pernicious heat, and the birds being cut into scattered parts on the hills, and on calling them they come in haste, whereas it can't be easily believed by knowledge and intellect; or that the blind and the leper being healed through only a wipe by "(the hand of)" Jesus ('a). Or rather even raising the dead, while all this cannot be well interpreted by knowledge and reason. All of these cases can be classified under the framework of the miracles that the Almighty Allah has made His prophets (peace be upon them) to do and show to people, in which Muslims, Jews and Christians believe.

Allah, the Glorified and Exalted, has appointed His prophets and messengers (upon whom be the best benediction and peace) to perform those miracles and supernatural acts, with the only aim to make people apprehend the fact that their minds being short of realizing and having full knowledge of everything, since He, the Glorified, has never given him but a little knowledge. In this fact may lie their interest and relative perfection, as so many people have been ungrateful toward Allah's bounties, with many even negating the Almighty's existence, and many others have held knowledge and reason so dear that they worshipped them other than Allah, despite their little knowledge and short-mindedness. How would it be then if He had granted them the knowledge of everything?!

Due to the importance of the creed and its centralism in the Muslim's faith, my book has covered an ample of Islamic doctrines cited in the Holy Qur'ān and Prophetic Sunnah that constituted a scene for the differences among the Islamic schools of thought. So, I have dedicated a complete chapter for the beliefs of Ahl al-Sunnah and the Shi'ah in the Holy Qur'ān and Prophetic Sunnah, then I exposed the issues on which they had long controversies, and each party was unjustifiably reviling the other, with the aim of exposing what I saw to be the truth, desiring to help all truth-seekers.All I hope is that my work will contribute in the establishment of the Islamic unity on a solid thought basis. I implore Allah to help us all to do what He likes and is pleased with, and that He keeps all Muslims in agreement on the right path, He is the Mighty, the Able.

THE QUR'ĀN IN THE PERSPECTIVE OF AHL AL-SUNNAH AND THE SHI'AH

The Holy Qur'ān is Allah's word revealed on His Messenger Muhammad (may Allah's benediction and peace be upon him and his Progeny), the book that falsehood cannot come at it from before it or from behind it. It is the superior reference for Muslims in all their rulings, rituals (*'ibādāt*) and doctrines (*'aqā'id*). Whoever doubts or affronts it will verily be out of the pale of Islam, as the Muslims as a whole are in agreement on sanctifying and revering it, with adhering strictly, in their worship, to all the teachings stated in it.

But Muslims differ concerning its exegesis and interpretation, in a way that the Shi'ah refer in this respect to the Prophet (s) and expositions of the Imāms of Ahl al-Bayt (peace be upon them), Ahl al-Sunnah wa al-Jamā'ah refer too to the Prophet's traditions, but they depend on the Sahābah (Companions) — without any distinction — or anyone of the four imāms, the leaders of the known four Islamic schools of thought, in reporting and exposing and interpreting the traditions.

Naturally, this led to the emergence of dispute and disagreement in opinions concerning so many Islamic — particularly *fiqhi* — issues. And when we can clearly find difference among the four Islamic schools of thought of Ahl al-Sunnah, it is not strange in any way to see the disagreement be more explicit between them and the school of Ahl al-Bayt (peace be upon them).

As I mentioned in the outset of the book, I would never refer but to a few examples for the sake of brevity, and anyone seeking more details must plunge into the depths of the ocean to extract as many as he can of the potential realities and hidden jewels.

Ahl al-Sunnah concur with the Shi'ah in believing that the Messenger of Allah (s) has verily exposed to the Muslims all the precepts of the Qur'ān, and interpreted its verses completely. But after the Prophet's demise the two sects differed regarding to whom they should refer, in order to have full knowledge of that exposition and interpretation. Thus Ahl al-Sunnah have determined to refer to the Sahābah — with no distinction — and after them to the four *imāms* and the *'ulamā'* of the Islamic *Ummah*. Whereas the Shi'ah held that the *Imāms* from among the Prophet's Household (Ahl al-Bayt) being competent alone for this status, beside just an elite of the selected Companions, since Ahl al-Bayt ('a) are the followers of the Remembrance (*Ahl al-dhikr*), whom Allah — the Exalted — commanded us to refer to when He — the Almighty and the Glorious — said:

"...so ask the followers of the Reminder if you do not know..." (16:43) [1]

They are too those whom Allah — the Exalted — has chosen and made them to inherit the knowledge of the books, when He — *Subhānahu* — said (in the Holy Qur'ān):

"Then we gave the Book for an inheritance to those whom we chose from among our servants..." (35:32).

Based on this, the Messenger of Allah (Allah's peace and benediction be upon him and his Progeny) has counted them the equal of the Qur'ān, and the second thaql (precious asset) of which he (s) ordered the Muslims to get hold, when he said: *"I am leaving behind among you two precious things. The Book of Allah and my kindred ('Itrah), as long as you hold on to them you shall never go astray."* [2]

In another narration reported by Muslim, he (s) said: "... *The Book of Allah and my Household (Ahl al-Bayt), I urge you to remember*

---

[1] *Tafsir al-Tabari*, vol. IXV, p. 109; *Tafsir Ibn Kathir*, vol. II, p. 570.

[2] It is reported by al-Tirmidhi in his *Sahih*, vol. II, p. 329, and also by *Sunan* al-Nasa'i and *Musnad* of Imām Ahmad Ibn Hanbal.

*Allah regarding my Ahl al-Bayt³ (He repeated the last statement three times)".*⁴

It is commonly known that Ahl al-Bayt (peace be upon them) were the most knowledgeable, piousl, godliest and best of people, in whose regard al-Farazdaq has said: When enumerating men of piety they be their leaders, or said who are the best of people, is replied they be.

I cite here one example just to show the nature of association between Ahl al-Bayt (peace be upon them) and the Holy Qur'ān, in which Allah, the Exalted said:

"But nay! I swear by the falling of stars; and most surely it is a very great oath if you only knew; most surely it is an honoured Qur'ān, in a book kept hidden, none shall touch it save the purified ones. " (56: 75 — 79).

These verses undoubtedly indicate that Ahl al-Bayt ('a) — headed by the Messenger of Allah (s) — are the only people entitled and able to realize the obscure meanings of the Qur'ān. When pondering upon the oath sworn by the Exalted and Glorious Lord, we will face this fact: When Allah — the Exalted — swears by the declining day, the pen, the fig and the olive, then the greatness of taking oath by the places of the stars shall be manifested due to the secrets and influence on the universe it implies, with Allah's permission. Confirming the oath in the negative and affirmative forms is explicitly observed, as after the oath the Almighty affirms by saying: *"That (this) is a noble Qur'ān. In a Book kept hidden."(56:77-78).* And what is hidden here means that which is internal and concealed, then Allah — the Mighty and Glorious — says: *"none shall touch it save the purified ones,"(56:79)* and 'none' (lā) here is

---

[3] For details on this topic please see author's book *'All Solutions are with the Prophet's Progeny'* at: https://www.al-islam.org/all-solutions-are-with-prophet-s-progeny-muhammad-al-tijani

[4] *Sahih Muslim*, vol. II, p. 362, "Bab fadā'il 'Ali ibn Abi Tālib".

a particle of negation, and "touches it"means, realizes and comprehends it, not meaning contacting by hand, as there is difference between contacting by hand (*lams*) and touching (*mass*). Allah, the Exalted, said:

"Surely those who guard (against evil), when a visitation from the Shaitan afflicts them they become mindful, then lo! they see."(7:201)

Allah, the Glorious, also said:

"Those who swallow down usury cannot arise except as one whom Shaitan has prostrated by (his) touch does rise.." (2:275).

"Touch' in these verses is relevant to '*Aql* (reason) and apprehension not to cantacting by hand (*lams*). And how is it possible that Allah swears that the Qur'ān should be touched only by who is purified, while several episodes in history books indicate that several tyrants have toyed with and torn it. Further we witnessed how the Israelis have trodden the Qur'ān under their feet — we seek protection with Allah, beside setting it to fire at the time of occupying Beirut during their ill-famed invasion, the event about which ugly and appalling pictures and films were transmitted by TV devices. So the meaning we conceive from Allah's saying is that the meanings of the Qur'ān can never be realized but only by an elite from among Allah's servants, whom He has chosen and cleansed with a thorough cleansing. The word "the purified" in the verse (56:79), is passive participle, i.e. those who were purified; and Allah — the Mighty and the Glorious — said:

"...Allah only desires to keep away the uncleanness from you, O People of the House! and to purify you a (thorough) purifying." (33:33)

The Almighty's saying: *"none shall touch it save the purified ones,"* indicates that the Qur'ān's reality can never be realized but only by the Messenger of Allah (s) and his Ahl al-Bayt (peace be upon them), so the Messenger (s) said in their regard: *"The stars are safety for inhabitants of the earth against drowning, and my Ahl al-*

Bayt are safety for my Ummah against disagreement, whenever being opposed by any Arab tribe, disagreement will prevail amongst them, after which they will turn to be party of Iblis (Satan)." ⁵

This idea that is held by the Shi'ah is derived from the Holy Qur'ān and the Messenger's traditions, which are reported even in Ahl al-Sunnah's *Sihah* (authentic collection of *Ahadith*) as we mentioned.

---

⁵ This *hadith* is reported by al-Hākim in *al-Mustadrak*, vol. III, p. 149, on the authority of Ibn 'Abbās, and said: This *hadith* is of authentic chain of narrators.

THE PROPHETIC SUNNAH IN THE PERSPECTIVE OF AHL AL-SUNNAH AND SHI'AH

The Prophetic Sunnah is whatever said or done or approved by the Messenger of Allah (God's peace and benediction be upon him and his Progeny), that is considered the second source after the Qur'ān for their rulings, rituals (*'ibādāt*) and doctrines (*'aqā'id*).

But Ahl al-Sunnah wa al-Jamā'ah add to it another source, which being the *sunnah* (conduct) of the four Rightly — Guided Caliphs (al-Khulafā' al-Rāshidun) who are Abu Bakr, 'Umar, 'Uthmān and 'Ali, according to a *hadith* narrated by them as follows:

"*Adhere to my sunnah and the sunnah of the rightly — guided successors after me. Hold on to it and cling to it stubbornly.*"[1]

The clearest evidence for this lies in their following of 'Umar ibn al-Khattāb's conduct (*sunnah*) in performing Salāt al-Tarāwih (amusement prayer) of which the Messenger of Allah (s) has forbidden. Sahih al-Bukhāri, vol. VII, p. 99, "bāb mā yajuz min al-ghadab wa al-shiddah li-amr Allāh"[2] Some of them even dare to add to the Prophetic Sunnah the *sunnah* of the Companions as a whole (whoever of them), according to a *hadith* narrated by them:

"*Verily, my Companions are like the stars (nujum) whichever of them you follow, you shall be guided rightly,*" beside the hadith: "*My Companions are safety for my Umma.*"[3]

But *Hadith al-Nujum* is verily incompatible with reason (*"aql*), logic (*mantiq*) and scientific reality since the Arabs were never

---

[1] Ahmad ibn Hanbal in his *Musnad*, vol. IV, p. 126.

[2] *Sahih al-Bukhāri*, vol. VII, p. 99, "bāb mā yajuz min al-ghadab wa al-shiddah li-amr Allāh"

[3] *Sahih Muslim*, "kitāb fadā'il al-Sahābah"; *Musnad* Ahmad, vol. IV, p. 398.

guided in their desert travelling, by merely following any one of the stars. But in fact they were guided by following certain specific stars, having known names. Besides, this *hadith* is not supported by the consequent events and practices that were exercised by the Companions after the demise of the Messenger of Allah (s), as some of them have apostatized,[4] beside differing in numerous issues that entailed disparagement between each other,[5] cursing each other,[6] and killing each other.[7]

Moreover some of the Companions were chastised for imbibing wine, perpetrating adultery and robbery, beside other crimes; so how can any sane man accept such a tradition commanding to follow such people? And can that one following Mu'āwiyah, who renegaded against Imām of the time — Amir al-Mu'minin 'Ali Ibn Abi Talib ('a), through warring against him ('a), be guided? How can he be guided while knowing that the Messenger (s) has called him the imam of the tyrant band (*al-fi'ah al-bāghiyah*)? [8] How can he be among those rightly-guided when he follows the example of 'Amr ibn al-'As, al-Mughirah ibn Shu'bah and Bisr ibn Arta'ah who murdered the innocent, for the sake of supporting the rule of the Umayyads? You also, the intelligent reader, when reading the *hadith* 'my companions are like the stars', will come to realize that it is fabricated, since it is addressed to the Companions, so is it reasonable that the Messenger(s) says:

"*O my Companions follow the guide of my Companions*"?

---

[4] In the case of those whom Abu Bakr fought, who were called later on the apostates (*Ahl al-Riddah*).

[5] It is obvious in the case of 'Uthmān, who was continuously reviled and defamed by most of the Sahābah, till being slain by them.

[6] It is exactly as done and practised by Mu'āwiyah, who kept on giving his orders to curse and slander 'Ali.

[7] Like the Battles of al-Jamal, Siffin and al-Nahrawān, and others.

[8] According to the *hadith*: "May God have mercy on 'Ammār, he shall be killed by the rebellious gang."

Whereas the *hadith* "*O my Companions, adhere to the Imāms from among my household, since they guide you after me*" is nearer to truth, due to having many evidences supporting it in the Prophetic Sunnah.

Besides, the Imāmiyyah Shi'ah hold that those meant by the *hadith* "*Adhere to my Sunnah and the Sunnah of the rightly-guided successors after me*" being the Twelve Imāms from Ahl al-Bayt (peace be upon them), to whom the Messenger of Allah (s) has commanded his *Ummah* to adhere and follow, in the same way they adhere to and follow the Book of Allah.[9]

And since I have committed myself not to argue except with the evidences used by the Shi'ah from the *Sihāh* of Ahl al-Sunnah wa al-Jamā'ah, so I sufficed with these examples, whereas the Shi'ah books are replete with many other evidences that are more explicit and indicative.[10]

But the Shi'ah never claim that Ahl al-Bayt Imāms ('a) are entitled to legislate, or that their Sunnah is of their *ijtihād*, but they hold that all the rulings and precepts they follow are derived from the Book of Allah and the Sunnah of his Messenger ... the Sunnah which the Messenger of Allah has taught to 'Ali, who in turn has taught to his sons, as it is a knowledge they inherit one from the other, having for this a large number of evidences reported by the '*ulamā*' of Ahl al-Sunnah in their *Sahihs*, *Musnads* and *Tarikhs*. The question that insistently raised all the time is: Why have al-Sunnah wa al-Jamā'ah

---

[9] *Sahih al-Tirmidhi*, vol. V, p. 328; *Sahih Muslim*, vol. II, p. 362; al-Nasā'i in al-Khasā'is and Kanz al-'ummāl, vol. I, p. 44; al-Imām Ahmad ibn Hanbal in his *Musnad*, vol. V, p. 189; al-Hākim in his *Mustadrak*, vol. III, p. 148; Ibn Hajar in *al-Sawā'iq al-muhriqah*, p. 148, Ibn Sa'd in *al-Tabaqāt al-Kubrā*, vol. II, p. 194; al-Tabarāni, vol. I, p. 131.

[10] I cite for this only one example: It is reported by al-Saduq in *al-'Ikmāl*, with his *sanad* reaching back to al-Imām al-Sādiq, from his father, from his grandfather, that he said: The Messenger of Allah (s) said: Verily, there will be twelve Imams after me, the first of them being 'Ali and the last one is al-Qāim (al-Mahdi). These are my (true) successors and executors.

never acted according to the content of those traditions, which they consider *Sahih* (veracious)...???

After all this, the Shi'ah and Ahl al-Sunnah disagree concerning the interpretation of the traditions that are authentically reported from the Messenger of Allah (s), as previously explained in the statement about the dispute between them in respect of the exegesis (*tafsir*) of the Qur'ān. They disagree in regard of who are meant by the rightly-guided successors (*al-Khulafā' al-Rāshidun*), that are referred to in the Prophet's *hadith* which is approved by both the sectts. Ahl al-Sunnah interpret it to mean the Four Caliphs who assumed the rostrum of caliphate after the Messenger of Allah, while the Shi'ah interpret it to mean the twelve successors, who are the Imāms of Ahl al-Bayt (peace be upon them).

So we see this disagreement so common concerning whatever is related to the persons that were exculpated by the Qur'ān and the Messenger, or whom he (s) commanded to follow, like the following *hadith* uttered by him (s):

"The 'ulamā' of my Ummah are superior to the prophets of Banu Israel," or *"The 'ulamā' are the inheritors of the prophets."*[11] Ahl al-Sunnah wa al-Jamā'ah take this tradition to include all the *Ummah 'ulamā'* as a whole, while the Shiah specify it to the Twelve Imāms, the reason making them to prefer them ('a) over the prophets, with the exception of Ulu al-'Azm (of resolution) among the messengers. In fact reason (*'aql*) inclines more to this specification, for:

First: the Qur'ān has made the knowledge of the Book be inherited by those whom Allah has chosen from among His bondmen, the fact indicating the specification. Besides, the Messenger of Allah (s) has specified his Ahl al-Bayt with particular traits, never making any partners to share them in these traits, when he called them Ark of Salvation, and Imāms of Guidance, and Beacons of Darkness, and

---

[11] *Sahih al-Bukhāri*, vol. I, "kitāb al-'ilm"; *Sahih al-Tirmidhi*", kitāb al-'ilm".

the Second Thiql (precious asset) that safeguards against deviation and astrayal.

The fact manifested from this is that the claim of Ahl al-Sunnah contradicts this specification that is confirmed by the Qur'ān and the Prophetic Sunnah. Besides, reason is never content with it due to its implying the obscurity and ignorance for the real '*ulamā*', far from Allah has removed cleanness and cleansed, and not distinguishing them from the (courtly) '*ulamā*' imposed upon the *Ummah* by the Umayyad and 'Abbāsid rulers. How far is it between those '*ulamā*' and Ahl al-Bayt Imāms, for whom history books never reported their learning under any teacher, except that the son was getting knowledge from his father. Despite this fact, Ahl al-Sunnah '*ulamā*' have reported in their books, wonderful narrations, especially concerning al-Imām al-Bāqir, al-Imām al-Sādiq, and al-Imām al-Ridā who managed, through his knowledge, in dumbfounding forty judges al-Ma'mum gathered for (debating with) him, while he was only a boy.[12]

The point affirming the distinguishment of Ahl al-Bayt from others, lies in the obvious disagreement among the four schools of thought of Ahl al-Sunnah, regarding numerous *fiqhi* issues, while no difference is there among the Twelve Imāms of Ahl al-Bayt concerning even one issue.

Second: If we approve the claim of Ahl al-Sunnah in generalizing these verses and traditions on all the *Ummah* '*ulamā*', this will necessarily lead to the multiplication of the opinions and schools of thought throughout long generations, to the extent that thousands of schools (*madhāhib*), would find way into the scene. Discerning the triviality of this view and its goal of disintegrating the unity of creed and faith, Ahl al-Sunnah hastened to close the door of *ijtihād* since time immemorial.

---

[12] *Al-'Iqd al-farid*, Ibn 'Abd Rabbih; *Al-Fusul al-Muhimmah*, of Ibn al-Sabbāgh al-Māliki, vol. III, p. 42.

Whereas the opinion held by the Shi'ah calls to the unity and to gather round known Imāms, upon whom Allah and the Messenger have imparted all sorts of knowledge that are necessary for all Muslims throughout all ages and times. After all this, no claimant can fabricate any lie against Allah and the Messenger, or innovate a new school compelling people to follow and believe in it. The two sects differ regarding this issue in the same way they differ concerning al-Mahdi, in whom they both believe. But for the Shi'ah he ('a) is known of definite father and grandfather while in the perspective of Ahl al-Sunnah he is still unknown, and will be born at the end of the Time. For this reason many of them have alleged to be al-Mahdi each, and al-Shaykh Isma'il the author of *al-Tariqah al-Mudaniyyah*, has said to me personally that he was the Awaited al-Mahdi, in front of a friend of mine, who was one of his followers, but he was enlightened and guided to truth afterwards.

But in the perspective of the Shi'ah, none of their newborn dares to claim this. And even if anyone of them names his son 'Mahdi,' he does so only for seeking auspiciousness and blessing, in the same way as done by anyone of us when calling his son Muhammad or 'Ali. Besides, the reappearance of al-Mahdi is considered by them in itself as a miracle, since he was born twelve centuries ago, and disappeared.

Then, after all these facts, disagreement may appear amongst Ahl al-Sunnah wa al-Jamā'ah, in respect of the meaning of the authentic veracious (*sahih*) *hadith* in the view of both the sects, even when the *hadith* being irrelevant to individuals, like the following one:

"The disagreement of my Ummah is a blessing," which is interpreted by Ahl al-Sunnah that any difference in the *fiqhi* rulings regarding one issue is a blessing for the Muslim individual, in a way that he can select any rule proper for him and keep pace with the solution he likes. In this way it will be a blessing (*rahmah*) for him since when finding al-Imām Mālik, for instance, being strict regarding one issue, it is permissible for the Muslim person to imitate (take the opinion of) Abu Hanifah, who being lenient in it.

But in the perspective of the Shi'ah, they interpret the *hadith* in another way, reporting that when al-Imām al-Sādiq ('a) was asked about the *hadith* "The disagreement of my *Ummah* is a blessing, he said: The Messenger of Allah said the truth! The inquirer then said: If their disagreement is a blessing, so their agreement should be indignation! Al-Sādiq replied: *It is not the way you think or they think (i.e. in this interpretation), but what the Messenger of Allah (s) meant is that: Their frequenting to each other, that is one of them travels to the other, going out and betaking himself to him to gain knowledge from him, inferring for this, as an evidence, Allah's saying:*

Of every troop of them, a party only should go forth, that they (who are left behind) may gain sound knowledge in religion, and that they may warn their folk when they return to them, so that they may beware." (9:122)

Then he added to it saying: *When they differ concerning religion, they will turn to be the party of Iblis (Satan). This, as can be clearly seen by all, being a reasonable and convincing interpretation, is inviting toward unity in creed and belief not disagreement in it.*[13]

Thereafter, the *hadith* as conceived by Ahl al-Sunnah is unreasonable, since it calls to disagreement, disunity and multiplicity of opinions and schools, the fact contradicting the Holy Qur'ān that calls us towards unity, agreement and to gather round one thing, when Allah, Subhānahu, says:

"Indeed this community of yours is one community, and I am your Lord, so be wary of Me." (23:52)

He also says:

---

[13] For example, saying Bismillah in the *salāt* is makruh (reprehensible) according to the Mālikis, obligatory according to the Shāfi'is, mustahabb (recommendable) according to the Hanafis, while the Hanbalis hold that it should be read inaudibly even in the audible (*jahri*) prayers.

"And hold fast, all of you together, to the cable of Allah, and do not separate." (3:103).

In another verse He says:

"...and dispute not one with another lest ye falter and your strength depart from you..." (8:46)

And is there a dispute or separation worse than dividing one *Ummah* into several schools, parties and sects, contradicting and deriding each other, or rather even charging each other with disbelief and infidelity to the extent that each deeming the blood (killing) of the other as lawful, the event that actually took place throughout consecutive ages, as recorded in history books. So we were warned by Allah — the Glorified — against the untoward consequences our *Ummah* will verily face when being separated and in dispute, when the Almighty said:

"And be ye not as those who separated and disputed after the clear proofs had come unto them." (3:105)

He also said:

"Lo! As for those who sunder their religion and become schismatics, no concern at all hast thou with them." (6:159).

In another place He said:

"...and be not of those who ascribe partners (unto Him). Of those who split up their religion and became schismatics, each sect exulting in its tenets." (30:31-32)

It is worth mentioning that the meaning of schismatics (*shiya'*) has nothing to do with the Shi'ah, as wrongly conceived by some naive and simple-minded people, when one of them came to advise me saying:"O brother, for God's sake! Forget about the Shi'ah, as Allah detests them and has warned His Messenger against being one of them! I said: How is that? He said: (the verse): "Lo! As for those who sunder their religion and became schismatics, no concern at all hast thou with them." I tried hard to persuade him that the word schismatics (*shiya''*) means clans or parties, and has nothing to do with Shi'ah. But he unfortunately insisted on his opinion and was never convinced, since his master, the mosque (prayers) leader has taught him in this way, warning him against the Shi'ah, so he was not ready to accept other than that.

Returning to the topic, I want to say that I was at a loss before being guided when reading the *hadith* "*The disagreement of my ummah is a blessing*" and comparing it with the *hadith*: "*My ummah will separate into seventy-two sects, all being in hellfire, except only one.*"[14] I used to wonder. How can the disagreement of the *ummah* be a blessing, while at the same time causing (people) to enter the fire??

But after reading the interpretation of al-Imām Ja'far al Sadiq ('a) for this *hadith*, my perplexity has vanished and the enigma was solved, with knowing afterwards that the Imāms of Ahl al-Bayt are the Imāms of guidance and beacons for darkness, being truly the interpreters of the Qur'ān and Sunnah, be meritorious for what the Messenger of Allah (s) said in their regard:

"*The parable of my Ahl al-Bayt among you is that of the boat of Noah; whoever gets aboard it is saved and whoever stays away from it is drowned. So don't outstrip them, for then you shall perish, and don't fall short of them, for then you shall perish. Don't teach them for they are more knowledgeable than you.*"[15]

Also al-Imām 'Ali ('a) said the truth when he uttered the following statement:

"Look at the people of the Prophet's family. Adhere to their direction

---

[14] *Sunan* Ibn Mājah, "kitāb al-fitan", vol. II, *hadith* No. 3993; *Musnad* Ahmad, vol. III, p. 120; al-Tirmidhi in his *Kitāb al-'Imān*.

[15] Ibn Hajar, *al-Sawā'iq al-Muhriqah*, pp. 136, 227; al-Suyuti, *al-Jāmi' al-Saghir*, vol. II, p. 132; Ahmad ibn Hanbal in his *Musnad*, vol. III, p. 17, and vol. IV, p. 366; *Hilyat al-'Awliyā'*, vol. IV, p. 306, *Mustadrak* al-Hākim, vol. III, p. 151; *Talkhis al-Dhahabi*; al-Tabarāni in *al-Mu'jam al-Saghir*, vol. II, p. 22.

and follow their footsteps, because they would never let you out of guidance, and never throw you into destruction. If they sit down you sit down, and if they rise up you rise up. Do not go ahead of them, as you would thereby go astray, and do not lag behind of them as you would thereby be ruined."[16]

In another sermon, he ('a) describes the position and worth of Ahl al-Bayt ('a) by saying:

"They are life for knowledge and death for ignorance. Their forbearance tells you of their knowledge, and their outward of their inward, and their silence of the wisdom of their speaking. They do not go against right nor do they differ (among themselves) about it. They are the pillars of Islam and the asylums of (its) protection. With them right has returned to its position and wrong has left its place, and its tongue is severed from its root. They have understood the religion attentively and carefully, not by mere heresy or from relaters, because the relaters of knowledge are many but its understanders are few."[17]

Al-Imām 'Ali has verily said the truth, as he is the gate of the city of knowledge. And there is a great difference between that who comprehends religion with consciousness and observance, and that who comprehends it through hearing and narrations.

Those who hear and narrate are so many, as a large number of Companions enjoyed the company of the Messenger of Allah (s), hearing and reporting from him numerous traditions unconsciously and unknowingly. This led to changes in the meaning of the *hadith*, in a way that it might give the opposite of what the Messenger (s) meant of it, or leading sometimes to disbelief due to the difficulty in realizing the real meaning of the *hadith* by the Companion.[18]

---

[16] *Nahj al-balāghah*, Khutbah No. 97.

[17] *Ibid.*, Khutbah No. 239.

[18] The example for this can be found in what is reported by Abu Hurayrah who said: *"Allah has created Adam with the same shape of him"* (in an

Whereas those who comprehend and observe knowledge being very few. Man may exhaust his entire life in seeking knowledge, but might not gain but only scanty of it, or may specialize in one of the fields of knowledge or one of its arts, without being able to have full command of its branches as a whole. But the fact commonly known is that Ahl al-Bayt Imāms ('a) were thoroughly acquainted with, and grasping miscellaneous sciences, as proved by al-Imām 'Ali, according to the reports confirmed by the historians. This fact is further proved by al-Imām Muhammad al-Bāqir, and Ja'far al-Sādiq too, under whom thousands of shaykhs have learnt different sciences and fields of knowledge, including philosophy, medicine, chemistry and natural sciences, and others.

---

incomplete and ambiguous way). But al-Imām Ja'far al-Sādiq ('a) elucidated the matter by saying: The Messenger of Allah (s) passed by two young men, and heard them reviling each other, one saying to the other: May Allah disfigure your face and that of whoever resembles you. Thereat the Messenger of Allah said to him: *"Allah created Adam with the same shape of him."* That is, with your slandering whoever resembling him, you have in fact defamed Adam as he is the one who is like him.

DOCTRINES IN THE PERSPECTIVE OF SHI'AH AND AHL AL-SUNNAH

My belief that the Imāmiyyah Shi'ah being the delivered sect, is even more strengthened by the fact that their beliefs are tolerant and flexible, that is, easily admitted by any wise sane man of sound adroitness. With them we can find for every question and creed, a satisfactory and sufficient solution given by any one of Ahl al-Bayt Imāms ('a) that can never be found with Ahl al-Sunnah or other sects.

In this chapter, I will follow up with details the most important beliefs of the two sects, trying to point out those ones which I have admitted, giving the reader the freedom of thought, choice, criticism and sarcasm.

I draw the attention to the fact that the original and genuine creed for all Muslims being only one, which is having faith in Allah— the Exalted — and His Angels and Scriptures and Messengers, without making any difference between His Messengers. All the Muslims also agree on the fact that Hell-fire is true, and Paradise is true, and that Allah will verily resurrect all the dead from graves, gathering them for the Day of Reckoning.

They concur too regarding the Qur'ān, believing that their Prophet being Muhammad the Messenger of Allah, and that their qiblah (direction for prayer) being one. But the difference lies in the conception of these doctrines and beliefs, which turned to be a stage for the theological schools, exposing on it miscellaneous opinions and madhāhib (religious doctrines)

Believing in Allah the Exalted by Both Sects

The most important point that can be referred to in this respect, is sighting Allah — the Exalted — which Ahl al-Sunnah have established in the Hereafter for all the believers. When going through the *Sihāh* of Ahl al-Sunnah, like those of al-Bukhāri and Muslim for instance, we shall find narrations proving the sighting really not figuratively.[1] Rather they contain even anthropomorphism to Allah — the Glorified — and that He laughs,[2] comes and walks and descends to this world (*dunyā*),[3] or even that He uncovers His leg that has a distinguishing sign.[4] Moreover, they say that He (Subhānahu) places His foot in hell, whereat it will be filled saying: at all, at all; beside other things and descriptions from which Allah — the Glorified and the Mighty — is free and far.[5]

One day I have passed by the City of Laamo in Kenya, at East Africa, finding a Wahhabi Shaykh giving a sermon in the mosque. He was telling the worshippers that Allah has two hands, two legs, two eyes and a face. When I disapproved this from him, he began to confirm his argument by citing some Qur'ānic verses, saying:

"The Jews say: Allah's hand is fettered. Their hands are fettered and they are accursed for saying so. Nay, but both His hands are spread out wide in bounty." (5:64)

He also said:

"Build the ship under Our eyes..." (11:37)

He further said:

"Everyone that is thereon will pass away; There remaineth but the Countenance of thy Lord..." (55:26-27).

I said: O brother, all these verses you cited and other ones, are all but metaphors and not real meanings! He replied by saying: All the Qur'ān is real and has no metaphor at all. Thereat I said: How do you interpret then the verse:

---

[1] *Sahih al-Bukhāri*, vol. II, p. 47, & vol. V, p. 179 & vol. VI, p. 33.

[2] *Ibid.*, vol. IV, p. 226 & vol. V, pp. 47-48; *Sahih Muslim*, vol. I, pp. 114-122.

[3] *Ibid.*, vol. VIII, p. 197.

[4] *Ibid.*, vol. VIII, p. 182.

[5] *Ibid.*, vol. VIII, p. 187, and on page 202 he confirms Allah's having a hand and fingers.

"Who so is blind here will be blind in the Hereafter..." (17:72),

Do you conceive it with the real meaning? Is every blind in the world will be blind in the Hereafter? The Shaykh replied: We are talking about Allah's hand and eye and face, and have nothing to do with the blind! I said: Forget about the blind. How do you interpret the verse I mentioned: "Everyone that is thereon will pass away; there remaineth but the Countenance of thy Lord...?" He turned his face to the attendants saying to them: Is there anyone among you who couldn't understand this verse? ...It is as clear and explicit as the Almighty's saying:

"Everything will perish save His Countenance..." (28:88)

I said to him: You have added fuel to the fire! My brother, we have disputed regarding the Qur'ān... you claimed that the Qur'ān has no figurative speech, and all is but reality! While I claimed that there is figurative speech in the Qur'ān, especially the verses having materialization or anthropomorphism. If you insist on your opinion, you have to say that the meaning of "Everything will perish save His Countenance" is that his two hands and legs, and all of His body will perish, and nothing will remain of Him but the face, above which Allah is highly elevated, and too far! I then turned my face toward those present in the meeting saying: Do you approve of such an interpretation? All of them kept silent, and even their shaykh could never say one word. So I bade them farewell, invoking Allah to guide and help them to know the truth.

This is the way they believe in Allah, as recorded in their *Siḥāh* and their sermons. I hold that some of our scholars deny this, but the majority of them believe in sighting Allah— the Glorified — in the Hereafter, and that they will see Him in the same way as seeing the moon at the night of full moon, with no cloud covering it, citing as a proof the verses:

"That day will faces be resplendent. Looking toward their Lord." *(75:22, 23)* [6]

But as soon as you be acquainted with the creed of the Imāmiyyah Shiah in this respect, your conscience will be at rest and your mind will submit to accept the interpretation of the Qur'ānic verses having incarnation or anthropomorphism to Allah — the Exalted — holding them to indicate figurative meaning and metaphor, not reality or the superficiality of utterances, as imagined by some people.

In this regard al-Imām 'Ali ('a) says: *"...Whom the height of intellectual courage cannot appreciate, and the divings of understanding cannot reach'; He for Whose description no limit has been laid down, no eulogy exists, no time is ordained and no duration is fixed..."* [7]

In refuting the anthropormorphists, al-Imām al-Bāqir ('a) says: *"Rather, whatever we have distinguished with our imagination, in its minutest meanings, is but a creature that is made like us, returning toward us..."* [8]

Further we should be sufficed in this respect with Allah's reply in His Holy Scripture: **"Naught is as His likeness,"** and His saying: **"Vision comprehendeth Him not"**, beside His saying to His messenger and conversationalist Musā ('a), when he asked to see Him"... He said: My Lord! Show me (Thy self), that I may gaze upon Thee. He said: **Thou wilt not see Me,**", and this *lan* (wilt not) in the verse, which is called Zamakhshari lan gives the meaning of *ta'bid* (neverness), as grammarians observe.

---

[6] Verse 23 of *Surah al-Qiyāmah* was interpreted by Ahl al-Bayt Imams (peace be upon them), that the faces at that Day (Doomsday) be resplendent (*nādirah*), to mean prettiness and splendour (*bahjah*), while looking at their Lord's mercy.

[7] *Nahj al-balāghah*, exposition (*sharh*) of Muhammad 'Abduh, vol. I, Sermon no. 1.

[8] *'Aqā'id al-'Imāmiyyah*.

All this being a decisive evidence proving the veracity of the opinions of the Shi'ah, who derive them from the traditions of Ahl al-Bayt Imāms — the source of knowledge and trustees of the Message, and whom Allah made to inherit the knowledge of the Scripture.

Whoever intends to go into details about this research, has to refer to the books elucidating this topic, such as *Kalimah hawl al-ru'yah* of al— Sayyid Sharaf al-Din, the author of *al-Murāja'āt*.[9]

Belief in Prophethood by the Two Sects

The dispute between the Shi'ah and Ahl al-Sunnah mainly lies in the issue of *'ismah* (infallibility). As the Shi'ah believe in the prophets' *'ismah* before and after their mission (*bi'that*), while Ahl al-Sunnah hold that their infallibility is confined only in Allah's words that they propagate, and other than this they, like all other people, may err and be correct. Their *Sihāh* are filled with narrations indicating that the Messenger of Allah(s) has mistaken in several places, and the Companions were correcting him and telling him the right. The examples they cite for this being the issue of the captives of Battle of Badr, in which the Prophet (s) has erred and 'Umar hit the mark, and without him the Messenger of Allah would have perished.[10] In another place, when he entered al-Madinah, he saw its people cutting the date-palms, whereat he said to them: *"Don't cut them as they will give dates"*, but they turned to be shays (unwanted bad dates). Then they came to him complaining about the matter, whereat he said to them: *"You are better aware of your world affairs more than me."* In another narration he said: *"I am just a human*

---

[9] *Al-Murāja'āt* is one of the books that should be read by whoever desiring to be acquainted with the Imāmi Shi'ah's beliefs and thoughts. Available at: https://www.al-islam.org/al-murajaat-shii-sunni-dialogue-sharaf-al-din-al-musawi

[10] *Al-Bidāyah wa al-Nihāyah*, of Ibn Kathir, who reported from al-Imām Ahmad, Muslim, Abu Dāwud and al-Tirmidhi.

being, if I command you to anything related to your religion you take it, and if I order you to do anything according to my opinion, I am but a human being."[11]

Another time they relate that he was bewitched, remaining so for several days not knowing what to do, to the extent that he was imagining of making sexual intercourse with women and not doing so,[12] or fancying to himself the doing of something and not doing it.[13]

Again they report that he once forgot in his prayer, being uncertain of the number of *rak'ahs* he performed,[14] and also he once slept so deeply that his snoring could be heard by all, and then he got up and prayed without taking ablution.[15] Once again they narrate that he be angry with, reviles and curses whoever undeserving that, saying *"O Allah I am no more than a human being, any of the Muslims I have cursed or reviled, You make this exculpatory and purifying fever for him..."*[16]

They also report that he once upon a time he was lying in 'A'ishah's house, with his thighs being uncovered, whereat Abu Bakr and then 'Umar entered upon him, conversing with him while he was on this condition... when 'Uthmān asked permission to enter, he (s) sat and made up his clothes. When asked by 'A'ishah about the reason, he said to her:

"Shouldn't I be ashamed of a man of whom the angels are ashamed."[17]

---

[11] *Sahih Muslim*, "kitāb al-fadā'il", vol. VII, p. 95; *Musnad* al-Imām Ahmad, vol. I, p. 162 and vol. III, p. 152.

[12] *Sahih al-Bukhāri*, vol. VII, p. 29.

[13] *Ibid.*, vol. IV, p. 68.

[14] *Ibid.*, vol. I, p. 123 and vol. II, p. 65.

[15] *Ibid.*, vol. I, pp. 37, 44, 171.

[16] *Sunan al-Dārimi*, "kitāb al-riqāq".

[17] *Sahih Muslim*, "bāb fadā'il 'Uthmān", vol. VII, p. 117.

They further claim that he sometimes would enter upon the morning ritually impure in the Month of Ramadān,[18] missing the dawn prayer... beside other strange traditions that no reason or religion or conscience is ready to accept or approve of.[19]

Whereas the Shi'ah — in accordance with Ahl al-Bayt Imāms — exculpate the prophets from such trifles and silly things, in particular our Prophet Muhammad (upon whom be peace and the best of benediction), holding that he is impeccable and immune against all minor and major sins, wrongs and insubordinations. They believe in his being infallible (*ma'sum*) against error, forgetfulness, absence of mind, sorcery and whatever causing mind to be disordered. And rather he is impeccable against practising any act contradictory to manliness and good morality, like eating on the roads, or giggling loudly, or joking with impropriety, or any reprehensible act disapproved by public norms. It is needless to refer to their claims that he used to place his cheek on his wife's cheek before people, sharing her in looking at the dancing of the Negroes,[20] or to let his wife go out in a battle, competing with her, in a way defeating her one time, and she defeating him the other, telling her then: "This one is versus that one."[21]

The Shi'ah consider all the narrations reported in this respect, that are incongruous with the prophets' *'ismah*, to be altogether composed and fabricated by the Umayyads and their supporters with these aims: First, for degrading the Messenger of Allah (s). Second, for seeking justification for their abominable deeds and unsightly wrongs recorded in history books. And if — supposedly — the Messenger of Allah (s) errs and be inclined to love and lust, as in the story they narrated of his passionate love for Zaynab bint Jahash, when he saw her combing her hair (while being the wife of Zayd ibn

---

[18] *Sahih al-Bukhāri*, vol. II, pp. 232, 234.

[19] *Ibid.*, vol. III, p. 114 and vol. VII, p. 96.

[20] *Ibid.*, vol. III, p. 228, and vol. II, p. 3, "kitāb al-'idayn".

[21] *Musnad* al-Imām Ahmad ibn Hanbal, vol. VI, p. 75.

Hārithah), exclaiming: *"Glorified is Allah Who changes the hearts."*[22] Or the story of his inclination toward 'A'ishah and his unjust treatment with his other wives, that they have delegated to him Fātimah once and Zaynab bint Jahash another time, asking and pleading him to deal equally between them.[23]

So if this be the state of the Messenger of Allah (s), no blame then is upon Mu'āwiyah ibn Abi Sufyān, or Marwan ibn al-Hakam, or 'Amr ibn al-'As, or Yazid ibn Mu'āwiyah, with all the caliphs who have perpetrated all kinds of abominations, and violated the sanctities and slaughtered the innocent.

This being the case, while the Imāms from Ahl al-Bayt (peace be upon them), the Imāms of the Shi'ah, believe in his *'ismah* (infallibility), interpreting the Qur'ānic verses which apparently indicate that Allah has admonished His Prophet, like

"He frown and turned away" (80:1),

or the verses containing confession of the sins like His saying:

"That Allah may forgive thee of thy sin that which is past and that which is to come" (48:2),

or His saying:

"Allah hath turned in mercy to the Prophet" (9:117),

and also:

"Allah forgive thee (O Muhammad)! Wherefore didnt thou grant them leave." (9:43).

They affirm that all these verses never derogate from his (s) *'ismah*, as some of them were not meant at him in particular, while some others have to be figuratively interpreted not according to the

---

[22] *Tafsir al-Jalālayn*, about interpretation of God's words: *"... And thou didst hide in thy self that which Allah was to bring to light."* (33:37).

[23] *Sahih Muslim*, vol. VII, p. 136, "bāb fadā' il 'A'ishah".

external meanings of the words, the method that is most often used in the Arabic language, and also by Allah-the Glorified — in the Holy Qur'ān.

Whoever seeking more information and intending to obtain certain knowledge of things, he has just to refer to the Shi'ah exegesis books, like *al-Mizān fi tafsir al-Qur'ān* of al-'Allāmah al-Tabātabā'i, and *Tafsir al-Kāshif* of Muhammad Jawād Maghniyyah, and *al-'Ihtijāj* of al-Tabrasi, beside other books. I haven't quoted from these books since I intended brevity and exposing the creed and belief of the two parties in general. And the aim of this is but to reflect my own beliefs in which I have conviction, and myself selecting a school believing in the infallibility of the prophets, and successors after them, to relieve my mind, dissipating my concern, and eradicating my suspicion and perplexity.

To claim that the Prophet's infallibility being confined in propagating Allah's words (Qur'ān), is just baseless nonsense, since no proof is there indicating which part of his speech is Allah's, and which one is his, so as to be ma'sum in the former and not ma'sum with being liable to err in the latter.

I seek protection by God from this contradictory utterance prompting to doubt and vilification in the sanctity of religions.

This fact recalls to my mind a conversation held between me — after being guided — and a group of friends, in which I tried my best to convince them that the Messenger of Allah (s) being infallible (*ma'sum*), while they were attempting to persuade me of his being ma'sum in propagating the Qur'ān alone. Among them there was a professor from Tozad (region of al-Jarid),[24] and they were known for wittiness, knowledge and crack jokes. He contemplated for a while and said: "O company I have an opinion regarding this issue," we all

---

[24] Region of al-Jarid is located south of Tunisia, with 92 kms from Qafsah, the birthplace of Abu al-Qāsim al-Shābi, the renowned poet, and al-Khidr Husayn, who was the head of al-'Azhar, beside many Tunisian *'ulamā'* who were born in this region.

exclaimed: Please give us what you have! He said: -What our brother al-Tijani says, as the Shi'ah hold, is the very truth, and we should believe in the Messenger's absolute *'ismah*, otherwise suspicion will find its way into our hearts in the Qur'ān itself!

-They asked: What for? He immediately replied:

-Have you seen any of the Qur'ānic verses with Allah's signature underneath??

By the signature he meant: The stamping with which the contracts and letters were sealed, denoting the identity of each party to the contract and sender of the letter. All those present laughed at this witty remark that was in fact of a deep meaning. Every unprejudiced person, contemplating attentively, will be shocked by the fact that: believing in the Qur'ān's being God's words is to believe in the absolute infallibility of its communicator, without partitioning it, since it is infeasible for anyone to claim of hearing Allah speak, and no one can allege that he saw Jabriel when descending with revelation (*wahy*).

The quintessence of the above-mentioned exposition, is that the Shiah's opinion about *'ismah* is an apposite opinion, making hearts feel assured, eliminating all whispers of the self and Satan, and closing all doors before the riotous, particularly enemies of religion from among the Jews, Christians, and infidels looking for gaps to sneak from. Their aim of this being to overturn our beliefs and religion from the foundation and to degrade our Prophet. So they most often dispute against us with what *Sahih al-Bukhāri* and *Sahih Muslim* reported of the deeds and sayings ascribed to the Messenger of Allah (s), from which he is far exempted.[25]

---

[25] In his *Sahih*, vol. III, p. 152, bāb shahādat al-'a'mā from "kitāb al-shahādāt", al-Bukhāri is reported to have said: Ibn 'Ubayd ibn Maymun narrated to us, saying, we are told by 'Isa ... from 'A'ishah who said: The Prophet (upon whom be God's peace and benediction) heard a (blind) man reciting the Qur'ān in a mosque. Thereat he (s) said: *"May Allah have mercy upon him, he reminded me of so and so verses I dropped from so and so surah ..."* —

How can we convince them that the books of al-Bukhāri and Muslim contain many lies and forged narrations, which being a dangerous speech of course, as it is never accepted by Ahl al-Sunnah, who consider *Sahih al-Bukhāri* as the most authentic book after the Book of Allah!

How is it wonderful, dear reader, such a messenger who forgets the verses (āyāt), and had not this blind man been there to remind him of them, they would have been buried in oblivion — I seek Allah's forgiveness of this hallucination.

BELIEF IN IMĀMATE BY BOTH SECTS

By Imāmate in this chapter, we mean the general Imāmate for Muslims, i.e. caliphate, rulership, leadership and *Wilāyah* (guardianship).

Since the main topic of my book being comparison between the school of Ahl al-Sunnah and that of the Imāmiyyah Shi'ah, I have to expose the principle of Imāmate in the perspective of both the sects, in order that the reader and researcher be acquainted with the foundations and principles upon which each sect depends, knowing consequently the convictions that led me to accept conversion and abandon my previous belief.

The Shi'ah view Imāmate as one of the principles of religion (*usul al-Din*), due to its great significance and seriousness, being the leadership of the best *Ummah* (community) that has been raised up for mankind. Beside the numerous virtues and unique characteristics upon which leadership is based, of which I refer to: knowledge, bravery, forbearance, honesty, chastity, asceticism (*zuhd*), piety (*taqwā*), and godliness...etc.

The Shi'ah hold that Imāmate being a Divine post with which Allah encharges whomever He chooses from among His upright bondmen, to undertake this critical role, being to lead and guide the world after the demise of the Prophet (God's peace and benediction be upon him and his Progeny).

On this basis, al-Imām 'Ali ibn Abi Tālib was the Imām and leader for Muslims in accordance with the election of Allah, Who has revealed to His Messenger to nominate him ('Ali) as the chief for mankind, the task that he (s) did, telling the *Ummah* to follow him as his successor, after returning from his last *Hajj* pilgrimage to Makkah (*Hajjat al-Wadā'*) at Ghadir Khumm, and people swore allegiance to him "as held by the Shi'ah."[1]

---

[1] *Sahih Muslim*, vol. VI, p. 24, "bāb khiyār al-'a'immah wa shirārihim".

Ahl al-Sunnah also believe in the necessity of the Imāmate for leading the *Ummah*, but they give the *Ummah* right to choose its Imām and leader. According to this, Abu Bakr ibn Abi Quhāfah became the leader for the Muslims through their electing him after the demise of the Messenger of Allah (s), who kept silent concerning the matter of successorship never declaring anything in its regard to the *Ummah*, leaving the issue to be determined according to the shurā (consultation) among people.

Where the Truth be?

When any researcher meditates in the sayings of the two sects, contemplating in their arguments without any fanaticism, he will undoubtedly approach the truth. Herewith I will review with you the truth I have attained as follows:

1. Imāmate in the Holy Qur'ān

The Almighty Allah said:

"And (remember) when his Lord tried Abraham with (His) commands, and he fulfilled them, He said: Lo! I have appointed thee a leader for mankind. (Abraham) said: And of my offspring (will there be leaders)? He said: My covenant includeth not wrong-doers." (2:124)

In this noble verse Allah tells us that Imāmate being a Divine post encharged by Allah to whomever He chooses from among His bondmen, when saying: "I have appointed thee a leader for mankind". The verse further elucidates that Imāmate is a covenant from Allah never including but the pious bondmen, whom Allah has elected for this task, due to denying it for the wrong-doers, who never deserve the covenant of Allah — the Glorified and the Exalted. The Almighty has said too:

"And We made them chiefs who guide by Our command, and We inspired in them the doing of good deeds and the right

establishment of worship and the giving of alms, and they were worshippers of Us (alone)." (21:73)

In another place, Allah, the Glorified, said:

"And when they became steadfast and believed firmly in Our revelations, We appointed from among them leaders who guided to Our command." (32:24)

He also said:

"And We desired to show favour unto those who were oppressed in the earth, and to make them examples and to make them the inheritors." (28:5)

Some may fancy that the denotation conceived from these verses being that the meant Imāmate here is prophethood and message, which is a wrong concept for Imāmate in general, as every messenger is a prophet and leader (Imām) but not every Imām being a messenger or prophet!

For this reason, Allah — the Glorified and Most High — has expressed in His noble Book that His godly bondmen are entitled to ask Him to grant them this reputable appointment, to have the honour of guiding people, and gaining out of this high reward. The Most High said:

"And those who will not witness vanity, but when they pass near senseless play, pass by with dignity. And those who, when they are reminded of the revelations of their Lord, fall not deaf and blind thereat. And who say: Our Lord! Vouchsafe us comfort of our wives and of our offspring, and make us patterns for (all) those who ward off (evil)." (25:72-74)

Besides, the Holy Qur'ān has used the word Imāmah to point to the oppressive leaders and rulers, who misguide their followers and nations, leading them toward corruption and torment in the world and Hereafter. Talking about Faraoh and his troops, the Almighty Allah said in His noble Scripture:

"Therefore We seized him and his hosts, and abandoned them unto the sea. Behold the nature of the consequence for evil-doers! And We made them patterns that invite unto the Fire, and on the Day of Resurrection they will not be helped. And We made a curse to follow them in this world, and on the Day of Resurrection they will be among the hateful." (28:40-42)

On this basis, the Shi'ah's claim is nearer to what the Holy Qur'ān has ordained, since Allah — the Glorified and the Mighty — has explicitly expounded with no doubt, that the Imāmate being a Divine appointment Allah imparts upon whomever He wills, and it is the covenant of Allah of which He deprived the oppressors. And since the Prophet's Companions other than 'Ali ('a) have ascribed partners unto Allah during the pre-Islamic era, thus they turn to be among the wrong-doers, being incompetent for Allah's covenant encharging them with Imāmate and caliphate. While the Shi'ah's claim stands firm that al-Imām 'Ali ibn Abi Tālib was the only one, from among all other Companions, having the right to Allah's covenant of Imāmah, due to the fact that he has never worshipped other than Allah, and never prostrated to any idol, the reason why Allah has granted him honour, out of the Companions. If it is said that Islam exonerates whatever is past before it, we never object, but there is a great difference between that who was a polytheist and repented afterwards, and that who used to be immaculate and pure, knowing none but Allah.

2. Imāmate in the Prophetic Sunnah

The Messenger of Allah (may God's peace and benediction be upon him and his Household) has disclosed several utterances regarding Imāmate, narrated by both the Shi'ah and Sunnah, in their books and Masānid (*Musnads*). Once he referred to it with using the expression Imāmah, and another time with the word successorship, and once again with the word '*wilāyah*' (guardianship) or *imārah* (princedom).

About the word Imāmah he (s) said: *"The best of your leaders are those whom you love and they love you, and whom you pray upon and they pray upon you (after death), while the most wicked of your leaders are those whom you detest and they detest you, and whom you curse and they curse you."* They (who were present) said: O Messenger of Allah, shall we declare war against them by the sword? He replied: *"No, as long as they are establishing prayer.*[2]

He also said: *"After me there will be leaders that can never follow my guide, and never adopt my sunnah, among whom will rise up men having hearts of the devils inside a body of a human being."*[3]

And about caliphate he (s) said: *"Religion remains established till the Doomsday or twelve successors rule over you, all being from Quraysh."*[4]

Jābir ibn Samurah is reported to have said: I heard the Messenger of Allah, may God's peace and benediction be upon him and his Progeny, say: *"Islam is still powerful as long as twelve successors are there,"* saying then a word I couldn't understand, so I asked my father: what did he say? He replied: All are from Quraysh."[5]

About princedom he (s) said: *"There will be emirs whom you recognize but deny. Whoever recognizes (them) will be acquitted and whoever denies will secure (against danger), but who admits and follows, (thereat) they said: Shall we fight them?* He replied: No, as long as they keep on establishing prayer."[6]

---

[2] *Sahih Muslim*, vol. VI, p. 24, "bāb khiyār al-'a'immah wa shirārihim".

[3] Sahih Muslim, vol. VI, p. 20, "bāb al-'amr bi-luzum al-jama'ah 'inda zuhar al-fitan".

[4] *Ibid.*, vol. VI, p. 4, "bab al-nās tubba'li-Quraysh wa al-khilāfah fi Quraysh".

[5] *Ibid.*, vol. VI, p. 3; and Sahih al-Bukhāri, vol. VIII, pp. 105, 128.

[6] *Ibid.*, vol. VI, p. 23, "bāb wujub al-'inkār 'alā al-'umarā."

Further, about the word princedom he (s) said: *"Verily there will be twelve emirs, all are from Quraysh."* [7]

He is also reported to have warned his Companions saying: *"You will covet eagerly for imārah (princedom, rule), and this will turn to be a regret on the Doomsday, so what an excellent nurse she is, and how bad the weaner is."*[8]

In another narration the word *wilāyah* is used instead of imārah.

The Messenger of Allah (s) said further: *"Whoever presides over subjects of Muslims, and dies after being dishonest with them, Allah shall verily forbid him the heavens."* [9]

In another place he (s) uttered a *hadith* about *wilāyah*: *"The affairs of people keep on running their course as long as being presided over by twelve men, all being from Quraysh."* [10]

That was a brief survey about the concept of Imāmate or caliphate, which I have displayed from the Holy Qur'ān and the genuine Prophetic Sunnah without exposition or interpretation. Rather I have mainly depended upon the *Sihāh* of Ahl al-Sunnah other than the Shi'ah, since this affair (i.e. caliphate of twelve men from Quraysh) is regarded by them as an irreproachable intuition, about which there is no slight difference between even two of them, despite the fact that the *'ulamā'* of Ahl al-Sunnah expressly declare that the Messenger of Allah (s) said:

"After me there will be twelve successors (ruling over you) who are all from Banu Hāshim."[11]

---

[7] *Sahih al-Bukhāri,* vol. VIII, p. 127, "bāb al-'istikhlāf".

[8] *Ibid.,* vol. VIII, p. 106, "bāb Ma yukrah min al-hirs 'alā al-'imārah".

[9] *Ibid.*

[10] *Sahih Muslim,* vol. VI, p. 3, "bāb al-Khilāfah fi Quraysh".

[11] *Yanābi' al-Mawaddah,* vol. III, p. 104.

Al-Shi'bi reports from Masruq that he said: "When we were in the house of Ibn Mas'ud offering him our codices (*masāhif*), a lad said to him: Did your Prophet make a covenant informing you how many successors will be after him? He replied: *"You are still so young, and no one other than you has ever asked me the question you have put forth... the answer is yes, our Prophet (s) has assured us that after him there will be twelve caliphs, the same number as that of the chiefs of Israel..."*[12]

After that, we have to review the opinions of the two sects, to know the veracity of the claim of each of them through the express texts. We will also discuss the interpretation of each of them for this critical issue that created disunity among the Muslims, dividing them into creeds and sects, and theological and thought schools, after being one *Ummah* (nation). And any dispute erupted among the Muslims, whether in regard of *fiqh* (jurisprudence), or tafsir (exegesis) of the Qur'ān, or in comprehending the Prophetic Sunnah, is traced back to and caused by the caliphate.No one is aware of the caliphate that — after the Saqifah — turned to be a factual affair due to which authentic traditions and express verses were disapproved and for whose establishment and confirmation many other traditions were composed and fabricated, that have no root or origin in the authentic Prophetic Sunnah. All this reminds me of Israel and the status quo, as the Arab Heads of State and Kings have met and reached an agreement that there should be no recognition of or compromise or peace with Israel, and whatever is taken by force can never be regained but by force. After only a few years they met again to sever, this time, their ties with Egypt due to its recognition of the Zionist Regime. After passage of some few years they resumed their relations with Egypt, never deploring its normalization of ties with Israel, though the latter had never recognized the right of the Palestinian people, and never changed its position. Rather it increased in its stubbornness and obstinacy, multiplying its repression against the Palestinian people. History is repeating itself

---

[12] *Ibid.*, vol. III, p. 105.

and events are recurred, and the Arabs are used to commit themselves to surrender to the status quo.

Ahl al-Sunnah's Opinion about Caliphate and its Discussion

The opinion of Ahl al-Sunnah about caliphate is known, being that the Messenger of Allah passed away without nominating anyone as a successor. But the influential magnates among the Companions have met in the Saqifah of Banu Saidah, and elected Abu Bakr al-Siddiq as their guardian (*wali al-'amr*) due to his position near the Messenger of Allah, and since he (s) made him his substitute in leading the congregational prayers during his illness. At that time people said. If the Messenger of Allah (s) recognizes him as a guardian of our religion affairs, so how can't we accept him as a guardian undertaking the affairs of our life?

The recapitulation of their belief is that:

1. The Messenger has never nominated any successor.

2. Caliphate can never be determined but through shurā (council).

3. Electing Abu Bakr as a caliph was made by the magnates of Sahābah (Companions).

This was also my opinion when I was a Māliki strongly defending him with argumenting by depending on the verses about shurā, trying my best to boast that Islam being a religion based on democracy in the rule, and the prior of other religions to invite toward this humane principle on which the civilized progressive countries are priding.

I say: While the Republican system was not known by the West but only during the nineteenth century, Islam realized and outstripped other religions in getting it since the sixth century.

But, after meeting the Shiah '*ulamā*' and reading their books and being acquainted with their convincing evidences, that can be found in our reference books, I changed my previous belief and converted when the argument (*hujjah*) showed itself clearly, since it is improper for the majesty of Allah— the Glorified — to forsake an *Ummah* without an Imām, while He says:

"Thou art a warner only, and for every folk a guide." (13:7).

It is also inappropriate for the mercy of the Messenger of Allah (s) to let his *Ummah* without a custodian, especially when knowing that he used to fear for his *Ummah* disunity,[13] turning back on their heels,[14] rushing madly upon the world,[15] smiting of the necks of each other,[16] and lastly following the systems (*sunan*) of the Jews and Christians.[17]

When knowing that Umm al-Mu'minin 'A'ishah, the daughter of Abu Bakr, delegated to 'Umar ibn al-Khattāb, when he was stabbed, someone to tell him: "Nominate someone as a successor over the *Ummah* of Muhammad, and never leave them discarded after you, as I fear they be inflicted with sedition."[18]

Also, when 'Abd Allāh ibn 'Umar entered upon his father, when he was stabbed, saying to him: "People have alleged that you have not designated anyone to succeed you, and if you have a camels or sheep shepherd who comes toward leaving his herd alone, verily you consider him as being neglectful of his duty, while taking care of people is much harder."[19]

---

[13] Al-Tirmidhi, Abu Dāwud and Ibn Mājah; *Musnad* Ahmad ibn Hanbal, vol. II, p. 332.

[14] *Sahih al-Bukhāri*, vol. VII, p. 209, "bāb al-hawd", and vol. V, p. 292.

[15] *Ibid.*, vol. IV, p. 63.

[16] *Ibid.*, vol. III, p. 112.

[17] *Ibid.*, vol. IV, p. 144, and vol. VIII, p. 151.

[18] *Al-Imāmah wa al-Siyāsah*, of Ibn Qutaybah, vol. I, p. 28.

[19] *Sahih Muslim*, vol. VI, p. 5, "bāb al-'istikhlāf wa tarkih".

Further, we observed how Abu Bakr himself, who was elected by Muslims through the shurā, breached this principle, rushing to nominate 'Umar as his successor, in order to eradicate any dispute, disunity and sedition. The fact that was foretold by al-Imām 'Ali ('a), when 'Umar exerted much pressure against him to swear allegiance to Abu Bakr, thereat he said to him:*"Prepare a scheme whose half shall be yours, and reinforce it for him today, he will reward you tomorrow."*[20]

While Abu Bakr was not believing in the *shurā* system, so how can we accept that the Messenger of Allah (s) has neglected the affair without nominating any successor, and was not aware of what was done by 'Abu Bakr, Aishah and Abd Allah ibn 'Umar, as known by people intuitively, including difference of opinions, scatterness of inclinations when they are encharged with the task of election, especially when it is related to headship and assuming the rostrum of caliphate. This has actually occurred even in electing Abu Bakr on the day of Saqifah, as we observed the dispute erupted between the Master of the Helpers (Ansār) Sa'd ibn 'Ubadah and his son Qays ibn Sa'd, 'Ali ibn Abi Tālib and al-Zubayr ibn al-'Awwām,[21] al-'Abbas ibn 'Abd Muttalib and Banu Hāshim with some of the Companions who were of the opinion that Ali ('a) was more entitled to caliphate, and lingered behind in his house refusing to swear allegiance (to Abu Bakr), until they were threatened with being burnt.[22]

On the other side, we find the *Imāmi* Shi'ah prove exactly the opposite of Ahl al-Sunnah's claim emphasizing that the Messenger of Allah has definitely nominated 'Ali to assume caliphate, confirming this in several occasions, the most known of which being in Ghadir Khumm.

---

[20] *Al-Imāmah wa al-Siyāsah*, of Ibn Qutaybah, vol. I, p. 18.
[21] *Sahih al-Bukhāri*, vol. VIII, p. 26, "bāb rajm al-hublā min al-zinā".
[22] *Tarikh al-Khulafā'*, of Ibn Qutaybah, vol. I, p. 18 and afterwards.

If equity necessitates of you to listen to your opponent to adduce his opinion and plea in controversial issue with you, how it would be when your opponent argues with you offering as a plea something the occurrence of which you yourself testify.[23]

The evidence given by the Shi'ah is not so feeble or unsubstantial that can be easily overlooked or forgotten, but rather it is relevant to Qur'ānic verses revealed in this respect. The care and importance given to these verses by the Messenger of Allah reached an extent that was propagated by caravans, and reported by all people, far and near, till filling books of history and traditions, and being recorded by the narrators, a generation from another.

'Ali's Guardianship in the Holy Qur'ān

Allah, the Exalted, said:

"Your guardian can be only Allah; and His Messenger and those who believe, who establish worship and pay the poor-due while bowing down (in prayer). And whoso taketh Allah and His Messenger and those who believe for guardian (will know that), lo! The party of Allah, they are the victorious." (5:55-56)

In his *al-Tafsir al-Kabir*, al-Imām Abu Ishaq al-Tha'labi[24] is reported, with his *isnād* (chain) reaching back to Abu Dharr al-Ghifāri, to have said: "I heard the Messenger of Allah (may God's peace and benediction be upon him and his Progeny) with my two ears, otherwise they be deaf, and saw him with my own eyes, otherwise they be blind, saying:

---

[23] This is according to the fact that no proof (*dalil*) can be found with the Shi'ah, but only when its application (misdāq) should be there in the Sunnah books.

[24] He is Abu Ishāq Ahmad ibn Muhammad ibn Ibrāhim al-Naysāburi al-Tha'labi (d. 337 H.). To him Ibn Khallikān referred by saying: *"He was the matchless of his time in science of exegesis ('ilm al-tafsir), of correct transmission, and trustable."*

'Ali is the leader of the pious, slayer of the disbelievers, victorious is that who helps him, and defeated is that who disappoints him."

"One day I was praying with the Messenger of Allah, when a beggar came to the Prophet's mosque. No one responded to his pleas. 'Ali ('a) was bowing down (in prayer) at that time. He pointed his little finger, on which was a ring, towards the beggar, who came forward and took away the ring. This incident occurred in the Prophet's presence, who raised his hands towards the Heavens and prayed My God! My brother Moses had begged of You saying: *"My Lord! Relieve my mind. And ease my task for me. And loose a knot from my tongue. That they may understand my saying. Appoint for me a henchman from my folk. Aaron, my brother. Confirm my strength with him. And let him share my task. That we may glorify Thee much. And much remember Thee. Lo! Thou art ever Seeing us."* Then you revealed to him: *"Thou art granted thy request, O Moses."* O Allah! I am your bondman and prophet, relieve my mind and ease my task for me, and appoint for me a henchman from my folk, 'Ali, and confirm my strength with him."

Abu Dharr then said: By God, the Messenger of Allah (s) had not yet finished his prayers, when Gabriel descended upon him revealing the following verse:

"Your Guardian can be only Allah; and His Messenger and those who believe, who establish worship and pay the poor-due, while bowing down (in prayer). And whoso taketh Allah and His Messenger and those who believe for guardian (will know that), Lo! the party of Allah, they are the victorious. (5:55,56)."[25]

There is no disagreement among the Shi'ah that this verse was revealed in 'Ali's regard, according to the reports of Ahl al-Bayt

---

[25] *Al-Jam' bayn al-Sihāh al-Sittah; Sunan al-Nasāi; Musnad* Ahmad; *al-Sawā'iq al-Muhriqah* of Ibn Hajar, and it was reported too by Ibn Abi al-Hadid in *Sharh Nahj al-Balāghah.*

Belief In Imamate by Both Sects

(peace be upon them), which being among the unanimously accepted *akhbār* (reports) that were referred to in many considerable Shi'ah books, like:

1. *Bihar al-Anwār*, by al-Majlisi.
2. *Ithbāt al-Hudāt*, by al-Hurr al-'Amili.
3. *Tafsir al-Mizān*, by al-'Allāmah al-Tabātabā'i.
4. *Tafsir al-Kāshif*, by Muhammad, Jawād Maghniyyah.
5. *Al-Ghadir*, by al-'Allāmah al-'Amini.

Beside numerous other books.

Its revelation in 'Ali's honor was reported too by a large number of Ahl al-Sunnah *'ulamā'*, among whom we refer only to the exegets:

1. *Tafsir al-Kashshāf* by al-Zamakhshari, vol.I, p.649.
2. *Tafsir al-Tabari*, vol.VI, p.288.
3. *Zād al-Masir fi 'ilm al-Tafsir*, by Ibn al-Jawzi, vol.II, p.383.
4. *Tafsir al-Qurtubi*, vol. VI, p.219.
5. *Tafsir al-Fakhr al-Rāzi*, vol, XII, p. 26.
6. *Tafsi Ibn Kathir*, vol.II, p.71.
7. *Tafsir al-Nasafi*, vol. I. p.289.
8. *Shawāhid al-Tanzil*, by al-Hasakāni al-Hanafi, vol. I, p.161.
9. *Al-Durr al-Manthur fi al-Tafsir bi al-Ma'thur*, by al-Suyuti, vol.II. p.293.
10. *Asbāb al-nuzul*, by al-Imām al-Wāhidi, p.148.
11. *Ahkām al-Qur'ān*, by al-Jassās, vol.IV. p.102.
12. *Al-Tashil li 'ulum al-tanzil*, by al-Kalbi, vol.I, p.181.

Beside other unmentioned Sunnah books, numbering more than those I referred to.

2) The Almighty Allah said:

"O Messenger! Make known that which hath been revealed unto thee from thy Lord, for if thou do it not, thou wilt not have conveyed His message. Allah will protect thee from people." **(5:67)**

It is reported by some exegetes from among Ahl al-Sunnah, that this verse was revealed in the early days of *Da'wah* (invitation), when the Messenger of Allah was having some bodyguards to protect him against murder and assassination. But when the verse *"and Allah will protect thee from people,"* was revealed, he (s) said: *"Go away, Allah has protected me."*

Ibn Jarir and Mardawayh have reported from 'Abd Allāh ibn Jarir that he said: "The Messenger of Allah (s) was pursued by some of his Companions, and when the words *"and Allah will protect thee from mankind,"* he came out and said:

"O people, go and reach your pursuants, as Allah has protected me from mankind." [26]

Ibn Hibbān and Ibn Mardawayh have reported from Abu Hurayrah that he said: When being in the company of the Messenger of Allah (s) on a journey, we used to dedicate for him the greatest and most shadowy tree to sit under. One day he sat under a tree, hanging his sword on it, when a man came and took it, saying: O Muhammad, who can protect you against me? The Prophet (s) replied: Allah protects me against you... put away the sword. So he returned it to its place. Thereat the verse *"and Allah will protect thee from mankind"* was revealed.[27]

Further, al-Tirmidhi, al-Hākim and Abu Nu'aym have reported from 'A'ishah that she said: The Prophet (s) used to be guarded till

---

[26] *Al-Durr al-Manthur fi al-Tafsir bi al-Ma'thur*, vol. III, p. 119.

[27] *Ibid.*

the words "*and Allah will protect thee from mankind*" were revealed, whereat he brought out his head from the dome saying: O people, go away, Allah has verily protected me.

Al-Jabarrāni and Abu Nu'aym in *al-Dalā'il*, narrate that Ibn Mardawayh and Ibn 'Asākir have reported from Ibn 'Abbās that he said: The Prophet (s) was having a bodyguard, and his uncle Abu jālib used to send with him every day some men from Banu Hāshim to safeguard him. One day he (s) said (to him) O uncle! Allah has protected me, so I am in no need any more for those you send.

When pondering upon these traditions and interpretations, we would realize their being incompatible with the denotation or even the context of the noble verse, as all these narrations show that they were revealed at the outset of the invitation (*da'wah*) to Islam. Some of them even declare their being revealed during the lifetime of Abu jālib that is, many years before the Hijrah (migration of the Prophet), and particularly Abu Hurayrah's narration in which he says: "*When being in the company of the Messenger of Allah on a journey, we used to dedicate for him the greatest tree... etc.*" This narration is explicitly fabricated, since Abu Hurayrah was never acquainted with Islam or the Messenger of Allah but only in the seventh year after Hijrah, as he himself testified.[28] So how can this be accepted, while all the exegetes, Sunnah and Shi'ah, unanimously concur that Surah al-Mā'idah (The Table Spread) was revealed at al-Madinah, and its being the last *surah* revealed of the Quran???

Ahmad and Abu 'Ubayd in *Fadā'il*, al-Nahhās in his *Nāsikh*, and al-Nisā'i, Ibn al-Mundhir, al-Hākim, Ibn Mardawayh and al-Bayhaqi in their *Sunan*, have reported from Jubayr ibn Nufayr that he said: I made the pilgrimage to Makkah, and when I entered upon 'A'ishah, she said: O Jubayr, do you read (*Surah*) *al-Mā'idah*? I said: Yes. Then she said: It is the last *surah* revealed (of the Qur'ān). Deem

---

[28] *Fath al-Bāri*, vol. VI, p. 31; *al-Bidāyah wa al-Nihāyah*, vol. VIII, p. 102; *Siyar A`lām al-Nubalā* of al-Dhahabi, vol. II, p. 436; Ibn Hajar's *al-'Isābah*, vol. III, p. 287.

lawful whatever you find lawful in it, and deem unlawful whatever you find unlawful (*harām*) in it.[29]

Also it is reported by Ahmad and al-Tirmidhi, and was improved and revised by al-Hākim, with Ibn Mardawayh and al-Bayhaqi in their *Sunan*, from 'Abd Allāh ibn 'Umar that he said: *Surah al-Mā'idah* is the last *surah* revealed of the Qur'ān.[30]

It is reported by Abu 'Ubayd, from Muhammad ibn Ka'b al-Qartani that he said: *Surah al-Mā'idah* was revealed unto the Messenger of Allah during *Hajjat al-Wadā'*, while being on his camel between Makkah and al-Madinah, whereat it (the camel) was cracked, and then the Messenger of Allah (s) got down.[31]

Ibn Jarir reports from al-Rabi 'ibn Anas that he said: *Surah al-Mā'idah* was revealed upon the Messenger of Allah (s) on his way back from his last pilgrimage, while being on his mount, and his mount kneeled down due to its (*surah's*) heavy burden.[32]

Abu 'Ubaydah reports from Damrah ibn Habib and 'Atiyyah ibn Qays that they said: The Messenger of Allah (s) said: "*Al-Ma'idah* (the Table spread) is the last of the Qur'ān in revelation, so deem lawful what it considers lawful (*halāl*) and deem unlawful what is considered unlawful (*harām*) in it.[33]

So, how can any sane equitable man accept then, the claim of one believing in its being revealed in the early days of the Prophetic mission (*al-Bi'thah al-Nabawiyyah*)? The aim of this move is clear, being to divert people from its real meaning. Added to this, the Shi'ah concur that *Surah al-Mā'idah* being the last *surah* revealed of the Qur'ān, and that the verse "O Messenger! Make known that

---

[29] Jalāl al-Din al-Suyuti's *al-Durr al-Manthur*, vol. III, p. 3.
[30] *Ibid.*
[31] *Ibid.*, vol. III, p. 4.
[32] *Ibid.*, vol. III, p. 4.
[33] *Ibid.*

which hath been revealed unto thee from thy Lord...", which is called *Ayat al-Balāgh* (Verse of proclamation), was revealed unto the Messenger of Allah on the eighteenth of Dhu al-Hijjah, in the wake of the last pilgrimage at Ghadir Khumm, before designating al-Imām 'Ali as a master for people and his successor after him. This incident was on Thursday, and Gabriel ('a) has brought it down after the elapse of five hours of the day, saying to the Prophet: O Muhammad Allah sends you His greetings and says to you.

"O Messenger! Make known that which hath been revealed unto thee from thy Lord, for if thou do it not, thou wilt not have conveyed His message. Allah will protect thee from people." (5:67)

But the Almighty's saying: *"...for if thou do it not, thou wilt not have conveyed His message"* explicitly indicates that the message has come to an end or was about to, though some very significant thing is left, without which religion can never be perfected. Further, the noble verse tells that the Messenger feared being belied by people, when inviting them to this serious affair. But Allah — the Glorified — has not respited him, since his hour has approached, and that was the best opportunity, of the greatest position since those who gathered around him (s) numbered more a hundred thousand, accompanying him in *Hajjat al-Wadā'*, whose hearts were still vivid through the offerings consecrated to Allah, recalling to mind the Messenger's telling them the approaching of his death hour.

Also we can refer to his saying to them: I may not meet you after this year, and imminently my Lord's messenger (death angel) is to come, so as to summon me and I should respond. And since after this awful situation all people will separate and return to their homelands, with a very little chance to meet such a huge multitude, and as Ghadir Khumm being a crossroad, so it was not, in any way, for Muhammad (s) to miss such an opportunity. How would he do so while it was revealed for him, in a threatening-like way that the message in a whole, was dependent upon this proclamation, with Allah's ensuring him protection from mankind, leaving no reason for him to fear his being belied by them. This was due to his awareness that many messengers before him were belied, but without being dissuaded from propagating that which was entrusted to them, since the duty of any messenger being only to convey the message. And had Allah known in advance that most of them were hateful unto the truth, and that some of them being the beliers (denying the message), He — the Glorified — would have never forsaken them without establishing an authority (*hujjah*) over them, that there might not remain any argument (excuse) for people against God (ref.4:165).

Whereas the Messenger of Allah (s) has a good example for his brethren the messengers who preceded him, and who were denied by their communities. Allah, the Exalted, said:

"If they deny thee (Muhammad), even so the folk of Noah, and (the tribes of) Ad and Thamud, before thee, denied (Our messengers). And the folk of Abraham and the folk of Lot. And the dwellers in Midian. And Moses was denied; but I indulged the disbelievers a long while, then I seized them, and how (terrible) was My abhorrence!" (22:42-44)

When abandoning the detested bigotry, and blind fanaticism, we would realize that this exposition being the reasonable one that keeps pace with the context of the verse and events that preceded and occurred after it.

Many of our *'ulamā'* have confirmed its revelation at Ghadir Khumm, in regard of designating al-Imām 'Ali for the post of caliphate, authenticating those narrations, concurring in this respect with their brothers among the Shi'ah *'ulamā'*. As an example I refer to some of the Sunni *'ulamā'*:

1. Al-Hāfiz Abu Nu'aym in his book *Nuzul al-Qur'ān*.

2. Al-Imām al-Wāhidi in his book *Asbāb al-Nuzul*, p.150

3. Al-Imām Abu Ishāq al-Thalabi in his *al-Tafsir al-Kabir*.

4. Al-Hakim al-Hasakani in his book *Shawāhid al-Tanzil li qawā'id al-tafdil*, vol.I, p.187

5. Jalāl al-Din al-Suyuti in his book *al-Durr al-Manthur fi al-Tafsir bi al-Ma'thur*, vol. III, p. 117.

6. Al-Fakhr al-Rāzi in his *al-Tafsir al-Kabir*, vol.XII, p.50.

7. Muhammad Rashid Ridā in Tafsir *al-Manār*, vol.II, p.86; vol. VI, p.463

8. Abu Asākir al-Shāfi'i in *Tarikh Dimashq*, Vo. II, p.86

9. Al-Shawkāni in *Fath al-Qadir*, vol.II, p.60

10. Ibn Talhah al-Shāfi'i in *Matālib al-Sa'ul*, vol.I, p.44

11. Ibn Sabbāgh al-Māliki in *al-Fusul al-Muhimmah*, p.25

12. Al-Qunduzi al-Hanafi in *Yanābi' al-Mawaddah*, p.120

13. Al-Shahristāni in *al-Milal wa al-Nihal*, vol.I, p.163

14. Ibn Jarir al-Jabari in *Kitāb al-Wilāyah*.

15. Badr al-Din al-Hanafi in *'Umdat al-Qāri fi Sharh al-Bukhāri*. vol.VIII, p.584

16. 'Abd al-Wahhab al-Bukhāri in *Tafsir al-Qur'ān*.

17. Al-'Alusi in *Ruh ma'āni*, vol. II, p.384

18. Ibn Sa'id al-Sijistāni in *Kitāb al-Wilāyah*.

19. Al-Hamwini in *Farā'id al-Simtayn*, vol.I, p.185

20. Al-Sayyid Siddiq Hasan Khān in *Fath al-bayān fi maqasid al-Qur'ān*, vol. III, p.63.

This is just a scanty modicum of what comes to my mind, beside a large number of other Ahl al-Sunnah *'ulamā'* referred to by al-'Allāmah al-'Amini in the book al-Ghadir. I wonder what did the Messenger of Allah (s) do when he was commanded by his Lord to deliver what was revealed unto him?

The Shi'ah hold that he (s) gathered the people from all strata in that place, being Ghadir Khumm, giving a long eloquent sermon, calling them to witness against themselves and they witnessed that he(s) certainly had more right on them than they themselves had. Thereat he took 'Ali's hand and declared: *"To whomever I am his master, this Ali also is his master (mawlā). My God befriend whoever him and be hostile to whoever is hostile to him, help whoever helps him, and forsake whoever forsakes him, and keep the haqq (truth) always with him."* [34]

Then he (s) made him wear his turban, arranging a ceremony for him, commanding his Companions to congratulate him for being the leader of the believers. And so they did, at the foremost of whom being Abu Bakr and 'Umar, who both said to 'Ali ('a): *"Congratulation, O son of Abu Tālib, within a day and a night you became a mawlā (master) of every believing man and woman."* [35] When the ceremony was over, the following verse was revealed unto him by Allah:

"This day have I perfected your religion for you and completed my favour unto you, and have chosen for you Islam (to be) the Religion." (5-3)

This notion is held by the Shi'ah, as an indisputable fact accepted by all. Do Ahl al-Sunnah ever refer to this incident? In order not to tilt toward them, or being pleased with their opinion, Allah — the Glorified — has warned us by saying:

"And among men there is he whose talk concerning the life here marveleth thee and he taketh God to witness as to what is in his heart yet he is the most violent of adversaries." (2:204)

---

[34] It is called *Hadith al-Ghadir*, and was reported by both the Shi'ah and Sunni *'ulamā'* at the same level.

[35] Ahmad ibn Hanbal in his *Musnad*, vol. IV, p. 281; al-Tabari in his *Tafsir*; al-Rāzi in his *al-Tafsir al-Kabir*, vol. III, p. 636; Ibn Hajar in his *Sawā'iq*; al-Dāraqutni al-Bayhaqi, al-Khatib al-Baghdādi, and al-Shahristāni, beside others.

We are asked then to be cautious, and to discuss this topic with much care, with looking honestly into the evidences given by the two sects, seeking only God's pleasure in this respect. The answer for the previous question is: yes, many of Ahl al-Sunnah *'ulamā'* refer to this incident with all its stages. The following are some of evidences quoted from their books:

1. Al-Imām Ahmad ibn Hanbal has reported a *hadith* narrated by Zayd ibn Arqam, saying: We got down with the Messenger of Allah (s) in a valley called Khumm Valley, and he ordered congregational prayer to be held, performing it in meridional heat. Then, while being shaded by a garment over a brown tree, from the sun, the Messenger of Allah addressed us saying:

"Aren't you aware, or don't you give witness that I have more right on every believer than he himself has? They said: Yea. Then he said: Of whomever I am his master (*mawlā*) 'Ali also is his master. O God, befriend whoever befriends him and be the enemy of whoever is hostile to him..." [36]

2. In *al-Khasā'is al—Imām al-Nasā'i* reports (from Abu al-Jufayl) from Zayd ibn Arqam that he said: "When the Messenger of Allah (May God's peace and benediction be upon him and his Progeny) returned from the last *hajj* pilgrimage and came down at Ghadir Khumm, he ordered (us) towards the big trees, and (the ground underneath them was swept. Then he declared: 'I am about to answer the call (of death). Verily, I have left two precious things (*thaqalayn*) among you, one of which is greater than the other: the Book of Allah and my *'Itrah*, my *Ahl al-Bayt*. So watch out how you treat them after me. For, indeed, they will never separate until they return to me by the side of the Pond." Then he said: 'Verily, Allah is my master (*wali*) and I am the master of every believer.' Then he took 'Ali's hand and declared: "*To whomever I am his wali, this one is also his wali. My God, befriend whoever befriends him and be hostile to whoever is hostile to him.*" Abu al-Jufayl says: "I said to Zayd: "Did

---

[36] *Musnad* Ahmad ibn Hanbal, vol. IV, p. 372.

you hear it from the Messenger of Allah?' He replied, "There was no one in the caravan who did not see it with his eyes and hear it with his ears." [37]

3. Al-Hākim al-Nayshāburi reports from Zayd ibn Arqam, through two *sahih* (correct) chains according to the requirements of the Shaykhayn (al-Bukhāri and Muslim), that he said: "When the Messenger of Allah (s) returned from the last *hajj* and came down at Ghadir Khumm, he ordered (us) towards the big trees, and (the ground) underneath them was swept. Then he said: '*I am about to answer the call (of death) Verily, I have left behind two precious things amongst you, one of which is greater than the other. The Book of Allah, the Exalted, and my 'Itrah (Kindred). So watch out how you treat these two after me, for verily they will not separate from each other until they come back to me by the side of the Pond.*' Then he said: '*Verily, Allah, the Almighty and the Glorious, is my master (mawlā) and I am the master of every believer (mu'min).*' Then he took Ali by the hand and said: "*This ('Ali) is the master of whomever I am his master. O God, love whoever loves him and be the enemy of his enemy*'..."[38]

4. This *hadith* was also narrated by Muslim in his *Sahih* with his sanad (chain) reaching back to Zayd ibn Arqam, in an abridged form, saying: "One day the Messenger of Allah upon whom be Allah's peace and benediction, addressed us near a pond called Khumm between Makkah and Madinah.

He praised God and extolled Him and preached and reminded (us). Then he said: "*Lo, O people, I am only a human being and I am about to respond to the messenger of my Lord (i.e. the call of death). I am leaving behind two precious things (thaqalayn) among you. The first of the two is the Book of Allah. In it is guidance and light. So get hold of the Book of Allah and adhere to it.*" Then he urged and motivated (us) regarding the Book of Allah. Then he said: "*And my*

---

[37] Al-Nasā'i in *al-Khasā'is*, p. 21.

[38] *Mustadrak* al-Hākim, vol. III, p. 109.

Ahl al-Bayt (family). I urge you to remember Allah regarding my Ahl al-Bayt. I urge you to remember Allah regarding my Ahl al-Bayt I urge you to remember Allah regarding my Ahl al-Bayt."[39]

A Commentary

Although Imām Muslim has briefed the incident, never relating it completely, but it is, thanks to Allah, so sufficient and conclusive. May be the abridgement was made by Zayd ibn Arqam himself when the polotical circumstances obliged him to conceal *Hadith al-Ghadir,* the fact conceived from the context of the tradition when the narrator says: "I Husayn ibn Sabrah and 'Umar ibn Muslim went to see Zayd ibn Arqam.When we sat down with him, Husayn said to him, "O Zayd, you have been greatly fortunate. You have seen the Messenger of Allah, upon whom be Allah's peace and benediction, heard his speech, fought with him in battles and have prayed behind him. Indeed, O Zayd, you have been enormously fortunate. Narrate to us what you have heard from the Messenger of Allah, may Allah's peace and benedictions be upon him.'

Zayd said: O brother, by God, I have become aged and old and I have forgotten some of what I used to remember from the Messenger of Allah, upon whom be Allah's peace and benediction. So accept what I narrate to you and as to what I don't, trouble me not regarding it.' Then he said: One day the Messenger of Allah, upon whom be Allah's peace and benediction, addressed us near a pond called Khumm..."

From the *hadith* context, it seems that Husayn has asked Zayd ibn Arqam about the Ghadir incident, putting him thus in a critical situation before all, undoubtedly knowing that giving express reply for this question would certainly create for him troubles with the Government that used to compel people to curse 'Ali ibn Abi Tālib. So he made apology to the inquirer with the excuse of being aged

---

[39] *Sahih Muslim*, vol. VII, p. 122, "bāb fadā'il 'Ali ibn Abi Tālib; and the *hadith* is reported too by Imām Ahmad Ibn Hanbal and al-Tirmidhi.

and old, and that he has forgotten some of what he used to remember, asking then the attendants to accept what he narrated to them, without troubling him regarding that he couldn't tell them.

Despite his fear, and abridgement of the details, but Zayd ibn Arqam (may Allah reward him) has exposed many facts, hinting at *Hadith al-Ghadir* without mentioning it by name. That was when he said: One day the Messenger of Allah, upon whom be Allah's peace and benediction, addressed us near a pond called Khumm between Makkah and Madinah, referring then to 'Ali's virtues and his being partner of the Qur'ān, as recorded in *Hadith al-Thaqalayn* (the Book of Allah and my Ahl al-Bayt). But he never mentioned the name of 'Ali, letting those present there to deduce with their wittiness, as it was commonly known for all Muslims that 'Ali being the doyen of the Prophet's Ahl al-Bayt.

Therefore we observed that al-Imām Muslim himself got the same meaning we got from the *hadith*, realizing what we realized, narrating then this *hadith* under the chapter of *Fadā'il* 'Ali ibn Abi Tālib, though no express reference was made in it to the name of 'Ali ibn Abi Tālib.[40]

5. In *al-Mu'jam al-Kabir*, al-Tabarani reports, through a correct chain (*sanad*), from Zayd ibn Arqam, from Hudhayfah ibn Asid al-Ghifāri, that he said: The Messenger of Allah, may Allah's peace and benediction be upon him and his Progeny, at Ghadir khumm under some trees saying: "O people, I am about to answer the call (of death). Verily I shall be answerable and you will be answerable, what do you say? They replied: We witness that you have delivered the message, and striven (on Allah's way) and given good advice, may Allah reward you good. Then he said: Don't you witness that there is no god but Allah and Muhammad is His bondman and messenger, and His heaven is truth, resurrection after death is truth, and the Hour (Doomsday) is certainly to come, and Allah resurrects the dead from graves? They said: Yes, we do witness so. He said: O

---

[40] *Sahih Muslim*, vol. VII, p.122 "bāb fadā' il 'Ali".

Allah be a witness. Then he said: O mankind, verily, Allah is my master (*mawlā*) and I am the master of every believer (*mu'min*), and I have more authority over the believers than they over themselves. Of whomever I am his master, this one also is his master — i.e. 'Ali O God, be the friend of whoever befriends him, and be the enemy of whoever is hostile to him.Then he said: O people, I am verily separating from you, and you are coming back to me by the side of the Pond (*Hawd*). A Pond that is wider than the space between my sight and San'ā', in which there are stars equalling two silver goblets. When you come back to me I will ask you about the *Thaqalayn*, how did you treat them after me. The greater thiql: the Book of Allah — the Almighty and the Glorious — which is a rope between Him and you, whose one end is in His hand and whose other end is in your hands. So get hold of it, as you shall never go astray and never be changed, and my '*Itrah* (kindred) my Ahl al-Bayt. The Subtile, the Aware informed me that the two will never part, until they come to me at the Pond (*Hawd*).[41]

6. Al-Imām Ahmad Ibn Hanbal narrates from al-Barā' ibn 'Azib, through two ways that he said: We were with the Messenger of Allah (s) and we came down at Ghadir Khumm, whereat a call for holding congregational prayer was made. People swept the ground under two trees for the Messenger of Allah, may Allah's peace and benediction be upon him and his Progeny, who performed the noon prayer (*salāt al-zuhr*). Then he took 'Ali's hand, saying: *'Don't you know that I have more right over every believer than he has over himself?* They replied: Yes (you do). Then he declared (taking 'Ali's hand): *'To whomever I am his master, 'Ali also is his master. My God, befriend whoever befriends him and be hostile to whoever is hostile to him.*" Then the narrator said: After that 'Umar met him ('a), and said to him: 'Congratulation, O son of Abi Tālib, within a day and a night

---

[41] Ibn Hajar in his *Sawā'iq al-Muhriqah*, p. 25, on the authority of al-Tabarāni and al-Hakim and al-Tirmidhi.

you became the mawlā (master) of every believing man and woman." [42]

In brief, *Hadith al-Ghadir* was narrated by numerous *'ulamā'* of Ahl al-Sunnah,[43] more than those we have mentioned. Among them are: al-Tirmidhi, Ibn Mājah, Ibn 'Asākir, *Abu* Nu'aym, Ibn al-'Athir, al-Khwarazmi, al-Suytti, Ibn Hajar, al-Haythami, Ibn al-Sabbāgh al-Māliki, al-Qundtzi al-Hanafi, Ibn al-Maghāzili, Ibn Kathir, al-Hamwini, al-Hasakani, al-Ghazāli, and al-Bukhāri in his *Tarikh*.

Further, al-'Allāmah al-'Amini, the author of the book *al-Ghadir*, has enumerated a large number of non Shi'i *'ulamā'*, who narrated *Hadith al-Ghadir* and recorded it in their books, from different classes and schools of law, since the first till the fourteenth Hijrah century, numbering more than sixty-three. Whoever wants to investigate and be more assured, can refer to the book *al-Ghadir*.[44]

After all this, is it possible for anyone to claim that *Hadith al-Ghadir* was fabricated by the Shi'ah?

The surprising and strange fact is that, when *Hadith al-Ghadir* is mentioned to most of the Muslims, they claim being unaware of it, or say, never hearing it. And even more surprising is that after this unanimously accepted *hadith*, how is it feasible for the Sunni *'ulamā'* to claim that the Messenger of Allah (s) has never designated anyone as his successor, leaving this matter to be determined through *shurā* (council) among Muslims.

---

[42] *Musnad* al-Imām Ahmad ibn Hanbal, vol. IV, p. 281; also in *Kanz al-'ummāl*, vol. XV, p. 117; and *Fadā'il al-Khamsah min al-Sihāh al-Sittah*, vol. I, p. 350.

[43] For complete list of Sunni Scholars reporting the incident of Ghadir, visit: https://www.al-islam.org/ghadir/books.htm

[44] The book *al-Ghadir* of Allamah Amini is written in 11 volumes. It is a valuable book in which the author has meticulously collected and compiled whatever was written about *Hadith al-Ghadir* from the Ahl al-Sunnah books. For internet database of the book, visit: https://www.al-islam.org/ghadir

O people! Is there any *hadith* more declarative and expressive than this one regarding caliphate?? I may refer to a conversation held between me and one of al-Zaytunah *'ulamā'* in my country. When I mentioned for him *Hadith al-Ghadir* as an evidence proving the successorship of al-Imām 'Ali, he admitted its veracity. He rather added fuel to the fire when making me acquainted with the interpretation he invented for the Qur'ān, with which he mentioned and rectified *Hadith al-Ghadir*, saying afterwards:

"The Shi'ah claim that this *hadith* is a text establishing the caliphate of our master 'Ali (may Allah grant him honour), while it is invalid in the perspective of Ahl al-Sunnah wa al-Jamā'ah, since it contradicts the caliphate of our master Abu Bakr al-Siddiq and our master 'Umar al-Faruq, and 'Uthmān Dhu al-Nurayn. So it is inevitable to interpret the word *mawlā* cited in the *hadith* to mean lover and helper, as referred to in the Holy Qur'ān. This being the same meaning conceived by the rightly-Guided Caliphs (al-Khulafā' al-Rāshidun) and honourable Companions (may Allah be pleased with them all), from whom the Tābi'un (followers) and Muslim *'ulamā'* have taken. So no sense is to be given to the interpretation given by the Rāfidah for this *hadith*, as they never recognize the successorship of the caliphs, speaking ill of the Messenger's Sahăbah. This being a sufficient proof to refute their lies and invalidate their allegations." (His speech in the book is over).

I asked him: Did the incident actually occur at Ghadir Khumm?

He replied: Had it not occurred, the *'ulamā'* and *muhaddithin* (traditionists) would have never related it!

I said: Is it appropriate for the Messenger of Allah (s) to gather his Companions under scorching sun's heat, addressing them with a protracted sermon, just to tell them that 'Ali was their lover and helper? Do you accept such an interpretation?

He replied: A number of the Companions have complained against 'Ali (to the Prophet), among whom there were some harbouring vindictive feelings against 'Ali and detesting 'him.

There after the Messenger, intending to eliminate their grudge, said to them: Ali is your lover and helper, so as to make them love him and never detest him.

I said: This never requires of him to make them all stop, and lead them in prayer, initiating his sermon by saying: Don't I have more right over you than you have over your own selves, for the sake of elucidating the meaning of *mawlā*. Had the case been as you claim, it was feasible for him to tell those complaining against 'Ali: "He is your lover and helper," and finished with it without any need to detain under the sun all those enormous multitudes, numbering more than a hundred thousand, among whom were old men and women. Any man having reason can never be content with this!

He then said: Does any sane man believe that a hundred thousand Companions have never apprehended what you and the Shi'ah apprehended??

I said: First of all, only very few of them were living in al-Madinah. Secondly: They apprehended exactly the same meaning I and the Shi'ah got. So it was narrated by the *'ulamā'* that Abu Bakr and 'Umar were among those congratulating 'Ali by saying: "Congratulations, O Ibn Abi Tālib, within a night and a day you became the *mawlā* of every believing man (and woman)."

He said: Why didn't they swear allegiance to him then, after the Prophet's demise? Do you think that they have disobeyed and contradicted the Prophet's commandment? I seek Allah's forgiveness for such claim.

I said: If Ahl al-Sunnah *'ulamā'* testify in their books that some of them — i.e. of the *Sahābah* — used to contradict the orders of the Prophet (s) during his lifetime and in his presence,[45] so it would be

---

[45] Al-Bukhāri and Muslim reported in their *Sahihs* several contradictions on the part of them (Sunni *'ulamā'*), as in the event of Hudaybiyyah Peace Treaty, and also the event of Thursday Misfortune, and many other events and cases.

no wonder to see them forsaking his orders after his demise. And when most of them vilify and disapprove of his appointment of Usāmah ibn Zayd as the commander of the army, due to his young age, despite the battalion being limited and for a short time, so how would they accept to be under the leadership of the young man 'Ali, and for life long absolute caliphate? And you yourself have testified that some of them were detesting and harbouring grudge against 'Ali!!

Feeling, upset, he replied: It was improper for al-Imām 'Ali, may (Allah grant him honour) and be pleased with him, to keep silent of his right, if being aware that the Messenger of Allah designated him as his successor, while being that brave man fearing no one and of whom all the Sahābah feeling awe.

I said: O Sayyid, this is another subject out of the scope of my discussion, since you were not convinced by the authentic (*sahih*) Prophetic traditions, trying to interpolate them and divert them from their true meanings with the aim of respecting the dignity of the good ancestors (*al-Salaf al-Sālih*). So how can I convince you with 'Ali's keeping silent or his arguing with them by his right to caliphate?

He smiled and said: By God, I am among those who consider our master 'Ali, may Allah grant him honour, superior to others. Had it been in my hand, I would have never preferred anyone of the Sahābah to him, as he is the gate of the city of knowledge and Allah's conquering lion, but it is the will of Allah, Who brings forward whoever He wills and keeps behind whoever He wills. He will not be questioned as to that which he does, but they will be questioned.

I, in turn, smiled and said: This is too another topic dragging us toward discussing the subject of *qadā'* and *qadar* (fate and destiny) that we have discussed earlier, with every one of us preserving his own viewpoint. I wonder, sir, why is that whenever I debate with any of Ahl al-Sunnah *'ulamā'*, presenting him a convincing strong argument (*hujjah*), he immediately tries to find outlet to change the course of discussion to another one irrelevant to the subject of debate. He said: I am still steadfast on my view, with no little change. So I bade him farewell and departed him. I remained contemplating attentively, about the reason behind the absence of anyone among our *'ulamā'*, to complete the task and confirm the debate with strong argumentation that settles the dispute.

There are some who commence the discussion, but when seeing themselves unable to establish any proof confirming their claims, they try to shirk the situation by saying: Those are people who have passed away. Theirs is that which they earned, and yours is that which you earn. Some others say: Keep us away from agitating seditions and grudges, as this is not our business. The important point is that the Sunnah and the Shi'ah believe in one God and one messenger, and that is enough. Some say, in brief: O brother, beware of Allah in regard of the Sahābah. After all that, is there any room for holding any scientific debate with such people, for the sake of enlightening them and illuminating the way for returning to the truth other than which only deviation is there? And how far are those from the style of the Qur'ān which invites mankind to present their evidences:

Say: Bring your proof (of what ye state) if ye are truthful. (2:111)

This, despite the fact that if they abstain from their vilification and criticism campaign against the Shi'ah, we have never resorted to dispute and controversy with them even by that which is good.

Verse of Perfection of Religion Relates to Caliphate Too

The Shi'ah unanimously agree that the saying of the Glorious and the Almighty*: "This day have I perfected your religion for you and completed My favour unto you, and have chosen for you Islam as a religion,"(5:3)* was revealed at Ghadir Khumm after the Messenger of Allah (s) had designated al-Imām 'Ali as his successor over the Muslims, as reported from the Pure *'Itrah* Imāms. That is why they consider Imāmah (Imāmate) as one of the principles of religion (*Usul al-Din*).

Many of our *'ulamā'* report its revelation at Ghadir Khumm, after the appointment of al-Imām 'Ali, of whom I may mention, as an example:

1. Ibn 'Asākir, in *Tarikh Dimashq*, vol.II, p.75.

2. Ibn al-Maghāzili al-Shāfi'i, in *Manāqib 'Ali ibn Abi Tālib*, p.19

3. Al-Khatib al-Baghdādi, in *Tarikh Baghdād*, vol.VIII, p.290.

4. Al-Suyuti, in *al-'Itqān,* vol.I, p.31.

5. Al-Khwārazmi al-Hanafi, in *al-Manāqib*, p.80

6. Al-Sibt ibn al-Jawzi, in *Tadhkirat al-Khawāss*, p.30.

7. Ibn Kathir, in his *Tafsir*, vol.III, p.14.

8. Al-'Alusi, in *Ruh al-Ma'āni*, vol.VI, p.55

9. Ibn Kathir al-Dimashqi, in *al-Bidāyah wa al-Nihāyah*, vol.V, p.213

10. Al-Suyuti, in *al-Durr al-Manthtr fi al-Tafsir bi al-Ma'thur*, vol.III, p.19.

11. Al-Qunduzi al-Hanafi, in *Yanābi'al-Mawaddah*, p.115.

12. Al-Hasakāni al-Hanafi, in *Shawāhid al-Tanzil*, vol.I., p.157.

I say, despite this fact, the Ahl al-Sunnah *'ulamā'* have no choice but to interpolate this verse to denote another occasion, in order to safeguard the dignity of good ancestors among the Sahābah. Because, had they admitted its revelation to be at Ghadir Khumm, this would have meant their tacit recognition that Allah has perfected the religion and completed His favour upon the Muslims, through the *wilāyah* (mastership) of 'Ali ibn Abi Tālib. Besides, this would have meant the abolition of the successorship of the three precedent Caliphs, with causing disruption for the Companions justice (*'adālah*), and dissolution of many well-known traditions like the dissolution of salt inside water. This being an impossible thing and blatant misfortune since it is relevant to the creed (*'aqidah*) of a huge coommunity (*ummah*) having its known history, and *'ulamā'* and glories. As it is infeasible for us to deny *'ulamā'* like al-Bukhāri and Muslim, who report that this verse was revealed at the night of 'Arafāt on Friday.

In this way, all the early narrations would turn to be only Shi'i baseless superstitions, and vilifying the Shi'ah would become more proper than speaking ill of the Sahābah who being (as regarded by Ahl al-Sunnah) immune against error (*ma'sumin*),[46] and it is impermissible for anyone to cirticize their acts or sayings. While the Shi'ah being only Majus (Magians), infidels, Zanadiqah and idolaters, and the founder of their school of thought (*madhhab*) being 'Abd Allāh ibn Saba',[47] who was a jew that embraced Islam during the reign of 'Uthmān, with the aim of conspiring against the Muslims and Islam. This being a much easier means to misguide the *Ummah*, that was brought up on glorifying and venerating the Sahābah (anyone of them even that who saw the Prophet only once). How can we be able to persuade them that those narrations are not Shi'i superstitions, but in fact traditions of the Twelve Imāms, upon whose Imāmate there are authentic texts. The Imāms who, the Islamic governments managed in the first century to grow the love and respect towards the Sahābah inside the hearts of people versus creating hatred and grudge against 'Ali and his sons, to the extent of cursing them from over pulpits, prosecuting their Shi'ah (followers)

---

[46] Because they (*Ahl al-Sunnah*) believe the *Sahāhbah* (Companions) to be like the stars "Whomever you follow you shall be guided rightly."

[47] Refer to the book *'Abd Allāh ibn Saba'* of al-'Allāmah al-'Askari, so as to realize that he had never existed at all, and that he was merely one of the fabrications of Sayf ibn 'Umar al-Tamimi, who was widely known for falsification and lying. Refer also to Tāhā Husayn's book *al-Fitnat al-Kubrā*, and the book *al-Silah bayn al-tasawwuf wa al-tashayyu'* of Dr. Mustafā Kāmil al-Shaybi, so as to know that this 'Abd Allāh ibn Saba' being in fact our master 'Ammār ibn Yāsir (may God be pleased with him).

and subjecting them to massacres and scatterness and homelessness. Out of this, strong destation and hatred against all the Shi'ah grew inside hearts of people, as a result of the rumours, superstitions and corrupt beliefs propagated by the mass media against the Shi'ah during the reign of Mu'āwiyah, as they were considered the opposition party, as called nowadays, in order to seclude and exterminate them.

Therefore, many writers and historians of those ages even call them al-Rawafid (Rafidites), charging them with impiety, deeming their blood (killing them) as lawful for the sake of showing sycophancy for the rulers. After the disintegration of the Umayyad State and coming of the 'Abbāsid State, some of the historians followed their suit, white some others realized the position of Ahl al-Bayt ('a) [48], trying to make compromise and equity through adding the name of "Ali to the Rightly-guided Caliphs, without daring to express his right and superiority. Therefore they don't report in their *Sihāh* but only very few of 'Ali's virtues that never contradict the caliphate of those who preceded him. Some of them have even composed traditions in the honour of Abu Bakr, 'Umar and 'Uthmān ascribing them to 'Ali himself, in order to close the door (as they claim) before the Shi'ah believing in his superiority.

Through research and investigation, I found out that men's fame and greatness being evaluated according to their hatred against 'Ali ibn Abi Tālib, so the Umayyads and 'Abbāsids used to bring near and glorify whoever fought or stood against al-Imām 'Ali by sword or tongue. Thus they were imparting high positions upon some Companions and belittling some others, expending much fortune on some poets, slaying others. 'A'ishah Umm al- Muminin might have

---

[48] This is due to the fact that the Imams of Ahl al-Bayt ('a) seized the hearts and assumed such fame through their morals and knowledge, which filled the East and the West. And also through their *zuhd* (asceticism), *taqwā* (piety), and the honour and virtues bestowed upon them by Allah

not enjoyed such good status among them, hadn't she harboured such detestation and animosity against 'Ali.[49]

Further, we also saw that the 'Abbāsids sublimate the position of al-Bukhāri, Muslim and al-Imām Mālik, since they have not recorded of 'Ali's virtues but only very few, or rather their books expressly state that 'Ali ibn Abi Tālib had no honour or merit at all. Al-Bukhāri in his *Sahih*, under the chapter "Manaqib 'Uthmān" (Excellences of 'Uthmān), reported from Ibn 'Umar who said: "During the lifetime of the Prophet, may Allah's peace and benediction be upon him and his progeny, we were never regarding anyone equal to Abu Bakr, and after him 'Umar and then 'Uthmān, leaving afterwards the Prophet's Companions with no preferentiability among them.[50]

That is, he considered 'Ali like all other common people (How astonishing is this)!!

Besides, there are other cults within the *Ummah*, such as the Mu'tazilah and *Khawārij* and others, who do not hold the same belief of the Shi'ah, due to the fact that the Imāmate of 'Ali and his sons after him, would verily curb them from attaining to caliphate, seizing the affairs of people and making of their fate, and properties as a plaything in their hands, as done by Banu Umayyah and Banu al-'Abbas during the era of the Sahābah and Tābi'un, to the present time. The reason behind this being that the time rulers who attained to power whether through heredity like kings and sovereigns, or even

---

[49] She ('A'ishah) could never endure hearing or mentioning 'Ali's name. Some historians say that when the news of his death reached her, she performed thanksgiving prostration with chanting some poetry verses. This was reported by al-Bukhāri in his *Sahih*, vol. I, p. 162; vol. VII, p. 18; and vol. V, p. 140.

[50] *Sahih al-Bukhāri*, vol. IV, pp. 191, 201. Also in vol. IV, p. 195 al-Bukhāri reported a narration ascribed to Muhammad ibn al-Hanafiyyah, that he said: I said to my father: Who is the best of men after the Messenger of Allah (S)? He said: Abu Bakr. I asked: Who is then? He said: 'Umar is the next. Thereafter, fearing him to say 'Uthmān (after 'Umar), I said: Then you. He said: I am no more than an ordinary man among Muslims.

Belief In Imamate by Both Sects

the presidents elected by their peoples, are averse to this dogma, i.e. the faithful's believing in the caliphate of Ahl al-Bayt. They even deride this theocratic notion, which is only held by the Shi'ah, especially when those Shi'ah having weak-mindedness and stupidity to the extent that they believe in the Imāmate of the Awaited al-Mahdi, who will fill the earth with equity and justice after being filled with oppression and tyranny.

We return to discuss, calmly and unfanatically, the ideas held by the two parties, to realize the occasion and purpose of the revelation of the verse of perfection of religion, so that truth be quite clear for us to follow. After that we have nothing to do with pleasure of these or displeasure of those ones, as long as we seek Allah's pleasure in the first hand, and deliverance from His chastisement on the way.

"When wealth and sons avail not (any man), save him who brings unto Allah a whole heart." (26:88-89).

On the Day when (some) faces will be whitened and (some) faces will be blackened, and as for those whose faces have been blackened, it will be said unto them;

"Disbelieved ye after your (profession of) belief? Then taste the punishment for that ye disbelieved. And as for those whose faces have been whitened, in the mercy of Allah they dwell for ever. (3.106-107).

Discussing the Claim that the Verse was Revealed on 'Arafāt

Al-Bukhāri is reported to have said in his *Sahih*:[51] 'Narrated to us Muhammad ibn Yusuf, from Sufyān, from Qays ibn Muslim, from Tāriq ibn Shahāb, who said: Some of the Jews said: Had this verse been revealed unto us we would have taken that day as a feast. 'Umar asked them: Which verse you mean? They replied: *"This day*

---

[51] *Ibid.*, vol. V, p. 127.

have I perfected your religion for you and completed My favour unto you, and have chosen for you Islam as a religion." (5:3)

'Umar said: I know the place where it was revealed. It was revealed while the Messenger of Allah, upon whom be Allah's peace and benediction, was halting at 'Arafāt.

Ibn Jarir reports from 'Isā ibn Hārithah al-'Ansāri, that he said: We were sitting in the *diwān* when a Christian man said: O followers of Islam, there is a verse revealed unto you, had it been revealed unto us we would have taken that day and that hour as a feast even only two of us survived, which is: "*This day have I perfected your religion for you.*" There at no one of us replied. Then I met Muhammad ibn Ka'b al-Qartani, and asked him about that, and he said: Couldn't you answer him? 'Umar ibn al-Khattāb then said: It was revealed unto the Prophet when he was halting on the Mount on the Day of 'Arafāt, and that day is still considered as a feast for Muslims as long as they live.[52]

First: Out of these narrations we observe that Muslims were unaware of the date of that memorable day, never celebrating it, the fact making the Jews once and the Christians another time to say to them: Had this verse been revealed unto us we would have celebrated that day as a feast. This prompted 'Umar to question: Which verse? When they said: *"This day have I perfected your religion for you"*, he said: I know where it was revealed, that was when the Messenger of Allah, upon whom be Allah's peace and benediction, was making a halt on (the Mount of) 'Arafāt. From this episode we can sense the smell of intrigue and opaqueness, realizing that those who forged this *hadith* and ascribed it to 'Umar ibn al-Khattāb during al-Bukhāri's lifetime, intended in fact to compromise between the belief of the Jews and Christians in the greatness of the day and necessity of regarding it as a feast, and their status quo of not celebrating that day and never remembering it at all till forgetting it. Whereas it is supposed to be held as the greatest of

---

[52] Jalāl al-Din al-Suyuti, *op. cit.*, vol. III, p. 18.

Muslims' feasts, as in it Allah, the Glorified, has perfected for them their religion, and completed His favour unto them and have chosen for them Islam as a religion.

Therefore, in the second narration, you find the narrator's saying when hearing the Christian's exclamation: 'O followers of Islam, there is a verse revealed unto you, had it been revealed unto us we would have taken that day as a feast, even only two of us survived. The narrator said that no one of them responded to him, due to their unawareness of the date, position and greatness of that day. The narrator, seemingly, is amazed as to how could the Muslims ignore celebrating such a day. So we observed that when he met Muhammad ibn Ka'b al-Qartani, he would question him about that matter, whereat the latter would reply that 'Umar ibn al-Khattāb reported its being revealed unto the Prophet (s) while he was making a halt on the Mount on the day of Arafāt.

Had that day been known among all Muslims to be a feast ('*Id*), it would have never been ignored by those narrators, whether being of the Sahābah or Tābi'un, as it is known and established amongst them that the Muslims have two feasts ('*idayn*), which are: '*Id al-Fitr* (feast at the end of Ramadan) and '*Id al-'Adhā* (feast on 10ᵗʰ Dhul Hijjah). This fact was so common that even the '*ulamā*' and traditionists, like al-Bukhāri and Muslim and others, mention in their books *Kitāb al-'idayn", Salāt al-'idayn and Khutbat al-'idayn,* with other similar idioms that are unanimously accepted among all people — far and near — with no existence for a third '*Id*.

It is widely thought that those believing in the principle of *shurā* in determining the caliphate, and the founders of this theory, being the same ones who diverted the revelation of the verse from its reality on the day of Ghadir Khumm, after designating al-Imām 'Ali as a master. Because diverting its revelation to the Day of 'Arafāt was much easier for those believing in it, since the Day of Ghadir could gather a hundred thousand pilgrims or more, and no occasion was there during *Hajjat al-Wadā'* nearer to Ghadir than the Day of 'Arafāt in comparison, as only during them the pilgrims would gather in that huge multitude. It is widely known that people are scattered in groups here and there during all *hajj* days, never meeting together in one place but at (mount of) 'Arafāt. That is why we notice those believing in the revelation of the verse on the day of Arafāt, hold that it was revelation directly after the well-known Prophet's sermon, which was reported by many traditionists.

And when witnessing how they have diverted the text of designating 'Ali ibn Abi Tālib to caliphate, far from its true sense, surprising people (including 'Ali himself and those who were busy preparing the messenger for burial) by swearing allegiance to Abu Bakr in the Saqifah of Banu Sa'idah all of a sudden, totally disregarding the texts of Ghadir, can anyone then argue with the revelation of the verse being on the Ghadir Day?

The concept of the verse is not more declarative than the *Hadith al-Wilāyah*, but rather it implies perfection of religion, and completion of favour, and the Lord's pleasure, besides its containing a notification to the occurrence of an incident that day for them leading to perfection of religion.

Our certainty in the veracity of this belief is even increased, when going through what is reported by Ibn Jarir, on the authority of Qubaysah ibn Abi Dhu'ayb that he said: Ka'b said: "Had this verse been revealed on other than this community, they would have taken the day of its revelation as a feast in which they meet."! Then 'Umar said: O Ka'b, which verse you mean? He replied: *"This day have I perfected your religion for you."* 'Umar said: I know the day and place in which it was revealed... that was on Friday, on 'Arafāt Day, and both of them are celebrated by us as a feast, thanks to Allah.[53]

Second: To believe that the verse *"This day have I perfected your religion for you"* was revealed on 'Arafāt Day, is contradictory with the verse of proclamation (*āyāt al-balāgh*): **"O Messenger! Make known that which hath been revealed unto thee from thy**

---

[53] Ibid., al-Suyuti's interpretation of the verse *"This day have I prefected your religion for you"* in Surah al-Mā'idah.

Lord,"(5:67) which commands the Messenger (s) to deliver a significant matter without which the Message is incomplete. The verse which we have discussed earlier, whose revelation was recorded to be in a place between Makkah and Madinah after the last *hajj* pilgrimage (*hajjat al-wadā'*), the event that was reported by more than a hundred and twenty Companions, and three hundred and sixty of Ahl al-Sunnah *'ulamā'*. So how can it be sensible that Allah perfects the religion and completes the favour on Arafāt Day, and after only one week He orders His Prophet (s), on his way back to al-Madinah to communicate a thing without which the Message is incomplete?? O men of understanding! How can this be correct and reasonable???

Third: If every investigating researcher ponders over the Messenger's sermon on 'Arafāt Day, he will never see in it anything new of which Muslims are unaware, or that can be regarded a significant matter with which Allah perfected the religion and completed the favour. It has nothing but an ample of precepts that are cited by the Holy Qur'ān and the Prophet (may Allah's peace and benediction be upon him and his Progeny), during several occasions, emphasizing on them on 'Arafāt Day. The following are the precepts stated in the sermon as recorded by all narrators;

• Allah has made inviolable for you your blood and properties as the inviolability of this month and this day you are in.

• Observe your duty toward Allah and wrong not mankind in their goods, and do not act corruptly, making mischief in the earth. Whoever has a trust (*amānah*) should restore it to its owner.

• People in Islam are equal, no favour is there for an Arab over a non-Arab but only through piety.

• Every blood consgnauinity that was in the pre-Islamic era (Jahiliyyah) is under my foot, and every usury that was made in the Jahiliyyah is under my foot.

- O Mankind, know that selling on credit is increasement in ingratitude... know that time is changed, returning to its first shape when Allah created the heavens and earth.

- Verily, the number of the months with Allah is twelve months by Allah's ordinance, four of them are sacred.

- I recommend you to treat women kindly, you have taken them as wives under Allah's trusteeship, and made their wombs lawful according to the Book of Allah.

- I recommend you to be kind to those whom your right hands possess, feed them of what you eat and make them wear of what you wear.

- The Muslim is the brother to the Muslim, he never cheats, betrays or backbites him; unlawful for him is his blood or anything of his properties.

- The Satan has been hopeless to be worshipped any more, but to be obeyed in other than the acts of you that you despise.

- The worst enemy for Allah is the one who avenges from other than his killer, and the beater of other than that who beat him. Whoever be ungrateful to the favour of his masters, is ungrateful to what Allah has revealed unto Muhammad. And whoever belongs to other than his (real) father, upon him will be the curse of Allah and the angels and all people.

- I am commanded to fight with people till they say: No god is there but Allah and I am the Messenger of Allah. And when they utter it (the witness), their blood and properties shall be protected from me except when it serves them right, and their reckoning is with Allah.

- Don't return after me as infidels, and misguided, smiting the neck of each other of you.

Those were all the points mentioned in the sermon of 'Arafāt during the *hajjat al-wadā'*, the chapters of which are collected from all the authentic sources so as not to leave any of his (s) precepts reported by the *muhaddithun*. Do they have anything new in relation to the Sahābah? Nay, whatever it contained is stated in the Qur'ān, and its verdict (*hukm*) is demonstrated in the Prophetic Sunnah. And the Messenger of Allah (s) has spent his whole life explaining for people whatever was revealed for them, teaching them all the minute details of affairs and necessities in life. So no sense then in the revelation of the verse of "perfection of religion, completion of favour, and 'Allah's approval", after these precepts (*wasāyā*) that are known by all Muslims, but reiterated by him (s) for the sake of emphasis, since this was the first time people could meet around him in that huge multitude, besides his informing them before going out to perform the *hajj*, that it was his last *hajj* pilgrimage, the fact obligating him to give them those precepts.

But when approving of the second notion, i.e. the revelation of the verse on the day of Ghadir Khumm, after designating al-Imām 'Ali as a successor to the Prophet (s) and lord of the faithful, the meaning will be more appropriate and congruous. Because to succeed the Prophet (s) being the most important affair, and it is improper for Allah to leave His bondmen aimless, and for the Prophet (s) to depart people without appointing a successor, leaving his *Ummah* without a custodian. This is more affirmed while knowing that he never used to depart al-Madinah but after designating someone as his successor, from among his Companions over it, so how can we believe that he passes away without thinking of the matter of caliphate??

And when the contemporary atheists believe in this rule, hastening to designate a successor to the President even before his death, to administer the people affairs, never forsaking them without a president! So how can it be reasoned that Islam, which is the most perfect and complete religion, with which Allah sealed all the legislations, may neglect such a critical issue?!

We have previously recognized that 'A'ishah and Ibn 'Umar, and before them Abu Bakr and 'Umar, altogether realized the necessity of designating a caliph or "otherwise a sedition might take place". This fact was realized by the caliphs who succeeded them, as all of them designated successors after them, so how is it possible that such a sagacity be ignored by Allah and His Messenger??!

To hold that Allah, the Glorified, has revealed to His Messenger in the first verse (verse of proclamation), when he was returning from *hajjat al-wadā'*, to designate 'Ali as his successor saying: *"O Messenger! Deliver that which hath been revealed unto thee from thy Lord, for if thou do it not, thou wilt not have conveyed His message. Allah will protect thee from people."(5:67)* That is: O Muhammad, if you don't deliver what I have ordered you, that 'Ali is the master of the faithful after you, it will be as if you have never completed the mission with which you were delegated, since to perfect the religion with Imāmate being something essential for all men of reason.

Seemingly the Prophet (may Allah's peace and benediction be upon him and his Progeny) was afraid of their objection against him or denying him. In some narrations the Prophet (s) is reported to have said: *"Gabriel has brought me the commandment of my Lord to stand in this place and inform every white and black that: "'Ali ibn Abi Tālib is my brother, executor (wasi), successor and the Imām (leader) after me. I asked Gabriel to seek my Lord's exempting me of this task, due to my awareness of the scarcity of the pious and multiplicity of those vexing and blaming me due to my long association to 'Ali and strong likeness to him, to the extent that they called me a hearer, whereat the Almighty revealed*: **"Among them are those who torment the Prophet, and say, 'He is an ear.' Say, 'An ear that is good for you...."** *(9:61). If I wish to mention their names I could do, but I had kindness through choosing to conceal them. But Allah never accepted save to proclaim the order regarding him. So be informed O multitudes of people, that Allah has* designated him as a guardian (wali) and Imām for you, making obedience to him incumbent upon everyone...(the sermon).[54]

When the words "and Allah will protect thee from mankind" were revealed unto him, he immediately hastened to comply to the commandment of his Lord, when he appointed 'Ali as a vicegerent after him, commanding his Companions to congratulate him for attaining the leadership of the believers, and so did they. Then this verse was revealed unto them: *"This day have I perfected your religion for you and completed My favour unto you, and have chosen for you Islam as a religon."*

Added to this, some of Ahl al-Sunnah *'ulama'* expressly admit that the verse of proclamation (*āyāt al-balāgh*) was revealed in regard of 'Ali's Imāmate. They have reported on the authority of Ibn Mardawayh, from Ibn Mas'ud that he said: During the lifetime of the Messenger of Allah (s), we used to read: "O Messenger, Deliver that which hath been revealed unto you from thy Lord—that 'Ali is guardian of the faithful—for if thou do it not, thou wilt not have conveyed His message. Allah will protect thee from mankind."[55]

When adding to this research the narrations of the Shi'ah, reported from the Pure Imāms, the fact be made clear will be that Allah has perfected His religion by Imāmate. That is why Imāmate is regarded in the perspective of the Shi'ah as one of the principles of religion (*Usul al-Din*).

With the Imāmate of 'Ali ibn Abi Tālib, Allah has completed His favour unto the Muslims, so as not to be left neglected, allured and affeted by desires, scattered by seditions, or be dispersed like sheep without a shepherd.

---

[54] The full text of the sermon is reported by al-Hafiî Ibn Jarir al-Tabari in the book *al-Wilāyah*. Jalal al-Din al-Suyuti has also reported a sermon with the same denotation and identical words, in his *al-Durr al-Manthur*, vol. II, p. 57.

[55] Al-Shawkāni in *Tafsir Fath al-Qadir*, vol. III, p. 57; and Jalāl al-Din al-Suyuti in *al-Durr al-Manthur*, vol. II, p. 298, on the authority of Ibn 'Abbās.

He approved Islam as a religion for them, as He chose for them Imāms, far from whom He removed uncleanness and cleansed a thorough cleansing, bestowing upon them wisdom, and causing them to inherit the knowledge of the Scripture, to be the executors of Muhammad (s). So it is incumbent upon Muslims to consent to Allah's judgement and choise, submitting with full submission, since the general concept of Islam being full submission to Allah as said by the Almighty Allah *"And thy Lord createth whatever He willeth and chooseth too; it is not theirs to choose; Glorified be Allah and Exalted High is He (far) above what they join (with Him). And thy Lord knoweth what concealeth their breasts and what they declare. And He is God, there is no god but He! His is all praise, in the first and (in) the last, and His is the authority, and unto Him (only) ye shall be returned". (28:68-70)*

From all this, it can be concluded that the Day of Ghadir was chosen by the Messenger of Allah (s) as a feast, as after designating al-Imām 'Ali, and revelation of the verse *"This day have I perfected your religion for you..."* unto him, he declared: All praise is Allah's for perfecting the religion, and completing the favour, and the Lord's approval of my message and the *wilāyah* (mastership) of 'Ali ibn Abi Tālib after me.[56] Then he arranged for him a congratulation meeting, sitting (s) inside a tent, making Ali to sit beside him, commanding all Muslims, including his wives, the mothers of the faithful, to enter upon him in crowds and congratulate him for his post, and greet him for receiving the leadership of the faithful. And so did people whatever they were commanded to, with Abu Bakr and 'Umar being among those congratulating Amir al-Mu'minin 'Ali ibn Abi Tālib on that occasion. They came to him exclaiming: Congratulations! O son

---

[56] Al-Hākim al-Hasakāni reported from Abu Sa'id al-Khudri his interpretation of the āyah; and al-Hafiz Abu Nu'aym al-'Isfahāni in his book: *Mā nazala min al-Qur'ān fi `Ali.*

of Abu Tālib, within a day and night you became our master, and mawlā of every believing man and woman.[57]

When Hassan ibn Thābit, the poet of the Messenger (may Allah's peace and benediction be upon him and his Progeny), came to know of the Prophet's gladness and delightness (of the good tidings) at that day, he said to him: Would you permit me, O Messenger of Allah, to recite on this occasion some (poetic) lines that you hear? He (s) said: Say, with Allah's blessing. You are still, O Hassan, supported by the sacred Essence as long as you keep on succouring us with your tongue.

Then he chanted, saying:[58]

On Ghadir Day their Prophet calls them.

At Khumm, so listen to the Messenger as he calls, ...

up to the other lines of the poem mentioned by the historians.[59]

But, despite this, Quraysh has chosen for itself (a caliph), disapproving that Prophethood and caliphate to be inside Banu Hāshim alone, so as they do injustice to their people by boasting and showing delightness, as was expressed by 'Umar ibn al-Khattāb during a conversation held between him and 'Abd Allāh ibn 'Abbās.[60]

---

[57] This episode was narrated by Imām Abu Hāmid al-Ghazāli in his book *Sirr al-'ālamin*, p. 5; and also by Imām Ahmad ibn Hanbal in his *Musnad*, vol. IV, 281; with Tabari in his Tafsir, vol. III, p. 428; beside al-Bayhaqi, al-Tha'labi, al-Dāraqutni, al-Fakhr al-Rāzi, and others.

[58] For complete poetry, visit: https://www.al-islam.org/ghadir/incident.htm

[59] Al-Hafiz Abu Nu'aym al-'Isbahāni, op. cit.; al-Khwārazmi al-Māliki in his *al-Manāqib*, p. 80; al-Kanji al-Shāfi'i in *Kifāyat al-tālib*; Jalāl al-Din al-Suyuti in his book *al-'Izdihār fimā 'aqadahu al-shu'arā'min al-'ash'ār*.

[60] *Tarikh al-Tabari*, vol. V, p. 31; *Tarikh Ibn al-'Athir*, vol. III, p. 31; *Sharh Nahj al-Balāghah*, of Ibn Abi al-Hadid, vol. II, p. 18.

No one tolerated to celebrate that feast (*'Id*) after its first anniversary, which was celebrated by the Prophet (s).

And when the text on caliphate is forgotten and ignored by people after lapse of only two months, with no one referring to it, so how about the anniversary of al-Ghadir that took place one year ago. But this *'Id* (feast) is related to that text regarding the caliphate (of 'Ali), in a way that when the text becomes oblivious and the cause vanishes, no trace of that feast will be left that can be mentioned.

This fact continued for long years, till right was restored to its owners after twenty-five years, when it was revived by Imām 'Ali anew after it was about to be obliterated totally. This was at Rahbah when he appealed to the Prophet's Companions, particularly those who attended *'Id al-Ghadir*, to stand up and bear witness before people concerning the *bay'ah* (swearing allegiance) of caliphate. Thereat thirty Companions, including sixteen Badris (those who participated in the Battle of Badr), stood up and gave testimony.[61] But whoever concealed the testimony and claimed forgetfulness—like Anas ibn Mālik, was inflicted by the prayer of 'Ali ibn Abi Tālib—could never leave his place but affected with leprosy, weeping and saying: I am befallen by the prayer of the upright bondman (*al-'Abd al-Sālih*) because I have concealed his witness.[62] In this way Abu al-Hasan established the proof upon this *Ummah*. Ever since to the present time, and upto the Doomsday, the Shi'ah celebrate the anniversary of the Ghadir Day, which they hold as the greatest feast (*al-'id al-akbar*). True, it is so, since it being the day in which Allah has perfected for us the religion, and completed unto us the favour, and chosen for us Islam to be the religion, being a day of great position with Allah, and His

---

[61] Ahmad ibn Hanbal in his *Musnad*, vol. IV, p. 370, and vol. I, p. 119; al-Nasā'i in *al-Khasā'is*, p. 19; *Kanzal-'ummāl*, vol. VI, p. 397; Ibn Kathir in his *Tarikh*, vol. V, p. 211; Ibn al-'Athir in *Usd al-ghābah*, vol. IV, p. 28; Ibn Hajar al-'Asqalāni in *al-'Isābah*, vol. II, p. 408; al-Suyuti in *Jam' al-jawāmi'*.

[62] Al-Haythami in *Majma' al-Zawā'id*, vol. IX, p. 106; Ibn Kathir in his *Tarikh*, vol. V, p. 211; Ibn al-'Athir in *Usd al-Ghābah*, Vol.

Messenger, and the faithful. Some of Ahl al-Sunnah *'ulamā'* are reported to have said on the authority of Abu Hurayrah that he said: When the Messenger of Allah (s) took 'Ali by the hand and said: Of whomever I am his master, 'Ali also is his master...up to the end of the sermon, Allah—the Almighty and the Glorious—revealed this verse: "This day have I perfected for you, your religion, and have completed My favour on you, and chosen for you Islam (to be) the religion", whereat Abu Hurayrah said: It is the Day of Ghadir Khumm; whoever fasts on the day of 18th of Dhu al-Hijjah, it will be recorded for him as if he fasted sixty months.[63]

Concerning the narrations of the Shi'ah reported from Ahl al-Bayt Imāms (peace be upon them), with regard to the excellences of that day, you can say what you like. And all the praise is Allah's for bestowing guidance upon us, when making us among those adhering to the guardianship (*wilāyah*) of Amir al-Mu'minin and celebrating the Feast of Ghadir *('Id al-Ghadir)*.

To sum up, the *Hadith al-Ghadir* (*of Whomever I am his master [mawlā], 'Ali also is his master. O Allah, befriend whoever befriends him and be the enemy of his enemy, and help whoever helps him and forsake whoever forsakes him, and keep the haqq (truth) always with him*) is a tradition, or rather a great historical event upon whose reporting all the Islamic *Ummah* has unanimously agreed. We have previously referred to three hundred and sixty of Ahl al-Sunnah *'ulamā'* with a far larger number from among the Shi'ah *'ulamā'*.

Whoever desires to get more details, is asked to refer to the book al-Ghadir of 'Allāmah al-Amini.

After this exposition, it is no wonder to see the Islamic *Ummah* divided into two sects: Ahl al-Sunnah and Shi'ah. The former adhering to the principle of *shurā* in the Saqifah of Banu Sa'idah, interpolating the express texts, contradicting thus the unanimously accepted *Hadith al-Ghadir*, and other texts.

---

[63] Ibn Kathir in his book *al-Bidāyah wa al-Nihāyah*, vol. V, p. 214.

Whereas the second sect adhered to those texts, never accepting any other alternative, and swore allegiance to the Twelve Imāms, never desiring to be removed from thence. True it is, as when I investigated into the school of Ahl al-Sunnah, especially the issue of caliphate, I saw the questions being based on surmise and exertion of opinion (*ijtihād*). All this is due to the fact that the rule of election is devoid of any definite evidence that the person we elect today being superior to others, since we are unaware of the traitor of the eyes, and that which the bosoms hide, And since we are combined in fact of emotions and partisanships and egoism harboured inside our hearts, which will play their effective role, when we are entrusted with the task of choosing one person from among many.

This thesis is not an imagination or an exaggeration, as anyone following up the idea of electing a caliph, will realize that this principle for which he propagates, has not been managed and will never succeed at all.

The example is clear in Abu Bakr, the head of shurā, who, despite attaining the post of caliphate (through choosing and *shurā*), rushed to appoint 'Umar ibn al-Khattāb as his successor, while being on deathbed, without resorting to the principle of *shurā*. Another example is 'Umar ibn al-Khattāb, who participated in founding the caliphate of Abu Bakr, announcing publicly, after Abu Bakr's demise, that swearing allegiance to Abu Bakr was a slip may Allah protect the Muslims against its evil.[64]

Then when 'Umar was stabbed, and was sure of his approaching hour, he hastened to nominate six persons to elect, in their turn, one from among them to the post of caliphate. He was certain that a dispute was to erupt among them despite their small number, companionship, precedence in embracing Islam, and extent of godliness and piety (*taqwā*) they had. Despite all this, it was evident that the act would arouse in them the human emotions against which no one being immune but the *ma'sum* (infallible). Therefore, for

---

[64] *Sahih al-Bukhāri*, vol. VIII, p. 26, "bāb rajm al-hublā min al-zinā".

settling the dispute, he preferred 'Abd al-Rahmān ibn 'Awf (over 'Ali) saying: When you differ, you should take the side of 'Abd al-Rahmān ibn 'Awf. But we observed afterwards that they chose al-Imām 'Ali to be a caliph over them, stipulating on him to rule according to the Book of Allah and the Sunnah of His Messenger and that of the Shaykhayn (Abu Bakr and 'Umar).Thereat 'Ali accepted the first condition, the Book of Allah and His Messenger's Sunnah, refusing the *sunnah* of the Shaykhayn[65] while both the conditions were accepted by 'Uthmān to whom they swore allegiance as a caliph. About this 'Ali said:

"...But good Heavens! What I to do with this 'Consultation'? Where was any doubt about me with regard to the first of them that I was now considered akin to these ones? But I remained low when they were low and flew high when they flew high. One of them turned against me because of his hatred and the other got inclined the other way due to his in-law relationship and this thing and that thing..."[66]

When these, though being the elect of Muslims and the upper class, are so affected by sentiments in a way they harbour grudge and partisanship between this thing and that thing, (in exposing this statement Muhammad 'Abduh says: Imām 'Ali refers to other purposes disdaining from mentioning them), say farewell to the world then.

But 'Abd al-Rahmān ibn 'Awf regretted later on his choice, being angry with 'Uthmān, charging him with breaking the promise, when noticing the bad consequences of his covenant. He was visited by the distinguished companions, then, who said to him: O 'Abd al-Rahmān, this is the making of your hands. He said to them: I have never thought him to be so, but I swear by Allah that I shall never talk to him at all. Then 'Abd al-Rahmān died while being at odds

---

[65] *Tarikh al-Tabari* and Ibn al-'Athir, after the death of 'Umar ibn al Khattāb and successorship of 'Uthmān.

[66] Muhammad `Abduh in *Sharh Nahj al-Balāghah*, Sermon no. 3.

with 'Uthmān, to the extent that it is reported that when 'Uthmān entered upon him to visit him in his illness, he ('Abd al-Rahmān) turned his face towards the wall, without talking to him.[67]

Then the known developments took place, which ended with the revolt against 'Uthmān that resulted in his murder, after which the *Ummah* returned again to elect another Caliph, when they chose 'Ali for this post. But what a pity for bondmen as the Islamic State faced a great turmoil, turning to be a stage for the hypocrites, and his ('Ali's) opposing and tyrannical foes who were covetous for assuming the rostrum of caliphate at any cost, and through any means, even by putting the innocent souls to death.

Throughout those twenty-five years (when 'Ali was deprived his right), the rules (*ahkām*) of Allah and His Messenger were changed, with Imām 'Ali finding himself in the midst of a tumultuous sea, clashing waves, pitchy darkness and overwhelming caprices. He spent the years of his caliphate in bloody wars imposed on him by the *Nakithin* (breakers of oath of allegiance), *Qasitin* (iniquitous) and *Mariqin* (renegades) that ended in his martyrdom. This while he was, feeling pity for the *Ummah* of Muhammad (s), for whom covetted the divorced (*taliq*) and son of the divorced, Mu'āwiyah ibn Abi Sufyān, and his likes such as 'Amr ibn al-'As, Mughirah ibn Shubah and Marwan ibn al-Hakam beside many others. The only thing that emboldened these people was the idea of consultation (*shurā*) and selection.

Thereat the *Ummah* of Muhammad (s) plunged into a sea of blood, with their insolents and wicked ones seizing their affairs, and the *shurā* turning to the mordacious king, and to Caesarism and Chosroism.

Then that era, which was called by them *al-Khilāfah al-Rāshidah* (the Rightly-guided Caliphate), and its four caliphs were called al-Rashidun (the Righty-guided) while in fact even those four did not

---

[67] *Tarikh al-Tabari* and Ibn al-'Athir, about the chronicles of the year 36 H.; Muhammad 'Abduh, *op. cit.*, vol. I, p. 88.

become caliphs through election and consultation (*shurā*), except Abu Bakr and 'Ali. Excluding Abu Bakr, since the oath of allegiance to him was a sudden lapse, without the presence of the opposition party as said nowadays, which was represented by 'Ali and the rest of Banu Hāshim, with those sharing their beliefs, no one to whom the oath of allegiance was sworn in the shurā and election, will be left but 'Ali ibn Abi Tālib, who was unwillingly acknowledged by Muslims, with some Sahābah remaining behind, but he neither imposed the allegiance upon them nor, threatened them.

It was Allah's will that 'Ali ibn Abi Tālib be the successor of the Messenger of Allah by a determination from Allah — the Glorified — and election by the Muslims, with the whole Islamic *Ummah* — Sunnah and Shi'ah-unanimously admitting his caliphate, with their disagreement concerning the caliphate of others as was commonly known. Alas, for people, had they accepted that which was chosen by Allah for them, they would have eaten from above their heads, and underneath their feet (ground), with Allah's bestowing over them blessings from the sky, and the Muslims' being the masters and leaders of the world, as willed by Allah if they follow Him:

"...for ye will overcome them if ye are (indeed) believers." (3:139)

But our manifest enemy, the accursed Iblis, addressed the Lord of Glory, by saying:

"Now, because Thou hast sent me astray, verily I shall lurk in ambush for them on Thy Right Path. Then I shall come upon them from before them and from behind them and from their right hands and from their left hands, and Thou wilt not find most of them beholden (unto Thee)". (7:16-17).

Any sane man observing nowadays the situation of Muslims all over the world, being obsequrious, unable to do anything, running after other countries, recognizing Israel which never recognizes them, nor even allowing them to enter Quds, that turned to be a capital for it. Making a glance at the homeland of Muslims today, we can see them being at the mercy of America and Russia, with their people being inflicted with poverty, starving to death, whereas the European dogs eating different kinds of meat and fish. There is neither might nor power but in Allah, the Most High, the Great.

The lady of women, Fātimah al-Zahrā' (may Allah's peace be upon her), when being at odds with Abu Bakr, delivering her famous sermon to the women of the Muhājirun (immigrants) and Ansār (helpers), prophesied at the end of her sermon about the fate of the *Ummah*, saying:

"By my life! Time is fecundated, so wait till it gives fruit, then milk pure blood and deadly poison, as much as that which fills up the vessel, and the followers of vanity will then be lost, and the latter shall recognize the consequence of what befell the earlier ones. Then renounce your world, and be undismayed for sedition, awaiting a sharp sword, and authority of a tyrannical aggressor, and an all-inclusive uproar, with despotism befalling you from the oppressors, rendering your shade so trivial, and your assemblage cut down. Alas for you, and where are you to go, while it has been made obscure to you, can we compel you to accept it when you are averse thereto."[68]

The lady of all women said the truth through her prophecy, as she is the offspring of Prophethood and source of message. Her words came true regarding the life of the *Ummah*, and it is not known that the destiny awaiting the *Ummah* may be uglier than the past, that is because they are averse to that which Allah has revealed, therefore made their actions fruitless.

The Significant Element in the Research

The important element to complement the research, that is worth mentioning and investigation and may be the sole objection that is raised most often is when the obstinates being dumbfounded by irrefutable arguments is when they resort to wondering and denying that a hundred thousand Companions attended the event of

---

[68] Al-Tabari in *Dalā'il al-'Imāmah*; Ibn Tayfur in *Balāghāt al-nisā*; 'Umar Ridā Kahhālah in *A'lām al-nisā*; Ibn Abi al-Hadid in *Sharh Nahj al-Balagha*

nominating Imām 'Ali (as a caliph). Did they all conspire to oppose and turn away from him, though some of them were the best of Companions, and most honourable of the *Ummah*! I was encountered with such a situation, in particular when carrying out my research, as I couldn't believe, nor would anyone, that the issue had its basis in this way. But when studying the issue with all its dimensions, no wonder will it remain in the minds, as the issue is not the way we imagine or as presented by Ahl al-Sunnah, as it is far from one hundred thousand Companions to contradict the Messenger's commandment, so how did the event got apparently lost in history?

First: Not all those who attended the oath of allegiance at al-Ghadir were living in al-Madinah, but only, as was supposed, three or four thousand of them. And when knowing that a large number among them were bondsmen, slaves and the oppressed (*mustad'fin*) who came to the Messenger of Allah (s) from numerous regions, having no tribe or clan in al-Madinah, like Ahl al-Siffah, only half of them, i.e. only two thousand are left, who themselves were faithful to and bounded by the chieftains and system of the clan to which they belonged. The Messenger of Allah took their recognizance on this, that whenever visited by any delegation he would entrust their head and master with their leadership. Thus a new term in Islam was found when they were called *Ahl al-Hall wa al-'Aqd* (men of resolution and decision).

Considering the meeting of al-Saqifah that was held immediately after the demise of the Messenger, we will come to know that those attending it who took the decision of electing Abu Bakr as caliph, were, at the most, less than one hundred in total. That was because none of the *Ansār*, people of al-Madinah, attended it except their masters and leaders. And this was true also for the Muhājirun, the Meccans: who migrated with the Messenger (s), of whom only three or four persons attended as the representatives for Quraysh. Sufficient be for us as a proof, is to imagine the size of al-Saqifah, as all of us are aware of the truth about al-Saqifah, that was present in every and each house, as it was not a hall for (holding) parties or a palace for convening conferences. We exaggerate when telling about the presence of a hundred persons at the Saqifah of Banu Sa'idah, so that the researcher may apprehend that hundred thousand companions were neither present nor had any knowledge of what happened in the Saqifah, but only after quite long time as there were neither telecommunications, nor wireless sets, nor satellites at that time.

Thus these chiefs concurred on nominating Abu Bakr, despite the objection of the Master of Ansār Sa'd ibn 'Ubādah, the head of Tribe of Khazraj, and his son Qays. But the overwhelming majority (as said nowadays) made pact and agreed on acknwoeldging him, though most of the Muslims of Madinah were absent at the Saqifah, with some of them being engaged in making preparations for the burial of the Messenger (s), or distracted by the news of his death, beside being threatened by 'Umar ibn al-Khattāb against announcing about his death.[69]

Added to this, the Messenger of Allah had mobilized most of the Companions under the command of Usāmah who were stationed at Jurf, neither attending the burial ceremonies of the Prophet (s) nor the gathering of al-Saqifah.

After all those events, is it reasonable that clan members dare to object their chieftain, especially that to him belongs the virtue and great honour with regard to the covenant he made, for which every tribe was striving and longing. Who knows, it is probable that they, one day, be honoured with the post of mastership over all Muslims, all over the world, since its legitimate owner was excluded, with the issue turning to be a *shurā*, of which they were frequently making use. So why wouldn't they be delighted at that or supporting it?

Second: When the men of resolution and decision, the Madinah dwellers, would confirm any matter, it would be infeasible for the distant far away people living in the outskirts of the Peninsula to declare any objection, while being unaware of what was going on

---

[69] *Sahih al-Bukhāri,* vol. IV, p. 1. 95.

during their absence, since the means of transportation in that era were primitive. Besides, they would imagine that as the Madinah-dwellers have lived during the lifetime of the Messenger of Allah, so they should be better aware of the new rulings and conditions that may be revealed at any hour and day. Then the chieftain who was far away of the capital had nothing to do with the caliphate, as for him it made no difference who is the caliph, would be whether Abu Bakr or 'Ali or anyone else, since the people of Makkah are better aware of its mountain passes. And that which mattered him more was preserving his post as the chieftain of his clan with no rival.

It is uncertain, whether someone of them did question about the matter looking up to the information but was silenced by the ruling system, either through temptation or intimidation. The incidence of Mālik ibn Nuwayrah, who refused to pay the *zakāt* (alms-due) to Abu Bakr, can be the best evidence proving it.

Anyone pursuing those events that took place in fighting the deniers of *zakāt*, during the caliphate of Abu Bakr, will certainly see many contradictions, never being convinced with what is reported by the historians, for the sake of safeguarding the dignity of the Sahābah, particularly the rulers among them.

Third: The element of surprise in the issue played a great role in admitting what is called today the "matter of act" or "status quo". We noticed how the meeting of al-Saqifah was held all of a sudden, away of the attention of the Companions who were busy arranging for the burial of the Messenger (s), among them were al-Imām 'Ali, al-'Abbas with the rest of Banu Hāshim, Miqdād, Salmān, Abu Dharr, Ammār and al-Zubayr, beside many others. When those who attended the Saqifah went out accompanying Abu Bakr to the mosque, calling for public oath of allegiance to him, and people were coming forward in groups and flocks voluntarily and forcibly, Imām 'Ali and his followers had not yet finished their Holy duty as prescribed by their sublime morals. It was improper for them to leave the Messenger of Allah without washing, shrouding and burial, hastening to the Saqifah to struggle for the caliphate.

As soon as they completed their obligation, the allegiance was already acknowledged for Abu Bakr, with whoever lingering behind being counted among those seditious renegading against the Muslims, that should be opposed or even killed by Muslims if necessary. Consequently, it is reported that 'Umar threatened to kill anyone refusing to swear allegiance to Abu Bakr, declaring: Kill him, he is seditious.[70] Then he threatened those who lingered in 'Ali's house to burn the house with whoever was inside it. Further, when we know the view of 'Umar ibn al-Khattāb regarding the oath of allegiance (*bay'ah*), we will come to recognize the solutions of many bewildering enigmas.

He held that the validity of allegiance could be established only when any of the Muslims manages to comply with it, whereat all the others should follow and obey him, and anyone lingering behind was considered out of the fold of Islam and so should be slain.

Herein his words about himself, when referring to *bay'ah* (allegiance), as reported by al-Bukhāri in his *Sahih*.[71] "He said: It is reported concerning what happened at the Saqifah:

Then there was a hue and cry among the gathering and their voices rose so that I was afraid there might be great disagreement, so I said, O Abu Bakr! Hold your hand out.' He held his hand out and I swore allegiance to him, and then all the emigrants swore allegiance and so did the Ansar afterwards. And so we became victorious over Sa'd bin 'Ubada (whom Al-Ansar wanted to make a ruler). One of the Ansar said, 'You have killed') Sa'd bin 'Ubada.' I replied, 'Allah has killed Sa'd bin 'Ubada.''

'Umar added, "By Allah, apart from the great tragedy that had happened to us (i.e., the death of the Prophet), there was no greater

---

[70] *Ibid.*, vol. VIII, p. 26; *Tarikh al-Tabari*; *Tarikh al-khulafā'* of Ibn Qutaybah.

[71] *Sahih al-Bukhāri*, vol. VIII, p. 28, Chapter 31, "bāb rajm al-hublā min al-zinā idhā uhsinat. Hadith # 6830.

problem than the allegiance sworn to Abu Bakr because we were afraid that if we left the people, they might give the allegiance after us to one of their men, in which case we would have given them our consent for something against our real wish, or would have opposed them and caused great trouble. So, if any person gives the allegiance to somebody (to become a caliph) without consulting the other Muslims, then the one he has selected should not be given the allegiance lest both of them should be killed."

Thus, the issue according to 'Umar's view is not election or nomination or consultation (*shurā*), but it suffices that one from among the Muslims hastens towards allegiance so as to be a proof for the others. So he said to Abu Bakr. Bring forth your hand O Abu Bakr. Then he (Abu Bakr) extended his hand and 'Umar swore allegiance to him without any consultation or meditation, for fear of that another one might hasten towards it. 'Umar has expressed this opinion by saying: That which made us worried was that people may depart us with no allegiance being sworn, so as to swear allegiance to a man from among them after that ('Umar feared that the *Ansār* [Helpers] might outstrip him and acknowledge someone from among them). This fact becomes even more explicit when he says: Thereat only two alternatives were left before us: either to acknowledge unwillingly the one they acknowledged (as a caliph), or to contradict them and cause corruption to prevail.[72]

To be equitable in our judgement and precise in investigation, we have to admit that 'Umar ibn al-Khattāb has changed his viewpoint concerning the oath of allegiance (*bay'ah*) in the last days of his life. That was when a man entered upon him, during his last *hajj* pilgrimage, with the presence of 'Abd al-Rahmān ibn 'Awf, and said: O Amir al-Muminin, have you heard so and so say: Had 'Umar died, I would have sworn allegiance to so and so. By Allah, the oath of allegiance to Abu Bakr was but a slip that was done. This aroused

---

[72] *Sahih al-Bukhāri*, vol. VIII, p. 26.

'Umar's anger who stood and addressed people, after returning to Madinah, saying in particular:

"I was informed that so and so among you says: By Allah had 'Umar died I would have acknowledged so and so. No one should be self-conceited to say that the acknowledgement to Abu Bakr was but a slip that was done, as even it was truly so but Allah safeguarded (us) against its evil...[73] Then he says: Whoever swears allegiance to anyone without consultation with other Muslims, neither be nor the one to whom he sworn allegiance will be acknowledged lest they should be killed..."[74]

Would that 'Umar ibn al-Khattāb was of this opinion on the Day of Saqifah, never overruling the Muslims by his swearing of allegiance to Abu Bakr, that was a slip against whose evil Allah has protected us, as he himself testified. But far it be for 'Umar to have such a new opinion, since he issued a death sentence against himself and his comrade, when disclosing it in his novel viewpoint: "Anyone swearing allegiance to some man without consulting the Muslims, neither he nor the one to whom he swore allegiance shall be acknowledged, lest they should be killed both."

That which we should know more, being the reason why had 'Umar, in the last days of his life, changed his opinion though he was aware, more than others, that his new opinion had blasted the acknowledgement to Abu Bakr outrightly. Since it was him who hastened to swear allegiance to him without any consultation with Muslims so as to be a slip, and he himself overturned his own acknowledgement, as he attained to caliphate through nomination by Abu Bakr on his deathbed, without consulting other Muslims. This act made some Companions enter upon Abu Bakr disapproving his decision in appointing a stern and rude man as a ruler over

---

[73] *Sahih al-Bukhāri*, vol. VIII, p. 26.

[74] *Ibid*.

them.[75] And when 'Umar went out to read for the people the letter of Abu Bakr, a man questioned him: O Abu Hafs, what does the letter contain? He replied: I know not, but I shall be the first to listen and obey. The man said: But, by Allah, I know what it does contain: You made him a ruler in the first year, and now he has appointed you ruler this year.[76]

This exactly resembles Imām 'Ali's saying to 'Umar (when observing him compelling people by duress to swear allegiance to Abu Bakr):

"Prepare a scheme whose half shall be yours, and reinforce it for him today, he will recompense you tomorrow."[77]

Of significance is to know the reason why 'Umar changed his opinion regarding allegiance! I think that he came to know that some of the Sahābah were intending to swear allegiance to 'Ali ibn Abi Tālib after the death of 'Umar, the fact that was never to be accepted by 'Umar, who contradicted the explicit texts, opposing the Messenger's writing them that order.[78] As he came to know its content, till he accused him (s) of hallucination, threatening people against disclosing his death[79] lest that the people should rush to swear allegiance to 'Ali. Then he arranged for acknowledging allegiance to Abu Bakr, forcing people to it by duress, threatening to kill whoever renouncing this allegiance,[80] all this for the only reason being excluding 'Ali from caliphate. So how would he accept

---

[75] *Tarikh al-Tabari*, the chapter on successorship of 'Umar ibn al-Khattāb; Ibn Abi al-Hadid in *Sharh al-Nahj al-Balagha*, vol. I.

[76] Ibn Qutaybah in *al-'Imāmah wa al-Sisāyah*, vol. I, p. 25, "bāb marad Abi Bakr wa istikhlāfihi 'Umar".

[77] Ibn Qutaybah, *op. cit.*, vol. I, p. 18.

[78] *Sahih Muslim*, vol. V, p. 75, kitāb al-wasiyyah; *Sahih al-Bukhāri*, vol. VII, p. 9.

[79] *Sahih al-Bukhāri*, vol. IV, p. 195.

[80] *Ibid.*, V ol. VIII, p. 28; *Tarikh al-khulafā'*, vol. I, p. 19.

someone to say that he would acknowledge so and so after the death of 'Umar, especially that this one (whose name was kept secret, and he might be among the great companions) might argue with what 'Umar did in swearing allegiance to Abu Bakr, when saying: By Allah, the swearing of Allegiance to Abu Bakr was but a slip and was done with. That is, despite its occurrence all of a sudden, without awareness of the Muslims or consulting them, but it was done and came true. That is why 'Umar allowed himself to do it with Abu Bakr, so how wouldn't it be permissible for him to do it in the same way with so and so. It is noticed here that Ibn 'Abbās, 'Abd al-Rahmān ibn 'Awf and 'Umar ibn al-Khattāb abstain from disclosing the name of that utterer with the name of the one he intended to swear allegiance to. And since these two were of great importance for the Muslims, so we observed how 'Umar got angry for this saying, embarking on the next Friday to address the people, by pointing out the issue of caliphate, surprising them with his new opinion, to close the door before that who wanted to repeat the same slip as this would be for the good of his foe. But out of this discussion, we understood that this statement being not only the opinion of so and so, but also of so many Companions. That is why al-Bukhāri is reported to have said: So 'Umar got angry and said: God-willing, I shall address people tonight, to warn those intending to usurp them their affairs...[81]

Then, 'Umar's changing his opinion concerning the oath of allegiance, was only a sign of objection against those intending to seize the people's affairs and swear allegiance to 'Ali, the fact that could never be accepted by 'Umar, since he was of the opinion that caliphate being one of people's affairs, and not a right for 'Ali ibn Abi Tālib. Had this belief been correct, why would he have allowed himself to usurp people of their affairs after the demise of the Prophet (s), rushing to swear allegiance to Abu Bakr without consulting the Muslims?

---

[81] *Ibid.*, vol. VIII, p. 25.

The stand of Abu Hafs ('Umar) toward Abu al-Hasan ('Ali) is widely known, being excluding him away from power. We have reached this conclusion not only through his previous sermon, but anyone following up the course of history can realize that 'Umar ibn al-Khattāb was the actual 'ruler even during Abu Bakr's caliphate. So we noticed how Abu Bakr sought permission of Usāmah ibn Zayd to let 'Umar ibn al-Khattāb stay with him to help him undertake the caliphate affair.[82] Nevertheless, 'Ali ibn Abi Tālib was kept away from any responsibility, as they have neither charged him with any post, or governorship, nor given him commandment of any army, nor entrusted him treasury, throughout the caliphate of Abu Bakr, 'Umar and 'Uthmān, and all of us know what was the status of 'Ali ibn Abi Tālib was during the life of Prophet of God (s).

Stranger than this, we are informed by history books that 'Umar, on his death bed, regretted the death of Abu 'Ubaydah ibn al-Jarrāh or Sālim the master of Abu Hudhayfah, and their absence so as to nominate them to succeed him. But, undoubtedly, on remembering that he changed his opinion regarding this *bay'ah* (oath of allegiance), considering it a slip and a usurpation of the Muslims' affairs, he would have no choice but to invent a new method for swearing allegiance, to be an intermediate compromise. So that no one would take the initiative and swear allegiance to whomever he considers competent for it, compelling people to follow his guide. That is, exactly as was done by him for Abu Bakr, and by Abu Bakr for him, or as intended to be done by so and so who was expecting 'Umar's death to swear allegiance to his favorite, but all this being impossible after it (*bay'ah*) was considered by 'Umar as a slip and usurpation. Also, it is infeasible for him to leave the affair to be determined through *shurā* among the Muslims, while he attended the meeting of al-Saqifah after the demise of the Prophet (s), witnessing by his own eyes the dispute which could result in taking away of lives and shedding of blood.

---

[82] As it is confirmed by Ibn Sa'd in his *Tabaqāt*, and most of the historians who referred to the contingent (*sariyyah*) of Usāmah ibn Zayd.

At last he contrived the idea of Ashab al-Shurā or the six men committee, who were entitled alone to elect the caliph, with no room for anyone to share them in this right. 'Umar was well aware that dispute would surely erupt among these six men, the fact prompting him to recommend them to be, in case of difference, on the side of 'Abd al-Rahmān ibn 'Awf even if this could lead to killing of those three opposing 'Abd al-Rahmān. This be in case of occurrence of split and the six being divided into two groups, which could never happen, since 'Umar knew well that Sa'd ibn Abi Waqqās being the cousin of 'Abd al-Rahmān, and both belong to Banu Zuhrah, and that Sa'd would never love 'Ali, harbouring grudge against him as 'Ali killed his uncles from 'Abd Shams. Further, 'Umar was quite aware that 'Abd al-Rahmān ibn 'Awf, being the brother-in-law of 'Uthmān, as his wife Umm Kulthum was 'Uthmān's sister, and that Talha having inclination toward 'Uthmān due to relations between them as reported by some narrators. The evidence proving his inclination toward 'Uthmān can be sought in his turning away from 'Ali, due to his belonging to the Tribe of Taym, and it was known that many disputes were there between Banu Hāshim and Banu Taym, due to Abu Bakr's ambition to attain caliphate.[83] 'Umar was aware of all this, the reason for which he chose these people in particular.

All these six people who were selected by 'Umar, were from Quraysh, and from among Muhājirun (Emigrants) with no one from the Ansār (Helpers), and each one of them represented and headed a tribe of great importance and influence. They were:

1. 'Ali ibn Abi Tālib, chief of Banu Hāshim

2. 'Uthmān ibn 'Affān, chief of Banu Umayyah

3. 'Abd al-Rahmān ibn 'Awf, chief of Banu Zuhrah

4. Sa'd ibn Abi Waqqās, from Banu Zuhrah and his uncles belonged to Banu Ummayyah

---

[83] Muhammad 'Abduh, *op. cit.*, vol. I, p. 88.

5. Talhah ibn 'Ubayd Allāh, the chief of Banu Taym

6. Al-Zubayr ibn al-'Awwām, the son of Safiyyah— the Messenger's aunt — and he was the husband of Asmā' the daughter of Abu Bakr.

These were the men of resolution and determination with their judgement being obligatory upon all Muslims, whether being inhabitants of the metropolis (centre of caliphate) or others from all over the Islamic world at that time. Then all Muslims had no choice but to adhere and obey, without any dispute, and death will be the fate of anyone refusing or contradicting the commandment. This is specifically the point we want the reader to be aware of, beforehand, with regard to concealing the news about the text of *Hadith al-Ghadir*.

Knowing the mentalities, emotions and ambitions of these six men, 'Umar had in fact nominated 'Uthmān ibn 'Affān for caliphate, as he was aware that the majority of them were averse to accepting 'Ali. Otherwise, why and according to which right he preferred 'Abd al-Rahmān ibn 'Awf to 'Ali ibn Abi Tālib?...While the Muslims have ever since been disputing about the superiority of 'Ali and Abu Bakr, with no one daring to make contrast between 'Ali and 'Abd al-Rahmān ibn 'Awf.

At this point I should make a halt to question Ahl a-Sunnah who believe in the Shurā principle, and all free-thinking men thus: How do you reconcile between the shurā (consultation) in its Islamic sense and this notion that indicates nothing but stubborness since it was him ('Umar) who chose those people not the Muslims? And if his attaining to caliphate be a slip, how would he permit himself to impose those six men upon Muslims?

It seems that 'Umar believed the caliphate to be a right for the *Muhājirun* (Emigrants) alone, without being disputed by others over this right. Moreover, 'Umar held, like Abu Bakr, that caliphate being a right owned by Quraysh alone, as among the *Muhājirun* some were found who didn't belong to Quraysh, or rather who were non-Arabs.

So neither Salmān al-Fārsi, nor 'Ammār ibn Yāsir, nor Bilal al-Habashi, nor Suhayb al-Rumi, nor Abu Dharr al-Ghifāri, nor thousands of the Sahābah who didn't belong to Quraysh, were entitled to be eligible for the post of caliphate.

This is not being just a claim! Never and far from that, but it is their belief as recorded in history books and reported by narrators from them directly. Let's refer to the very sermon reported by al-Bukhāri and Muslim in their *Sahihs*:

'Umar ibn al-Khattāb is reported to have said: I intended to speak, when forging an article I wanted to lay before Abu Bakr, with showing some cajolery. As I intended to begin my speech, Abu Bakr said: Take it easy, so I didn't like to arouse his anger, and kept silent. Then Abu Bakr spoke, showing more clemency and solemnity than me. By Allah, he never spared any word I liked in my falsification but mentioning the like of or better than it through his intuition, till he paused for a while and then said: You truly deserve all the good traits I did mention to be owned by you (addressing the Ansār), and this matter is never realized but to belong to this locale of Quraysh.[84]

Thus, it becomes explicit that Abu Bakr and 'Umar were never believing in the principle of shurā and election. Some historians are reported to have said that Abu Bakr argued with the *Ansār* (Helpers) about the Messenger's *hadith*: "Verily caliphate is in Quraysh", which being a *sahih* (correct) tradition whereof there is no doubt, whose real text (as reported by al-Bukhāri and Muslim and all *Sihāh* of the Sunnah, and the Shi'ah books) being thus:

The Messenger of Allah (s) said: *"The successors after me are twelve ones, all being from Quraysh."*

More explicit than this *hadith*, is the following saying uttered by the Messenger (s):

---

[84] *Sahih Muslim*, "bāb al-wasiyyah".

"This matter (caliphate) will verily continue to be in Quraysh as long as only two men survive,"[85] and his saying: *"Mankind being only followers of Quraysh in good and evil."*[86]

If all Muslims totally believe in these traditions, how would anyone dare to claim that he (s) had left the issue to be determined through consultation (*shurā*) among Muslims, to choose whoever they wish to appoint?

There is no way to get rid of this contradiction but through adherence to the sayings of Ahl al-Bayt Imāms and their followers (Shi'ah), with some of Ahl al-Sunnah *'ulamā'* who affirm that the Messenger of Allah (s) has determined the caliphs, defining them by number and names. Henceforth we can also conceive the position of 'Umar and his endeavour to confine caliphate within Quraysh, as 'Umar was known for exerting his opinion (*ijtihād*) against the clear orders, even during the lifetime of the Prophet (s). The best evidences that prove our claim can be sought in the Peace Treaty of Hudaybiyyah,[87] performing prayer (*salāt al-mayyit*) on hypocrites,[88] the Thursday misfortune,[89] and his forbidding announcement of the good tidings of Paradise.[90] So no wonder to see him impose his opinion, after the demise of the Prophet (s), regarding the *hadith* text of the caliphate, seeing no obligation in accepting the determination of 'Ali ibn Abi Tālib who was the youngest of Quraysh, and restricting the right to successorship in Quraysh alone. This fact prompted 'Umar to choose, before his death, six men from among the masters of Quraysh to reconcile between the Prophet's traditions and his own viewpoint regarding the right of Quraysh alone to

---

[85] *Ibid.*, vol. VI, pp. 2, 3; *Sahih al-Bukhāri*, vol. VIII, p. 27.

[86] *Ibid.*, vol. VI, pp. 2, 3; *Sahih al-Bukhāri*, vol. VIII, p. 27.

[87] *Sahih al-Bukhari*, vol. III, p. 182

[88] *Sahih al-Bukhāri*, vol. II, p. 76.

[89] *Ibid.*, vol. I, p. 37.

[90] *Ibid.*, vol. I, "bāb man laqiya Allāh bi al-'imām wa huwa ghayr shākk fih dakhala al-jannah, p. 45.

caliphate. Including 'Ali among the other men, with pre-knowledge that they would never elect him, was a plan contrived by 'Umar to force 'Ali to agree with them in the political trickery, as called nowadays, and so that no argument (*hujjah*) would be left for his ('Ali's) followers and supporters believing in his superiority and precedence. But all this was later elucidated by Imām 'Ali ('a) in a sermon before the public, saying in this regard:

"...Nevertheless, I remained patient despite length of period and stiffness of trial, till when he went away (of death) he put matter (of caliphate) in a group and regarded me to be one of them. But good Heavens! What had I to do with this consultation"? Where was any doubt about me with regard to the first of them that I was now considered akin to these ones? But I remained low when they were low and flew high when they flew high. One of them turned against me because of his hatred and the other got inclined the other way due to his in-law relationship and this thing and that things..." [91]

Fourth: Imām 'Ali (peace be upon him) has argued and reasoned with them by everything, but all was in vain. Should 'Ali beg allegiance from the people who turned their faces away from him, and whose hearts inclined toward other than him. Either out of envy for the favours Allah has bestowed upon him, or out of grudge against him because he killed their valiants and relatives, shattered their heroes, coercing them to kneel down, subduing them and destroying their pride through his powerful sword and bravery till making them surrender and embrace Islam. Nevertheless, he remained lofty, defending his cousin, fearing no censure in Allah's way, from those who censure, never being frustrated by any of the vanities of the world. The Messenger of Allah (s) was fully aware of all this, extolling, throughout opportune times, the virtues of his brother and cousin, so as to make them love him, saying in this respect:

---

[91] *Nahj al-Balāgha*, Sermon no. 3. Available at: https://www.al-islam.org/nahjul-balagha-part-1-sermons

To love "'Ali is faith and hating him is hypocrisy." [92]

And: *"'Ali is from me and I am from him."* [93]

He also said: *"'Ali is the wali (guardian) of every believer after me."* [94]

Further: *"'Ali is the gate of the city of my knowledge and the father of my children."* [95]

He said too: *"'Ali is the master of the Muslims and Imām of the pious, and leader of the immaculate pure ones."* [96]

But all these traditions have, unfortunately, increased them in jealously and rancour, the fact prompting the Messenger of Allah (s) to summon him, before his death, embracing him and weeping, with saying: *"O 'Ali, I know that there are vindictive feelings harboured inside the bosoms of people which they will divulge for you after me. If they swear allegiance to you, accept it, otherwise you should forbear till you meet me while being wronged."* [97]

So Abu al-Hasan's keeping patient, after acknowledging Abu Bakr (as a caliph), was only in response and submission to the Messenger's order to him, the fact implying unconcealed wisdom.

Fifth: Added to all this, any Muslim, when reading the Holy Qur'ān, contemplating in its verses, will verily recognize, out of its stories dealing with the earlier nations and peoples, that they were inflicted with more calamites than us. He can witness how Qābil (Cain) killed Hābil (Abel) out of injustice and maltreat; with Noah,

---

[92] *Sahih Muslim*, vol. I, p. 61.
[93] *Sahih al-Bukhāri*, vol. III, p. 168.
[94] *Musnad Ahmad*, vol. V, p. 35; *Mustadrak al-Hākim*, vol. III, p124
[95] *Mustadrak al-Hākim*, vol. III, p. 126.
[96] *Muntakhab Kanz al-'ummāl*, vol. V, p. 34.
[97] Al-Tabari, *al-Riyād al-nādirah fi manāqib al-'ashrah*, "bāb fadā'il 'Ali ibn Abi Tālib".

the grandfather of prophets, could never find from among his folk but a very few, after a total of a thousand years of struggle and strival, with his wife and son being among the disbelievers. Besides, in the village of Lot only one family of believers could be found, and the folk of Pharaoh who were haughty in the land and enslaved mankind, when one believer among them is found, he would conceal his faith, and the brothers of Joseph, the sons of Jacob, though being many, conspire to kill their younger brother not due to any sin he perpetrated but out of jealousy since he was dearer to their father than them. Moreover, another example is in the children of Israel, whom Allah has delivered through Moses, cleaving for them the sea and causing their enemies — Pharaoh and his hosts — to drown, without charging them the pains of fighting. As soon as going out of the sea and before their feet being dried, they came toward some people devoted unto idols, worshipping them, saying to them: O Moses! Make for us a god even as they have gods. He said: *Lo! You are a folk who know not.*

On his going to the appointed tryst of his Lord, making his brother Harun (Aaron) as a successor over them, they contrived a plot against him intending to slay him, declaring disbelief in Allah and worshipping the calf, killing after that Allah's prophets, whereat Allah the Exalted said:

"What! (and yet) whenever (thereafter) an apostle came unto you with that which yourselves desired not, swelled ye with pride, some (of the apostles) ye belied (as imposters) and some ye slew." (2:87)

Also we witness our master Yahyā ibn Zakariyyā, despite his being a prophet (of Allah) and a chaste from among the virtuous ones, being slained and his head being gifted to one of the strumpets of Banu Israel.

And again, the Jews and Christians conspired to slaughter and crucify our master Jesus, and the *Ummah* of Muhammad (s) mobilize an army of thirty thousand to kill al-Husayn, the basil (*rayhānah*) of the Messenger of Allah (s) and master of the youth of Heavens, who was accompanied with only seventy of his companions. Then they slew them all, including even his suckling children in Karbala.

So what causes wonder after all this? Is there any wonder after the Prophet's saying to his Companions: *"You shall verily follow the sunan (conducts) of those who were before you span-by-span and cubit-by-cubit, and even if they enter the lizard hole you will certainly go inside it."* They asked: *Do you mean the Jews and Christians?* He replied: *But who would be then (other than them)??"* [98]

Where from to come the wonder while we read what is reported by al-Bukhāri and Muslim from the Messenger of Allah (s): *"On the Doomsday my Companions will be brought unto the left, whereat I would inquire: Whereto (are they brought)? The reply will come: To the Hellfire, and I will say: O my lord, these are my Companions, then it will be said to me. You are unaware of what they have done after you. Thereat I will say: Remote be whoever changed after me, and I can't see anyone delivered from among them except as few as the forsaken cattle."* [99]

What wonder when listening to the *hadith* uttered by the Prophet (s): *"My Ummah will be divided, after me, into seventy-three sects, all will go to Hellfire except only one."* [100]

And the Most High, the Lord of Glory, and Exaltness, Who knows what is kept in bosoms, disclosed the truth when saying:

"And most believe (it) not, though thou desire it." (12:103)

"Nay! he hath brought unto them the Truth, but most of them hate the Truth." (23:70)

---

[98] *Sahih al-Bukhāri*, vol. IV, p. 144, and vol. VIII, p 151.
[99] *Ibid.*, vol. VI, p. 117, Bab al-Tafsir; *Sahih Muslim*, "bāb al-hawd".
[100] *Sunan Ibn Mājah*, "kitāb al-fitan", vol. II, *hadith* No. 3993; *Musnad Ahmad*, vol. III, p. 120; *Sunan al-Tirmidhi*, "kitāb al-'imān".

"Indeed have We brought unto you with the truth but most of you unto the truth were hateful." (43:78)

"Be it known verily God's is what is in the heavens and the earth; Be it (also) known, verily, God's promise is true, but most of them know not." (10:55)

"...They allure you with (the sweet words of) their mouths while their hearts are averse (from you), and most of them are transgressors." ((Tawbah, 9:8)

"...Verily, God is the Lord of grace for mankind, but most of them thank not." (10:60)

"They recognize the bounties of God, and yet they deny them, and most of them are infidels." (16:83)

"And indeed We distribute it (water) to them that may be (thankfully) mindful, but content not the great number of the people but to be thankless." (25:50)

"And believe not most of them, in God, except as polytheists." (12:106)

"...Nay! most of them know not the truth, so they turn aside." (21:24)

"What Wonder ye then at this statement? And laugh ye and not weep? And yet sport ye (negligently)?" (53:59-61)

Grief and Sorrow

How shouldn't I be grieved? Or rather why shoulnd't every Muslim sigh when looking into these realities, demonstrating the losses that befell the Muslims as a result of excluding al-Imām 'Ali from the post of caliphate, for which the Messenger of Allah has designated, depriving the *Ummah* from his sagacious leadership and abundant sciences.

When any Muslim considers the matter without any fanaticism or prejudice, he will see him ('Ali) to be the most knowledgeable man after the Messenger (s). History records and testifies that all the *Sahābah 'ulamā'* have asked him the solution of the judicial questions for which they couldn't find answers, and it is reported that 'Umar ibn al-Khattāb said more than seventy times: "Had 'Ali not been there, 'Umar would have perished,"[101] whereas he ('a) has never asked anyone of them, at all.

Further, history admits that 'Ali ibn Abi Tālib was the bravest and strongest among the Sahābah, and in many times the valorous among the Companions fled the fighting and battle-fields, while he resisted and took a firm stand throughout all the incidents and wars. A sufficient evidence would be the badge of honour granted to him by the Messenger of Allah (s) saying: *"Verily I shall give my standard to a man who loves Allah and His Messenger and is loved by Allah and His Messenger, bearing down upon the enemy, not runaway, whose faith was put to test by Allah,"*[102] Each one of the Companions longed and desired to be the one meant by this tradition, but he (s) handed it to 'Ali ibn Abi Tālib.

To sum up, the traits of knowledge, power and bravery distinguishing al-Imām 'Ali, being a fact known by all people, near and far, with no any dispute. Regardless of all the texts indicating his Imāmah, expressly and allusively, the Holy Qur'ān recognizes no one to be competent for leadership and Imāmah except the bold, strong scholar (*'alim*). Regarding the obligation of following the 'ulamā', Allah the Glorified and Exalted, said:

---

[101] *Manaqib al-Khwārazmi*, p. 48; *al-'Isti'āb*, vol. III, p. 39; *Tadhkirat al-Sibt*, p. 87; *Matālib al-sa'ul*, p. 13; *Tafsir al-Naysāburi, on Surah al-'Ahqāf; Fayd al-Qadir*, vol. IV, p. 357.

[102] *Sahih al-Bukhāri*, vol. IV, pp. 5, 12, and vol. V, pp. 76, 77; *Sahih Muslim*, vol. VII, p. 121, "bāb fadā'il Ali ibn Abi Tālib."

"...Is then He Who guideth unto truth more worthy to be followed or he who himself goeth not aright unless he is guided? What then hath befallen you? How (ill) ye judge?" (10:35)

And as regards the obligation of the leadership of the valiant powerful scholar, the Almighty said:

"...They said, "How can the kingdom be his, over us, whereas we are more rightful for it than he while he is not gifted with abundance of wealth." he said" "Verily, God hath chosen him over you and hath increased him abundantly in knowledge and physique; and verily, God granteth His kingdom unto whomso He pleaseth; God is Omniscient and All-Knowing." (2:247)

Allah — the Glorified — has increased al-Imām 'Ali, other than all the Sahābah, abundantly in knowledge, making him truly 'the gate of the city of knowledge,' and the sole reference for the Sahābah after the demise of the Messenger of Allah (may Allah's peace and benediction be upon him and his Progeny). And whenever the Companions felt unable to find a solution for any questin, they used to say: "No problem is there but to be solved by Abu al-Hasan." [103]

He increased him abundantly in physique, in a way he was the conquerring lion of Allah, and that his might and bravery became an example to be followed by all generations. This fact reached an extent that historians reported miracle-like stories, such as pulling out Khybar Gate, which twenty Companions failed to move later on[104] and extracting the great Idol of Hubal,[105] from over the roof of the Ka'bah, and shifting the huge rock which all the army stood unable to displace,[106] beside other well-known narrations.

---

[103] *Manāqib al-Khwārazmi*, p. 58; *Tadhkirat al-Sibt*, p. 87; Ibn al-Maghāzili, *Tarjumat 'Ali*, p. 79.

[104] *Sharh al-Nahj*, Ibn Abi al-Hadid, in the introduction.

[105] *Sharh al-Nahj*, Ibn Abi al-Hadid, in the introduction.

[106] *Sharh al-Nahj*, Ibn Abi al-Hadid, in the introduction.

Belief In Imamate by Both Sects

The Prophet (s) has, time and again, extalted his cousin 'Ali manifesting his honour and virtues throughout all occasions, referring to his traits and merits. Once he said:

"This man ('Ali) is my brother, and executor and successor after me; so you should adhere to and obey him."[107] Once again he said: *"Your position to me is exactly like that of Aaron to Moses, except that there is no prophet after me."*[108]

Another time he said:

"Whoever desires to live my life, and to die my death, and dwell the Land of the Leal (Paradise) with which my Lord promised me, he should follow the guide of 'Ali ibn Abi Tālib, as he would either take you out of guidance nor bring you into misguidance (*dalālah*)."[109]

Anyone following out the conduct (*sirah*) of the Holy Messenger (may Allah's peace and benediction be upon him and his Progeny), will verily realize that he was not satisfied with only disclosing sayings and traditions, but also his words were incarnated in his acts and deeds. This is evident through the fact that he never made anyone of the Sahābah a commander over 'Ali, though investing with authority some of them over others, as in the case of giving commandment to Abu Bakr and 'Umar over 'Amr ibn al-'Aæ during the Battle of Dhāt al-Salāsil.[110]

Another example also, is when he made the young man, Usāmah ibn Zayd, a commander over all of them, within the battalion of Usāmah before his (s) death.

But concerning 'Ali ibn Abi Tālib, he was never sent in a mission but only as a leader and commander. Once upon a time he (s)

---

[107] *Tarikh al-Tabari*, vol. II, p. 319; *Tarikh Ibn al-'Athir*, vol. II, p. 62.
[108] *Sahih Muslim*, vol. VII, p. 120; *Sahih al-Bukhāri*, "bāb fadā'il 'Ali".
[109] *Mustadrak al-Hākim*, vol. III, p. 128; *al-Mu'jam al-kabir*, al-Tabarāni.
[110] *Al-Sirah al-Halabiyyah*, Ghazwat Dhāt al-Salāsil; *Tabaqāt Ibn Sa'd*, beside others who referred to this Ghazwah (invasion).

delegated two armies, giving the commandment of one of them to 'Ali and the other to Khalid ibn al-Walid, saying to them: When being separated each one of you can undertake the commandment of his army, but when meeting together 'Ali should be the commander of the whole army.

From the aforementioned, we conclude that 'Ali being the *wali* (guardian) of the believers after the Prophet (s), and no one is entitled to outstrip him or be preferred over him. But unfortunately and with much regret, the Muslims have undergone a heavy loss, suffering much to the present time reaping the fruits of what they have sown. The latters have recognized the (ill) consequences of what was founded by the earliers.

Can anyone imagine a rightly-guided caliphate as that of 'Ali ibn Abi Tālib, had the *Ummah* followed the one chosen by Allah and His Messenger. 'Ali was quite competent to lead the *Ummah* so symmetrically throughout thirty years, exactly in the same way as the Messenger of Allah led it with no little change. Whilst we see on the other hand that Abu Bakr and 'Umar have changed everything, exerting their opinions against the texts in a way that their acts turned to be a *sunnah* to be followed. And when 'Uthmān came to power, he perverted more and more to the extent that he contradicted the Book of Allah and Sunnah of His Messenger and that of Abu Bakr and 'Umar. This practice was disapproved by the Companions, and a violent people revolt was launched against him, taking away his life, and creating a great sedition amongst the *Ummah*, whose bad consequences could never grow sound till nowadays.

But on the other hand, 'Ali ibn Abi Tālib used to adhere to the Book of Allah and Sunnah of His Messenger, without a bit deviation from them. The best evidence for this being his refusing the post of caliphate when they stipulated that he should rule according to the Book of Allah and Sunnah of His Messenger, and *sunnah* of the Two Caliphs (Abu Bakr and 'Umar).

One may wonder: Why should 'Ali abide by the Book of Allah and Sunnah of His Messenger, while Abu Bakr and 'Umar and 'Uthmān were obliged to exert their opinions (*ijtihād*) and interpolation?

The reply for this being that the knowledge owned by 'Ali was not possessed by any of them, and also the Messenger of Allah distinguished him with a thousand gates of knowledge, for every gate a thousand gates open,[111] saying to him:

"O 'Ali, you will verily demonstrate for my Ummah all that which they differed regarding it after me."[112]

Whereas the caliphs were ignorant of a large number of the apparent precepts and rules of the Qur'ān, beside being unable to interpret it. Al-Bukhāri and Muslim are reported to have said in their *Sahihs*, in the chapter on *Tayammum,* that: A man questioned 'Umar ibn al-Khattāb when he was a caliph, saying: O Amir al-Mu'minin, I found myself ritually impure and couldn't find water (for bathing), so what should I do? 'Umar said to him: Do not perform prayers!! Furthermore, he was unaware of the judgement concerning *Kalālah* till the time of his death, keeping on saying: I wished I had asked the Messenger of Allah about its judgement, while it is stated in the Holy Qur'ān. When 'Umar, whom the Ahl al-Sunnah used to consider among the inspired men, be at this level of knowledge, so what about the others who added many a heresy into the religion of Allah with no knowledge, or guidance or illuminative book, but out of personal *ijtihādāt* (exertions of opinion).

A question may be raised that: If this be the case why hasn't al-Imām 'Ali demonstrated for the *Ummah* the points of difference and dispute among them after the demise of the Messenger (s)?

---

[111] *Kanz al-'Ummāl*, vol. VI, p. 392, *hadith* No. 6009, *Hilyat al-Awliyā'*; *Yanābi' al-mawaddah*, pp. 73, 74; *Tarikh Dimashq of Ibn 'Asākir*, vol. II, p. 483.

[112] *Mustadrak al-Hākim*, vol. III, p. 122; Ibn 'Asākir, op. cit., vol. II, p. 488.

The answer would be: Al-Imām 'Ali has spared no effort in exposing and clarifying the problematic matters, with being the reference for the Sahābah regarding whatever they couldn't find a solution for. He used to come to them, elucidating and giving counsels, of which they would take that which be appropriate for them and not contradictory to their policy, neglecting whatever be other than this, and history be the best witness for our claim.

The truth lies in that: Had 'Ali ibn Abi Tālib and the Imāms among his sons not been there, it would have been impossible for people to realize whatever is related to their religion. But people, as the Qur'ān informed us, never like truth, so they followed their desires inventing new *madhāhib* (schools of thought) versus the Ahl al-Bayt Imāms, who were kept under strict surveillance by the time governments, which would never grant them freedom of movement and direct contact with people.

'Ali used to assume the pulpit and address the people: Ask me before you loose me. Sufficient be for him is the valuable book *Nahj al-balāghah* that 'Ali left for us, and the knowledge left by Ahl al-Bayt Imāms ('a) which filled the East and the West, the fact testified by Sunni and Shi'i leaders (*imāms*) of Muslims.

Returning to the topic, I would say: Based on this, had it been destined for 'Ali to have the lead of the *Ummah* for thirty years in accordance with the sirah (conduct) of the Messenger (s), Islam would have prevailed everywhere, and creed ('*aqidah*) would have penetrated hearts of people much more and in a deeper way, and no minor or major sedition, nor Karbala and Ashura' would have been there. Further, if we imagine the *Ummah* being led by the Eleven Imāms after 'Ali, who were determined by Allah from the Messenger of Allah (s), and whose lives extended for three centuries, no homeland would be left on the earth for other than Muslims, and the world today would be different of what it actually is, and our life would be humane in its true sense, but Allah, the Exalted, said:

"Alif Lam Meem. What! Do people imagine that they will be left off on (their) saying: "We believe!" and they will not be tried?" (29:1,2)

And verily the Islamic *Ummah* failed the trial as did the previous nations, as emphasized by the Messenger of Allah,[113] through many occasions, and confirmed by the Holy Qur'ān through numerous verses.[114]

Other Evidences for 'Ali's Guardianship

All evidences indicate that it was Allah's will that 'Ali's guardianship be the trial for the Muslims, as it was the reason behind every dispute and controversy erupted. And since Allah is subtile toward His bondmen, never taking the latters to task for what the earliers did, therefore He made His wisdom apparent and encompassed that incident (of Ghadir Khumm) with other splendid miracles-like events, so as to be an incentive for the *Ummah*, and the contemporary people would convey them and the followers would take an example of them, hoping that they might be guided to truth through searching and investigation.

First Evidence

It is related to punishing whoever denying 'Ali's guardianship, after the prevalence of the news of Ghadir Khumm, and designation

---

[113] Like the *hadith*: Hold on to the *sunnah* of the Jews and that of the Christians, and abide by it in a way that even when they enter a hole of a lizard, you should enter it." This *hadith* is reported by al-Bukhāri, and a reference to it was made previously. And also like the *hadith al-hawd* (pond) in which the Messenger of Allah (s) says: "I never believe anyone of them to be delivered but those who are like abandoned cattle (very few)."

[114] As in the Holy verse: "...Therefore if he dieth or be slain, will ye turn upon your heels?" (3:144). And also the verse: "And shall say (out) the Apostle (that Day) "O my lord! Verily my people have held this Qur'ān as a vain forsaken thing!" (25:30).

of al-Imām 'Ali as a caliph over the Muslims, with the Messenger's telling the people: The attendant should inform the absent.

When this news reached al-Hārith ibn al-Nu'mān al-Fahri, it displeased him.[115] So he rushed toward the Messenger of Allah, made his camel kneel down before the Mosque door, and entered upon the Prophet (s). After saluting him, he said: O MuHammad! You ordered us to witness that no god is there but Allah and you are the Messenger of Allah, and we accepted this from you. You also commanded us to perform five prayers day and night, fast the Month of Ramadān, perform pilgrimage to Allah's House, and pay the alms-due out of our money and properties and so we did. But you were not satisfied with all this, till you one day surprised us with raising the hand of your cousin; preferring him over other people, and said: "Of whomever I am a master, 'Ali also is his master." Is this from you or ordained by Allah?

The Messenger of Allah (s), whose eyes turned red, replied: By Allah, Who no god is there but He. It is ordained by Allah, and not from me (repeating it three times)

On standing up, al-Hārith said: "O Allah, if what is uttered by MuHammad being true, send against us stones from the sky or bring us a painful doom."

Then he (s) said: By Allah, before reaching his camel, Allah pelted him with a stone from the heaven, which fell upon the top of his head and went out from his posterior, causing his death. Thereat these verses were revealed by Allah the Almighty:

---

[115] This incident reveals the presence of some of bedouins living outside al-Madinah, who detest 'Ali ibn Abi Tālib and never like him, beside disliking Muhammad (S). As a consequence we can notice how did this fool enter upon the Prophet, and, without greeting him, called him: O Muhammad! He thus proved to be among those meant in the Holy Qur'ānic verse: *"The (rustic) Arabs (of the desert) are very hard in infidelity and hypocrisy, and more inclined not to know the limits of what Allah hath sent down unto His Apostle ..."* (*Tawbah, 9:97*)

"Demanded, a demander, the chastisement inevitable. For, the disbelievers against it, there is no repeller." (70:1-2)

This episode is reported by a large number of Ahl al-Sunnah *'ulamā'*, other than those we referred to.[116] Whoever desires to go through more references, can refer to the book al-Ghadir of al-'Allāmah al-'Amini.

Second Evidence

It is related to the punishment of anyone concealing the witness regarding the incident of *al-Ghadir*, and was inflicted by the imprecation uttered by al-Imām 'Ali. That was when al-Imām 'Ali, during a memorable day, rose up, and gathered people at al-Rahabah, proclaiming from over the *minbar*:

I appeal to every Muslim who heard the Messenger of Allah (s), saying on the day of Ghadir Khumm. *"'Ali is the master of whomever I am his master"*, to stand up and give witness of what he heard, provided that he saw him by his own eyes and heard him by his own ears."

Thereat thirty Companions, among whom sixteen Badrites (those who attended Battle of Badr), stood up and witnessed that he(s) took him by hand and addressed people, saying: *"Do you know that I have more authority over the believers than they have over themselves? They said: Yes, you do. He said: Of whomever I am his master, this one ('Ali) is also his master. O Allah, befriend whoever befriends him, and be the enemy of his enemy..."*

But jealousy and hatred harboured inside the hearts of some Companions who attended the Incident of *al-Ghadir*, withheld them

---

[116] Al-Hasakāni, *Shawāhid al-tanzil*, vol. II, p. 286; *Tafsir al-Tha'labi*, on the *Surah al-Ma'ārij*. *Tafsir al-Qurtubi*, vol. XVIII, p. 278; *Tafsir al-Manār*, by Rashid Ridā, vol. VI, p. 464; *Yanābi' al-mawaddah*, by al-Qunduzi al-Hanafi, p. 328; *Al-Mustadrak 'alā al-Sahihayn*, by al-Hākim, vol. II, p. 502; *Al-Sirah al-Halabiyyah*, vol. III, p. 275; *Tadhkirat al-khawāss*, by Ibn al-Jawzi, p. 37.

from standing and giving witness. Among them being Anas ibn Mālik, toward whom al-Imām 'Ali descended the *minbar* (pulpit) and said to him: O Anas, what is the matter with you? Why don't you rise up together with the Messenger's Companions and give witness of what you heard on that day as they did? He replied: O Amir al-Mu'minin! I became old and forgot (that incident). Then al-Imām 'Ali said: If you are proved to be a liar I invoke Allah to afflict you with leprosy in a way that no turban can cover. Then as soon as he stood up, his face turned white out of leprosy, after which he began to lament himself, weeping and saying: I am inflicted with the curse of the upright man because I concealed the witness to his benefit.

This episode is widely known, and was reported by Ibn Qutaybah in the book *al-Ma'ārif*, [117] in which he counted Anas among the cripple persons under bāb al-baras (leprosy), and also by al-Imām AHmad ibn Hanbal in his *Musnad*,[118] when he said: They all stood up except three, who didn't rise up, so they were afflicted with his imprecation.

It is noteworthy to mention here that these three men were referred to by al-Imām AHmad as reported by al-Baladhuri,[119] when saying: After citing al-Imām 'Ali's appeal to witness, Anas ibn Mālik, al-Barā' ibn 'Azib and Jarir ibn 'Abd Allāh al-Bajali were sitting near the pulpit. Al-Imām repeated his appeal, but received no response from any of them, whereat he('a) said: My Lord, whoever hides this witness while knowing it. You should never let him die and leave the world without branding him with a sign distinguishing him for all people. After that, Anas ibn Mālik was affected with leprosy, al-Barā' ibn 'Azib turned blind, and Jarir was converted to a bedouin after his migration, and on coming al-Shurāt he died inside his mother's house.

---

[117] Ibn Qutaybah al-Dinawari, *Kitāb al-ma'ārif*, p. 251.
[118] Al-'Imām Ahmad ibn Hanbal in his *Musnad*, vol. I, p. 119.
[119] Al-Balādhuri in *Ansāb al-'Ashrāf*, Vols. I & II, p. 152.

This story is famous, reported by a large number of historians.[120]

"So Learn a Lesson, O ye who have eyes."

Any truth-seeker can recognize, out of this incident,[121] that was revived by al-Imām 'Ali after elapse of twenty-five years and was about to be obliterated, the real value, greatness, sublimity and self serenity of al-Imām 'Ali ('a). While he showed extreme forbearance, being true counseller to Abu Bakr, 'Umar and 'Uthmān as long as knowing that advising them being for the interest of Islam and Muslims, nevertheless he kept on holding in mind the Incident of *al-Ghadir* with all its denotations, besides its being remembered in his conscience throughout all of his life moments. As soon as finding an opportune time to resurrecting and reviving it, he would immediately embark on compelling others to give witness with it publicly and before all people.

Anyone can contemplate in the way of reviving this blessed memory and its implied extreme wisdom for establishing the proof against all Muslims, whether those attended the incident and others. If al-Imām said: "O people, the Messenger of Allah has committed caliphate to me at Ghadir Khumm", this wouldn't have that influence and impression upon the hearts and minds of the attendants, and they

---

[120] *Tarikh Ibn 'Asākir*, which is called *Tarikh Dimashq*, vol. II, p. 7 and vol. III, p. 150;

– *Sharh Nahj al-balāghah*, of Ibn Abi al-Hadid, verified by Muhammad Abu al-Fadl, vol. XIX, p. 217;

– *'Abaqāt al-Anwār*, vol. II, p. 309;

– *Manāqib 'Ali ibn Abi Tālib*, of Ibn al-Maghāzili al-Shāfi'i, p. 23;

– *Al-Sirah al-Halabiyyah*, vol. III, p. 337.

[121] The incident occurred on the Rahbah Day when al-'Imām 'Ali asked the Sahābah to give witness about *Hadith al-Ghadir*. This incident is reported by a large number of traditionists and historians, to whom a reference was made previously, like Ahmad ibn Hanbal, Ibn 'Asākir and Ibn Abi al-Hadid, beside others.

would have surely disputed with him due to the silence he kept throughout all that period.

But when he said: I appeal to every Muslim, who heard what the Messenger of Allah (s) declared on the day of Ghadir Khumm, to stand up and give witness, so as to make the incident reported through a tradition from the Messenger of Allah (s), by thirty Companions among whom were sixteen men attending Badr (Battle). In this way al-Imām closed the door before the deniers and skeptics, and those protesting against his keeping silence all that period, since keeping silence by these thirty men, who being the magnates among the shaābah, would be a strong evidence indicating the perilousness of the situation, and that silence implying the interest of Islam as known by all.

A Comment about Shurā

Out of what is mentioned, it became clear for us that caliphate, in the perspective of the Shi'ah, being according to Allah's will and choice, and determination by the Messenger of Allah (s) through a revelation revealed to him. This claim is quitely in line with the philosophy of Islam in all its rulings and legislations, as Allah, the Glorified, is He Who

"...createth whatever He willeth and (also) chooseth too; it is not theirs to choose."... (28:68)

And since Allah, the Glorified, willed that the *Ummah* of Muhammad to be the best community that has been raised up for mankind, so it should have a leader who being wise, sagacious, knowledgeable, powerful, valiant, pious, ascetic, and having the highest level of faith. All these traits can never be enjoyed but by that who being chosen by Allah, the Glorious and the Mighty, distinguishing him with special characteristics qualifying him for the post of leadership and headship. The Almighty Allah said:

"Allah chooseth from the angels messengers, and (also) from mankind. Lo! Allah is Hearer, Seer." (22:75)

The executors have been chosen by Allah exactly as in the case of the prophets. The Messenger of Allah (s) said in this respect: "For every prophet there is an executor (wasi), and my executor is 'Ali ibn Abi Tālib.[122]

In another haadith, he (s) said:

"I am the seal of the prophets and 'Ali is the seal of the executors."[123]

On this basis, the Shi'ah submitted totally to Allah and His Messenger, with no one left among them claiming caliphate for himself or covetting to it, neither through text (*nass*) nor through election: first, because the *nass* negates the election and *shurā* (council), and secondly due to the fact that the *nass* was made by the Messenger of Allah (may Allah's peace and benediction be upon him and his Progeny) upon particular and specific persons[124] by their names, so as no transgressor could lift a hand against it, and otherwise he would be considered a debauchee and an apostate.

While caliphate in the perspective of Ahl al-Sunnah being through election (*ikhtiyār*) and council (*shurā*). In this way they opened a door that couldn't be closed before anyone, arousing the greediness of all, far and near, and bad and good for it, till it was handed over from Quraysh to the *mawāli* and slaves, then to the Mamalik and lastly to the Turkish and Moguls.

Thereat, all the values and conditions they stipulated to be possessed by the caliph, have been neglected since anyone other than the Infallible was merely a human being full of passions and instincts, who as soon as attaining to power, feels uncertain of being

---

[122] *Tarikh Ibn 'Asākir al-Shafi'i*, vol. III, p. 5; *Manāqib al-Khwārazmi*, p. 42; *Yanābi' al-mawaddah*, p. 79.

[123] *Yanābi' al-mawaddah*, vol. II, p. 3, on the authority of al-Daylami, *Manāqib al-Khwārazmi* and *Dhakhā'ir al-'uqbā*.

[124] The number was reported by al-Bukhāri and Muslim, while the number and names were reported by the author of *Yanābi' al-mawaddah*, vol. III, p. 99.

converted and turned to be worse than he was. And the Islamic history is replete with many evidences confirming our claim.

Some readers may think that I am exaggerating, and I ask them to go through the history of the Umayyads with the 'Abbāsids and others, to realize that who called himself 'Amir al-Mu'minin' used to show openly the habit of imbibing wine, frolic with the apes, clothing them with gold. And that the so-called (Amir al-Mu'minin) used to clothe his bondmaid his clothes to lead Muslims in prayers, turning mad due to the death of his slave-girl Habbabah, being delighted at a poet whereat he kisses his penis. Why do we occupy our minds in talking about those whom the Muslims judged to be representing only the mordacious kings, not the (real) caliphate, as referred to by the *hadith* narrated by them, which is the utterance of the Messenger (s). "Verily successorship after me shall last for thirty years, after which it will be only a mordacious rule."

This point is out of scope of our discussion, and anyone desiring to have information about that is asked to refer to *Tarikh al-Tabari, Tarikh Ibn al-'Athir, Tarikh Abi al-Fidā' and Tarikh Ibn Qutaybah*, and others.

What I intended to say was to demonstrate the disadvantages of election, and futility of the theory from its foundation, as against the one whom we elect today we may harbour malice, and it, will be manifested for us that we were mistaken and have gone wrong in election. This is exactly like the case of 'Abd al-RaHmān ibn 'Awf when he chose 'Uthmān ibn 'Affān for the post of caliphate, after which he felt so regretful, but that was of no use for the '*Ummah* after putting it in trouble. When a reputable Companion belonging to the first vanguard like 'Uthmān, breaches the covenant he gave to 'Abd al-RaHmān ibn 'Awf, and when the latter, though being a companion of fame among the predecessors, being unable to choose properly, it would be impossible then to any sane man to be satisfied with this barren theory that produced nothing but turmoil, instability and bloodshed. And while swearing allegiance to Abu Bakr being a slip Allah protected Muslims against its evil, as described by 'Umar ibn al-Khattāb, with a large number of Companions opposing and renouncing it, and when allegiance to 'Ali ibn Abi Tālib being sworn publicly with presence of some Companions violating the allegiance, leading to eruption of the Battles of al-Jamal, Siffin and al-Nahrawan, in which innocent people were killed, how would wisemen be pleased then, with that rule which was put to test and exorbitantly failed from the beginning, being a mischief for the Muslims. This fact is more ascertained when knowing that those who believe in the principle of shurā, elect the caliph having no authorization after that to substitute or depose him. The Muslims tried their best to depose 'Uthmān, but he disdained, saying: "I never take off a garment Allah has clothed me with."

That which increases even our aversion to this theory, being what is seen nowadays in the civilized democracy-claiming Western countries, in regard of electing the Head of State, with various parties struggling, bargaining and competing for attaining to power at any cost, spending for this purpose billions of money allocated for publicity in all its means. Further huge potentials and resources being squandered on the cost of the oppressed among the people who badly needing them.As soon as any of them assumes the headship, sympathy overwhelms him, making him designate his supporters, party members, friends and relatives in the posts of ministers, high-ranking responsibilities, and significant positions in administration, leaving the others busy in the activities of the opposition throughout his reign period, upon which it is agreed too. In this way, they would create problems and obstacles for him, doing their utmost to disgrace and topple him, entailing thus a heavy loss for the downtrodden people. Consequently, many humane values were devoluted and numerous Satanic depravitives were elevated with the titles of freedom and democracy, and under bombastic slogans, in a way that sodomy was practised as a lawful and legitimate act, and adultery turned to be a progress and advancement as a substitute for marriage, about which you can say what you like.

How great the Shi'ah's belief in holding that successorship (*khilāfah*) being one of principles of religion, and what sublime is their belief that this post be according to the Will and choice of Allah, the Exalted. It is really on apposite saying and sensible opinion, admitted by reason (*'aql*) and with which the conscience is pleased, being supported by texts from the Qur'ān and (Prophetic) Sunnah, coercing the tyrants, dominants, kings and sovereigns, imparting upon the society tranquillity and stability.

DISAGREEMENT ABOUT AL-THAQALAYN

We have already conceived, through the aforementioned discussions, the viewpoints of the Shi'ah and Ahl al-Sunnah regarding the caliphate, and the acts and conduct of the Messenger (s) toward the *Ummah*, as held by the two sects.

Has the Messenger of Allah (s) then left anything for his *Ummah*, upon which it depends and to which it refers regarding any controversial matter entailing inevitable dispute, that was stated by the Holy Qur'ān, when the Almighty said:

"O ye who believe! Obey God and obey the apostle and those vested with authority from among you; and then if ye quarrel about anything refer it to God and the Apostle if ye believe in God and in the Last Day (of Judgement). This is the best and fairest way of ending (the dispute)" (4:59).

True, the Messenger has to leave behind for the *Ummah* a foundation and basis upon which it relies and to which it refers, since he was sent as a blessing for the worlds and he is so keen and concerned that his community be the best of communities, and never be in disagreement after him. Hence his Companions and the traditionists reported that he said "I am leaving behind among you two precious things (*Thaqalayn*), as long as you adhere to them you will never go astray after me. The Book of Allah and my *'Itrah*, my Ahl al-Bayt. They will never separate till they come unto me near the pond (*hawd*), so look how you are going to treat them after me."[1]

This *hadith* is *sahih* (correct) and authentic, and was reported by both the sects Sunnah and Shi'ah. It was narrated in the *Musnads* and *Sahihs* of Ahl al-Sunnah, through more than thirty Companions.

---

[1] *Mustadrak al-Hākim*, vol. III, p. 148.

Since I, as usual, never argue by the books of the Shi'ah or sayings of their *'ulamā'*, who have reported the *Hadith al-Thaqalayn,* acknowledging its veracity, so that the discussion be objective, fair and square (though fairness and equity necessitating that a reference should be made too to the Shi'ah). Hereinafter a brief list of the narrators of this *hadith* from among the Sunni *'ulamā'*.

1. *Sahih Muslim*: "kitāb fadā'il 'Ali ibn Abi Tālib". vol. VII p.122

2. *Sahih al-Tirmidhi,* vol.V.p.328

3. Al-Imām al-Nasā'i in his book *al-Khasā'is.* p.21

4. Al-Imām Ahmād ibn Hanbal. in his *Musnad*, vol.III,p.17

5. *Mustadrak al-Hākim*, vol.III, p.109

6. *Kanz al-'ummāl*, vol.I, p.154

7. Ibn Sa'd in *al-Tabaqāt al-Kubrā*, vol. II, p.194

8. Ibn al-'Athir in *Jāmi' al-Usul*, vol.I, p.187

9. Al-Suyuti in *al-Jāmi' al-Saghir*, vol.I, p.353

10. Al-Haythami in *Majma' al-Zawā'id*, vol.IX, p.163

11. Al-Nabhāni in *al-Fath al-Kabir,* vol.I, p.451

12. Ibn al-'Athir in *Usd al-ghābah fi ma'rifat al-Sahābah*, vol.II, p.12

13. *Tarikh Ibn 'Asākir* vol.V, p.436

14. *Tafsir Ibn Kathir*, vol.IV,p.113

15. *Al-Tāj al-Jāmi' li al-Usul,* vol.III,p.308

Added to these, Ibn Hajar who mentioned it in his book *al-Sawā'iq al-Muhriqah,* acknowledging its veracity, beside al-Dhahabi in his *Talkhis* admitting its correctness provided that it be accepted by the Shaykhayn, Ibn al-Maghāzili al-Shāfi'i and al-Tabarrāni in his Mu'jam, with the author of *al-Sirah al-Nabawiyyah fī Hāmish al-Sirah al-Halabiyyah,* and the author of *Yanābi' al-Mawaddah,* beside others.

Can anyone claim, after this, that *Hadith al-Thaqalayn* "The Book of Allah and my *'Itrah*": being unknown by the Sunnis, and appertaining to the Shi'ah alone?? May Allah curse fanaticism, thought inaction and Jahiliyyah fervour.

Hence *Hadith al-Thaqalayn* in which the Messenger (s) recommended to hold fast to the Book of Allah and his Pure kindred (*'itrah*), is a correct *hadith* in the perspective of Ahl al-Sunnah as mentioned before, and it is regarded by the Shi'ah more authentic and having stronger chains going back to the Pure Imāms.

So why do some raise doubts about this *hadith*, trying their best to substitute it with the Book of Allah and my Sunnah"? And though the author of *Miftāh Kunuz al-Sunnah* reports from al-Bukhāri, Muslim, al-Tirmidhi and Ibn Mājah, in page No.478 under the heading; "His (s) recommendation with the Book of Allah and His Messenger's Sunnah." But when going into these four books we can never see any hint or reference to this *hadith*. True, you may find within *Sahih al-Bukhāri* the chapter titled "Kitāb al-'i'tisām bi al-Kitāb wa al-Sunnah,"[2] but you never find such a *hadith* at all.

That which can be found in *Sahih al-Bukhāri* and the aforementioned books being a *hadith* saying:

"Talhah ibn Musarraf is reported to have said: I asked 'Abd Allāh ibn Ubayy Awfā (may God be pleased with them): Has the Prophet (may God's peace and benediction be upon him and his Progeny) committed to anyone's charge? He replied: No. I said then: So how was bequest (*wasiyyah*) prescribed for people, or how were they

---

[2] *Sahih al-Bukhāri,* vol. VIII, p. 137.

commanded to write a will? He said: He recommended with the Book of Allah."[3]

So no reference is there to a *hadith* uttered by the Messenger of Allah, saying in it: "I am leaving behind among you two precious things (*Thaqalayn*): the Book of Allah and my Sunnah." And if supposedly such a *hadith* is there in some books, it would be to no avail since unanimity was, as mentioned before, to the contrary. Further, should we investigate the *hadith*. "The Book of Allah and my Sunnah," we will verily see it not congruous with truth, neither through quoting (*naql*) nor reason ('*aql*). For refuting it there are several causes:

First Cause: The historians and traditionists concur that the Messenger of Allah (s) has forbidden anyone from writing down his traditions, and no one could claim that he was inscribing the Prophetic Sunnah during his lifetime. The Messenger's saying "I am leaving behind among you the Book of Allah and my Sunnah" then can never be reasonable. And concerning the Book of Allah, it is inscribed and preserved in the bossoms of men, in a way that any Companion can refer to the Qur'ān, even though being not among the memorizers. But as regards the Prophetic Sunnah, there is nothing inscribed or compiled during the Prophet's lifetime, and the Prophetic Sunnah as is widely known and agreed upon, being whatever said, or done or determined by the Messenger (s). And as is known too, the Messenger never used to gather his Companions for teaching them the Prophetic Sunnah, but rather he used to address them, in all occcasions, with the attendance of some or only one of his Companions. In this case, how would the Messenger say to them, I am leaving behind among you my Sunnah??

Second Cause: When the Messenger of Allah became in a low state of health, three days before his death, he asked to bring him the scapula and inkhorn, so as to write a book after which they would

---

[3] *Ibid.*, vol. III, p. 186; *Sahih al-Tirmidhi*, "Kitāb al-wasāyā"; *Sahih Muslim*, "kitāb al-wasāyā"; *Sahih Ibn Mājah*, "kitāb al-wasāyā".

never go astray. Thereat 'Umar ibn al-Khattāb said: The Messenger of Allah is hallucinating, and we are sufficed with the Book of Allah. [4]

Had the Messenger (s) told them previously: I am leaving behind among you the Book of Allah and my Sunnah, it would have been infeasible for 'Umar to say: The Book of Allah is sufficient for us!, as in this case he with the Sahābah sharing his opinion, would be renegading against the Messenger of Allah, the fact that would never be approved of by Ahl al-Sunnah.

Thus it can be realized that this *hadith* was only fabricated by some of the latters who harbour animosity against Ahl al-Bayt, especially after excluding them away from caliphate. It was as if that who composed the *hadith* "the Book of Allah and my Sunnah" was astonished to see people adhering to the Book of Allah, forsaking the *'Itrah* and following the guide of other than them, so he thought that he would, through fabricating this *hadith*, rectify their course, removing any criticism and sarcasm far from the Sahābah who contradicted the testament of the Messenger of Allah (s).

Third Cause: It is known that the first incident Abu Bakr faced during the first days of his caliphate, was his decision to fight those refusing to pay the *zakāt* (poor-due), despite opposition on the part of 'Umar ibn al-Khattāb, beside quoting the Messenger's *hadith* (as an evidence):

"Whoever says, there is no god but Allah and Muhammad is the Messenger of Allah, his property and blood will be immune against me except when it is due, and his accountability is with Allah."

Hence, if the Messenger's Sunnah was publicly known, it was not to be ignored by Abu Bakr while he was supposed to be the most entitled to recognize it.

---

[4] *Sahih al-Bukhāri*, "bāb marad al-Nabi wa wafātih" (The Prophet's sickness and death), vol. V, p. 138; *Sahih Muslim*, "kitāb al-wasiyyah", vol. II, p. 16.

But thereafter 'Umar was satisfied with Abu Bakr's interpretation for the *hadith* he narrated, and his saying that zakāt being the levy on money (*māl*). They were unaware, or neglected the Messenger's actual and non-interpreted Sunnah, being the story of Tha'labah who refused to pay the *zakāt* to the Messenger of Allah (s), and a Qur'ānic verse was revealed in his regard. Nevertheless, the Messenger neither fought him, nor forced him to pay it. Another example can be seen in Abu Bakr and 'Umar's displeasure concerning the Messenger's delegating Usāmah ibn Zayd as a commander of a battalion. When he defeated the disbelievers, he pursued one of them and as he caught him, he (the enemy) said: There is no god but Allah! Whereat Usāmah killed him. When this news reached the Prophet(s), he said to Usāmah: O Usāmah, did you kill him after uttering *'lā ilāha illā Allāh*?' He replied: He was seeking protection through his saying, and he kept on repeating it till I wished I had never embraced Islam before that day.[5]

However, this can never be a proof making us to believe in the *hadith* "The Book of Allah and my Sunnah", since the Companions were the first in ignoring the Prophetic Sunnah, so how about those who succeeded them, and those whose houses were distant from al-Madinah?

Fourth Cause: It is known also that so many of the Sahābah's deeds after the Messenger's demise, were contradictory to his Sunnah. Those Sahābah either were aware of his Sunnah and contradicted it deliberately, out of exerting their opinion against the Prophet's texts, the fact making them to be among those addressed by the Almighty's saying:

"And it is not for a believer man or woman to have any choice in their affair when God and His Apostle have decided a matter; and whoever disobeyeth God and His Apostle, indeed he hath strayed off a manifest straying." (33:36)

---

[5] *Sahih al-Bukhāri*, vol. VIII, p. 36, and "kitāb al-diyāt"; *Sahih Muslim*, vol. I, p. 67.

Or they were unaware of the Prophet's Sunnah, the case in which the Messenger of Allah would not be entitled to tell them: I am leaving behind among you my Sunnah, while knowing that his Companions and nearest people to him having no knowledge of it, so what about those succeeding them who neither recognized nor seen the Prophet (s).

Fifth Cause: It is known further that the (Prophetic) Sunnah was never inscribed but only during the era of the 'Abbāsid State, and the first book written on *hadith* was *al-Muwatta'* of al-Imām Mālik. That was after the great sedition, Battle of al-Harrah and proscription of al-Madīnah, with slaying the Sahābah forcibly. After all that, how would anyone have confidence in narrators trying to make advances to the Emperor for gaining worldly lusts? For this reason, there was great confusion and disagreement in between the traditions, with the *Ummah* being divided into several *madhāhib* (schools of thought), in a way that whatever was approved by this school was negated by the other ones, and vice versa.

How would we believe that the Messenger of Allah said (I am leaving behind among you the Book of Allah and my Sunnah) while knowing that the hypocrites and deviants would be lying against him, when he said: "The liars against me have multiplied. Whoever lies against me should occupy his abode in fire."

So if liars did increase in number during his lifetime, how would he charge his *Ummah* to follow his Sunnah, while they having no knowledge of it, or be able to distinguish the sound from the unsound and the weak from the authentic ones.

Sixth Cause: Ahl al-Sunnah report in their *Sihāh* that the Messenger of Allah (s) has left behind two precious assets (*thaqalayn*), or two caliphs, or two things. Once they narrate (that he (s) said) the Book of Allah and Sunnah of His Messenger, and another time that he said: I ask you to adhere to my Sunnah and the *sunnah* of the Rightly-guided caliphs after me. It should be known that the latter *hadith* adds the *sunnah* of the caliphs to the Book of

Allah and His Messenger's Sunnah, so as to make the sources of legislation three instead of two ones, the fact contradicting the correct version of *Hadith al-Thaqalayn,* upon which there is agreement between the Sunnah and Shi'ah, which says: "the Book of Allah and my *'Itrah"*, for which we introduced more than twenty sources from among the authentic Sunni references,, beside the Shi'ah sources that we didn't mention.

Seventh Cause: If the Messenger of Allah (s) knew for certain that his Companions, with whose language and dialects the Qur'ān was revealed (as they claim) had no good knowledge of its *tafsir* or *ta'wil* (interpretation), so what about those to succeed them, and how would be the case of those embracing Islam from among the Romans, Persians, Abyssinians and all the non-Arabs who neither comprehend nor speak the Arabic.

It is confirmed in the books of *hadith* that Abu Bakr was once asked about the meaning of the Holy verse: "And fruits and the herbage," he said: Which sky can overshadow me, and which land can bear me, when I claim something I know not regarding the Book of Allah.[6] 'Umar ibn al-Khattāb also was unaware of the meaning of this verse, as Anas ibn Mālik is reported to have said: Once upon a day 'Umar ibn al-Khattāb ascended the *minbar* (rostrum) and recited: "and caused We to grow therein the grain. And grapes and the vegetables. The Olive and the Palm. And gardens enclosed, thick with trees. And fruits and the herbage."

He said: All these things are known for us, but what is meant by *"abbā"*? Then he said: *By God, this is the affectation in itself. What happens if you know not the meaning of "abb", you can follow and apply what was exposed and demonstrated from the Book and whatever is not known for you, leave it to its Lord."*[7]

---

[6] Al-Qastallāni in *Irshād al-Sāri*, vol. X, p. 298; Ibn Hajar in *Fath al-Bāri*, vol. XIII, p. 230.

[7] *Tafsir Ibn Jarir*, vol. III, p. 38; *Kanz al-'Ummal*, vol. I, p. 287. *Mustadrak al-Hākim*, vol. II, p. 14: *Talkhis al-Dhahabi*; al-Khatib in his *Tarikh*, vol. II, p. 468;

Whatever is said here in interpreting the Book of Allah, is said also in explaining the Holy Prophetic Sunnah. Many a Prophetic *hadith* remained a topic of controversy between the Sahābah, and among the schools, and also between the Sunnah and Shi'ah, either due to confirming or weakening the *hadith*, or because of interpreting and comprehending it. For elucidation, I supply the dear reader with some examples in this regard:

Disagreement among Sahābah about Veracity or Fabrication of *hadith*:

This case has actually happened for Abu Bakr during the first days of his caliphate, when Fātimah al-Zahrā' came toward him demanding to hand her Fadak, which he seized from her after the demise of her father. But he denied her claim that her father the Messenger of Allah donated it to her during his lifetime. And when she demanded from him the inheritance of her father, he told her that the Messenger of Allah said once: "We, the folk of prophets, never give as inheritance what we leave as alms."

She, in turn, denied the ascription of this *hadith* to her father, arguing with the Book of Allah. The dispute and debate heated between them, till she passed away while being wrathful against him, forsaking and never talking to him, as reported in both *Sahih al-Bukhāri* and *Sahih Muslim*.

Added to this the dispute between 'A'ishah and Abu Hurayrah concerning the ruling of who entered upon the morning while being ritually impure (*junub*) during the month of Ramadān. She opinioned that his fasting being valid with keeping on his condition, whereas Abu Hurayrah's view was that: whoever enters upon the morning in a state of ritual impurity, he should break his fasting. Hereafter the incident in details:

---

al-Zamakhshari in his *al-Tafsir al-Kashshāf*, vol. III, 253; *Tafsir al-Khāzin*, vol. IV, p. 374; Ibn Taymiyyah in *Muqaddimat usul al-tafsir*, p. 30; Tafsir Ibn Kathir, vol. IV, p. 473.

Al-Imām Mālik in *al-Muwatta'* and *al-Bukhāri* in his *Sahih*, report from 'A'ishah and Umm Salamah, the Prophet's wives, that they said: The Messenger used to enter upon the morning in the Month of Ramadān in a state of ritual impurity, out of copulation not out of having a venereal (wet) dream (*ihtilām*), and was keeping on his fasting. Abu Bakr reports from 'Abd al-Rahmān that he said: I and my father were in a gathering near Marwan ibn al-Hakam, the Emir of al-Madinah, when someone told him that Abu Hurayrah holds that: whoever enters upon the morning (in Ramadān) in the state of *janābah*, he should break the fasting of that day. Thereat Marwan said: O 'Abd al-Rahmān, I take an oath by God upon you to betake your self toward the two mothers of believers, 'A'ishah and Umm Salamah, and inquire about this from them. Then I and 'Abd al-Rahmān went together till we entered upon 'A'ishah, when he saluted her and said: O Umm al-Mu'minin, we were near Marwan ibn al-Hakam, and he was told that Abu Hurayrah holds that whoever enters upon the morning as *junub* (ritually impure), he should break the fasting of that day. 'A'ishah said: O 'Abd al-Rahmān, it is not as Abu Hurayrah claims. Do you want to turn away from what was done by the Messenger of Allah? 'Abd al-Rahmān replied: No, by God. Then 'A'ishah said: He witnessed against the Messenger of Allah (s) that he used to keep on fasting the day on which he would enter upon its morning in the state of ritual impurity out of copulation not out of having a venereal dream. He said: We went out and entered upon Umm Salamah, when he asked her the same question and she gave the same reply as that of 'A'ishah, and then we went to Marwan ibn al-Hakam, to whom 'Abd al-Rahmān mentioned what these two (women) said. Thereat Marwan said: O Abu Muhammad, would you get on my mount at the door, and betake yourself to Abu Hurayrah who is in his land of al-'Aqiq, and inform him about this. So 'Abd al-Rahmān and I got on the mount and went to Abu Hurayrah, when 'Abd al-Rahmān talked to him for an hour, telling him about the matter, whereat Abu Hurayrah said: I have no knowledge of this but I was told by someone.[8]

---

[8] *Sahih al-Bukhāri,* vol. II, p. 232, "bāb al-sā'im yusbihu junuban; Muwatta'

Look, Dear reader, to a Companion like Abu Hurayrah, who is considered by the Sunnis as the Islam narrator; how he issues religious verdicts according to surmise, ascribing them then to the Messenger of Allah (s), without being aware of who has appraised him with them.

Another Self-Contradictory Story by Abu Hurayrah

'Abd Allāh ibn Muhammad reports from Hishām ibn Yusuf, from Mu'ammar, from al-Zuhri, from Abu Maslamah, from Abu Hurayrah that he said: The Prophet (s) said: There is neither contagion, nor paleness, nor vermin. An Arab said: O The Messenger of Allah, what is the matter with the she-camels that being in the sand like the deers, and then when being associated with the mange camel, they be infected with mange? The Messenger of Allah replied: Who has infected the former.

Abu Salamah also reports that he heard Abu Hurayrah say: The Prophet (s) said: No diseased should be brought unto a healthy one. Then Abu Hurayrah denied his first *hadith*, and we said: Haven't you narrated that no contagion is there? Thereat he jargonized in the Abyssinian language. Abu Salamah said: I never saw him forgetting any other *hadith* than it.[9]

So, that is, O intelligent reader, the Sunnah of the Messenger, or say, what is ascribed to the Messenger. As Abu Hurayrah that he has no knowledge of his former *hadith*, but he was told by some newsteller, and another time when he is confronted with his contradiction, he can't give a reasonable reply but only jargonizes in the Abyssinian dialect so as no one be able to understand his speech.

Mālik fi tanwir al-hawālik, vol. I, p. 272; "mā jā'a fi alladhi yusbihu junuban fi Ramadān".

[9] *Sahih al-Bukhāri*, vol. VII, p. 31, "bāb lā hāmmah"; *Sahih Muslim,* vol. VII, p. 32, "bāb lā 'adwā wa lā tiyarah".

The Dispute between Aishah and Ibn Umar

Abu Jarih is reported to have said: I heard 'Atā' informing and said: 'Urwah ibn al-Zubayr told me, saying: I and Ibn 'Umar were leaning onto 'A'ishah's room, hearing the sound of brushing her teeth with the toothbrush. He says: I said: O 'Abd al-Rahmān, did the Prophet (may Allah's peace and blessing be upon him and his Household) perform the *'umrah* in Rajab? He replied: Yes. I said to 'A'ishah: O bondmaid, don't you hear what Abu 'Abd al-Rahmān say: She said: What does he say? I replied: He says that the Prophet performed 'umrah (minor pilgrimage) in the Month of Rajab. She said: "May Allah forgive 'Abu 'Abd al-Rahmān. By my life the Prophet has never performed 'umrah in Rajab, and he never made 'umrah but only when being accompanied by him." He said. And Ibn 'Umar was hearing, but he said neither 'no' nor 'yes', and kept silent.[10]

Disagreement among Schools about the Prophetic Sunnah

When there is disagreement regarding the Prophetic Sunnah between 'Umar and Abu Bakr, between Abu Bakr,[11] and Fātimah ('a),[12] among the Prophet's wives[13], and between Abu Hurayrah and

---

[10] *Sahih Muslim*, vol. III, p. 61; *Sahih al-Bukhāri*, vol. V, p. 86.

[11] It is an indication to their disagreement in regard of fighting those abstaining from paying out the zakāt (poor-due). The readers are asked to see the references to which were stated before.

[12] This being an indication to the issue of Fadak, and the *hadith* "We, the folk of prophets, never leave behind any inheritance". The references were stated before.

[13] An indication to the narration of fostering the full-grown men *(ridā'at al-kabir)*, which was reported by 'A'ishah, but was contradicted by the other wives of the Prophet (S).

Disagreement about Al-Thaqalayn

'A'ishah with contradiction,[14] and between Ibn 'Umar and 'A'ishah,[15] and also between Abd Allāh Ibn 'Abbās and Ibn al-Zubayr,[16] and further between 'Ali ibn Abi Tālib and 'Uthmān ibn 'Affān.[17] And when the Sahābah differ among themselves concerning the Prophetic Sunnah[18] to the extent that the Tābi'un (followers) after them were left with more than seventy creeds (*madhhabs*). Hence Ibn Mas'ud had his own madhhab, and so had Ibn 'Umar, Ibn Abbas, Ibn al-Zubayr, Ibn 'Uyaynah, Ibn Jarih, al-Hasan al-Basri, Sufyān al-Thawri, Mālik, Abu Hanifah, al-Shāfi'i, and Ahmad ibn Hanbal beside many others. But the political developments have done away with all of them, with only the four schools of thought are left, which are known for Ahl al-Sunnah.

Despite the small number of the schools of thought, but they differ regarding most of the *fiqhi* questions, due to their disagreement as regards the Prophetic Sunnah. One of them, for instance, may establish his judgement on some question according to what he approved from the Messenger's *hadith*, while another one may exert his opinion or makes analogy (*qiyās*) with another issue, due to the non-existence of the text and hadith on its regard.

---

[14] An indication to the *hadith* saying that "the Prophet used to wake up in the morning of Ramadān in the state of ritual impurity (*junub*), but keeping the fasting of that day," which was denied by 'A'ishah.

[15] An indication to the narration claiming "that the Prophet (s) performd *'umrah* (short pilgrimage) four times, one of which during the Month of Rajab", which was negated by 'A'ishah.

[16] An indication to their dispute regarding the lawfulness and prohibition of *mut'ah* (temporary marriage). (See *Sahih al-Bukhāri*, vol. VI, p. 129).

[17] An indication to their controversy concerning the *mut'at al-hajj* (enjoyment of pilgrimage). See *Sahih al-Bukhāri*, vol. II, p. 153.

[18] They (Sahābah) differed regarding countless issues some of which a reference can be made like: *basmalah*, *wudu'* (ablution), *salāt* during travel, and so many other jurisprudential (*fiqhi*) issues and questions.

Difference between Ahl Al-Sunnah and Shi'ah about the Prophetic Sunnah

The disagreement between the Sunnah and Shi'ah regarding this question, may be due to two main reasons: One of them being unauthenticity of the *hadith* in the view of the Shi'ah if one of its narrators being of those whose justice being vilified, though being among the Sahābah. That is due to the fact that the Shi'ah never believe in the justice of the Companions as a whole, as Ahl al-Sunnah do.

Added to this, they reject any *hadith* contradicting the reporting of Ahl al-Bayt Imāms, since they give it priority over narration of others, however high their position be, introducing for this strong proofs from the Qur'ān and (Prophetic) Sunnah, which being confirmed even by their opponents, to which reference was made before.

The second reason for disagreement betwen them stems from the concept meant by the *hadith* itself, as it may be interpreted by Ahl al-Sunnah contrarily to the interpretation of the Shi'ah, as in the case of the afore-mentioned *hadith*, uttered by the Prophet (s) thus: "Difference of my *Ummah* is a blessing."

Ahl al-Sunnah interpret it to mean that difference among the four schools of thought in respect of *fiqhi* affairs being a blessing for the Muslims. Whereas the Shi'ah interpret it to mean visiting each other and caring for acquiring knowledge with alike benefits (being a blessing).

Or it may mean disagreement between the Shi'ah and Sunnah, not regarding the interpretation of the Prophetic *hadith*, but regarding the person or persons meant by it, like the Messenger's saying: "Adhere to my Sunnah and the *sunnah* of the Rightly-guided Caliphs after me." Ahl al-Sunnah interpret it to mean the four caliphs, whereas the Shi'ah take it to mean the Twelve Imāms, beginning with 'Ali ibn

Abi Tālib and ending with al-Mahdi Muhammad ibn al-Hasan al-'Askari (peace be upon them all).

Or the *hadith* uttered by him (s):

"The successors after me are twelve, all belonging to Quraysh."

The Shi'ah mean by it the Twelve Imāms of Ahl al-Bayt (peace be upon them), whereas Ahl al-Sunnah can't find a satisfactory interpretation for this *hadith*. Moreover, they have differed even in respect of the chronicles related to the Prophet (s), as in the case of the day of his birth. Ahl al-Sunnah celebrate the Prophet's birth on the twelfth of Rabi al-'Awwal while the Shi'ah celebrate it on the seventeenth of the same month.

By my life, this difference concerning the Prophetic Sunnah is an inevitable natural matter, during the absence of a religious authority (*marji'*) to whom all people refer, with his judgement being efficacious, and his opinion accepted by all, as the Messenger (s) was. He used to root out all the disputes and settle any conflict, judging according to Allah's revelation, so they Muslims were but to submit though feeling, annoyed in their bossoms. So the presence of such a person is a necessity for the *Ummah* as long as it exists on earth! Such is determined by reason, and it is impossible for the Messenger of Allah to neglect this fact while knowing that his *Ummah* will pervert Allah's words after his demise. Therefore it was incumbent upon him to prepare and bring up for it a competent able teacher, so as to lead it to the right path whenever it trying to deviate or go astray. And he has actually prepared for his *Ummah* a great leader, doing his utmost in bringing him up and educating and teaching him all kinds of knowledge, from, birth till attaining perfection and gaining near him a position which being the same as Aaron had to Moses. So he entrusted him the following mission by saying:

"I fight them regarding revelation of the Qur'ān and you fight them regarding its interpretation."[19]

And also his saying:

"O 'Ali, you will verily demonstrate for my *Ummah* all that they differed about after me."[20]

So, when the Qur'ān, Allah's noble book, requires someone to fight for interpreting and exposing it, since it is a silent book that cannot speak, having numerous and various meanings and denotations, and containing the visible (*Zahir*) and unvisible (*bātin*) or hidden (meanings), so how would be the case with the Prophetic traditions?

When this be the truth about the Book and Sunnah, it would be improper for the Messenger (s) to leave behind for his *Ummah* two silent and dumb *thaqalayn* (weighty assets), in a way that those in whose hearts is doubt would feel no compunction in explaining them allegorically for a (hidden) purpose. Pursuing, forsooth, that which is allegorical seeking (to cause) dissension, and seeking (to gain) worldly lusts, so as to mislead those succeeding them, since they thought of them well, believing in their justice, and being then repentful on the Doomsday, to be among those meant by Allah's saying

"On that day when their faces shall be turned into the fire, they shall say: "Oh would that we had obeyed God and obeyed the Apostle! And they shall say L"O our Lord~! verily we obeyed our chiefs and our elders, and they led us astray from the path.:" O our

---

[19] *Manāqib al-Khwārazmi,* p. 44; *Yanābi' al-mawaddah,* p. 233; Ibn Hajar al-'Asqalāni, *al-'Isābah,* vol. I, p. 25; *Kifāyat al-tālib,* p. 334; *Muntakhab Kanz al-'Ummāl,* vol. V, p. 36; *Ihqāq al-Haqq,* vol. VI, p. 37.

[20] *Mustadrak al-Hākim,* vol. III, p. 122, Ibn 'Asākir in *Tarikh Dimashq,* vol. II, p. 488; al-Khwārazmi in *al-Manāqib,* p. 236; al-Manāwi in *Kunuz al-haqā'iq Muntakhab Kanz al-'Ummāl,* vol. V, p. 33; *Yanābi' al-Mawaddah,* p. 182.

Lord! give them a double chastisement, and curse them a great curse." (33:66-68).

And His saying:

"Everytime a (new) people entereth (it) it shall curse its sister (people); until they have all come together into it, the later of them shall say about the former of them; "O our Lord! These are they who led us astray, therefore give them a double chastisement of the fire," He will say: "For every one (of you) double, but ye know not." (7:38)

Has deviation ever stemmed from other than this? No nation (*Ummah*) was left without an apostle sent by Allah, with the mission of showing them the path, and enlightening the route for them, but on the demise of every prophet, his people embarked on perverting, changing, and allegorically explaining Allah's words according to their desires! Does any sane man imagine that the Messenger of Allah Jesus ('a) claimed deity for himself before the Christians? Verily not, and it is too far from him. He addressed the Almighty saying: "I never told them anything other than what You commanded me with." In fact, the desires, avarices and worldliness altogether have prompted and pushed the Christians to such a practice. Hasn't Jesus, and before him Moses, given them good tidings of the advent of Muhammad? But they explained the name Muhammad and Ahmad allegorically to mean the "savior", and they are still awaiting him.

Thus *ta'wil* (allegorical explanation) was verily the only reason that caused the *Ummah* of Muhammad to be divided into different numerous sects and schools of thought (seventy-three sects, all going to fire except only one). Now we are living amongst these sects and cutts; does anyone of them ascribe astrayal (*dalālah*) to itself? Or in other words: Is there one cult claiming to have contradicted the Book of Allah and Sunnah of His Messenger? The contrary is true, as each one of them claims to be the only cult adherring to the Book and Sunnah. What will be the solution then??

Could the solution be far from the reach of the Messenger of Allah, or rather from Allah? I seek God's forgiveness, as He is Subtile toward His bondmen, seeking their good, so it is inevitable for Him but to set for them a solution, so that he who perished might perish by a clear proof (of His sovereignty). And it is not His business — the Glorified — to neglect His creatures, leaving them without guidance, only that when we believe that it is Him Who desired disunity and pervertion for them so as to throw them into His fire, which is a void and invalid belief. I seek God's forgiveness and turn to him from such an utterance that never fits Allah's Glory, Wisdom and Justice.

So the Messenger's saying that he has left behind the Book of Allah and Sunnah of His Prophet can never be the reasonable solution for our issue, but rather it increases in our complexity and interpolation, and can never root out the rioters and deviants. The evidence for this can be seen clearly when they revolted against their Imām, proclaiming the slogan: Rule (*hukm*) belongs to Allah not to you, O 'Ali! It is really a glistening slogan infatuating the mind of any hearer making him to believe the utterer to be so anxious to apply Allah's precepts and rulings (ahkām), and rejecting the judgements of others than Him from among the human beings. But this is not true at all. Allah — the Exalted — said:

"And among men there are those who talk concerning the life here marveleth thee and he taketh God to witness as to what is in his heart yet he is the most violent of adversaries." (2:204)

True, we most the time are beguiled by the bombastic slogans, being unaware of what they keep behind, while such fact could never be kept from al-Imām 'Ali, as he being the gate of the city of knoweldge, so he answered them by saying: "It is a word of truth intended to denote falsehood."

Right, many words of truth are there, meant to indicate falsehood (*bātil*), how is that? When the *Khawārij* say to al-Imām 'Ali: "Rule belongs to God not to you, O 'Ali," does this mean that Allah will appear on the earth and settle the dispute between them? Or they know that Allah's judgement is stated in the Qur'ān, but 'Ali has explained it according to his opinion? What proof they have, and how can't one believe that it was them who explained God's judgement allegorically? In fact he is more knowledgeable, truthful and precedent to Islam than them, and is Islam incarnated in other than him?

So it is just a seductive slogan used by them to overlay (the truth) before the naive people, with the aim of gaining their support to seek their help for fighting him and achieving victory against him (Ali), as occurring nowadays. Every time has its men, and shrewdness or cunningness can never stop, but rather it grows and increases since the contemporary shrewd people benefit from formers' experiences. How many truth words are there intended to denote batil (falsehood), in the time-being? Glittering and bombastic mottos, like those proclaimed by the Wahhabis against the Muslims, such as "monotheism and non-polytheism", so is there any Muslim rejects it? Or one Muslim community calling themselves "Ahl al-Sunnah wa al-Jamā'ah, so is there anyone among the Muslims who never likes to be with the company (Jama'ah) following the Prophet's Sunnah? Or the banner raised by the Ba'thists: "One Arab Nation with Immortal Message", and who can escape the beguilment of such a banner, before recognizing what is hidden by the Ba'th Party and its founder Michael Aflaq?

May Allah help you O 'Ali ibn Abi Tālib, your wisdom remained and still will be resounding throughout time, as many words of truth intended to indicate falsehood. Once upon a day a scholar ascended the oration rostrum and exclaimed loudly: Whoever says: I am a Shi'i we would say to him: You are a disbeliever, and whoever says I am a Sunni, we would say to him: You are a disbeliever. We need neither Shiah nor Sunnah, but we only seek Islam. It is a truth word meant to indicate falsehood, as which Islam is wanted by this scholar? In our present time there is a multifarious Islam, and it was so even in the first century. As there was Islam of 'Ali and Islam of Mu'āwiyah with both of them having supporters and followers, being so fanatic to the extent of fighting each other. Further there was Islam of al-Husayn and Islam of Yazid who murdered Ahl al-Bayt in the name of Islam, claiming that al-Husayn has renegaded from Islam when revolting against Yazid. Moreover there is the Islam of Ahl al-Bayt and their Shi'ah (followers), and Islam of the rulers and their subjects. Throughout the course of history we see disagreements among the Muslims, as there may be the indulgent Islam, as called by the West, since its followers showed affection and friendship to the Jews and Christians, kneeling down to the two Superpowers. Lastly, there is also the fundamentalist Islam, which is labelled by the West as the Islam of fanaticism and petrification (*tahajjur*), or madmen of Allah.

After citing all this, no room is left for us to believe in the *hadith* "the Book of Allah and my Sunnah", for the aforementioned reasons.

The truth remains so clear and evident concerning the second *hadith*, upon which all Muslims unanimously concurred, that is: "the Book of Allah and my '*Itrah*, my Ahl al-Bayt", since this *hadith* solves all the problems leaving no room for any difference or dispute in interpreting any verse of the Qur'ān, or in confirming and explaining any Prophetic *hadith*. That can be achieved through referring to Ahl al-Bayt, to whom we are commanded to refer, particularly when realizing that those who were determined by the Messenger of Allah (s) being verily competent for such mission. No Muslim can have any doubt in the profundity of their knowledge, and *zuhd* (asceticism) and *taqwā* (piety). They are those far from whom Allah has removed uncleanness and cleansed with a thorough cleansing, making them to inherit the knowledge of the Book, in a way that they neither contradict it nor differ regarding its interpretation, and rather never separate from it till the Doomsday.

The Messenger of Allah (s) said:

"I am leaving behind among you two successors the Book of Allah a rope extended from the heaven to the earth, and my kindred

('*Itrah*) my Ahl al-Bayt. They will never separate till coming unto me at the Pond (*hawd*)."²¹

"So to be with the truthful, I should utter the truth never fearing on this way the blame of those who have authority to blame, with the only objective of seeking God's pleasure, and pleasing my conscience before gaining consent of people."

The truth in this discussion is verily on the side of the Shi'ah, who adhered completely to the Messenger's recommendation regarding his '*Itrah*, giving them priority upon themselves, taking them as Imāms and leaders, seeking nearness to Allah through showing love to them, and following their guide. So may it give them pleasure by winning the world and Hereafter, where everyone will be resurrected and gathered with whoever he loved (in the world), and what a pleasure would be to gain the company of those whom he adored and followed their guidance.

In this respect al-Zamakhshari said:

Suspicion and difference multiplied and,

Each one claims to be the right path,

So I adhered to lā ilāha illā Allāh,

And to my love toward Ahmad and Ali,

A dog triumphed through loving men of cave,

So how would I be miserable by loving the Prophet's Progeny.

O God, make us among those committed and adherant to the rope of their loyalty, and those following their course and method, getting

---

²¹ *Musnad* Ahmad, vol. V, p. 122; *al-Suyuti's al-Durr al-Manthur*, vol. II, p. 60; *Kanz al-'Ummāl*, vol. I, p. 154; *Majma' al-Zawā'id*, vol. IX, p. 162; *Yanābi' al-Mawaddah*, pp. 38, 183; *'Abaqāt al-Anwār*, vol. I, p. 16; *Mustadrak al-Hākim*, vol. III, p. 148.

in their ark, believing in their Imāmate, and resurrected with their company. You guide whoever You will to a straight path

FATE AND DESTINY
(In the View of Ahl Al-Sunnah)

The topic of fate and destiny (*al-qadā' wa al-qadar*) remained in the past a complicated engima for me, as I could not find a satisfactory and sufficient explanation, at which I feel assured. I remained perplexed, with two alternatives: between what I learned in the school of Ahl al-Sunnah, that man is determined (*musayyar*) in all of his acts, having no free will to do what he likes: "Everyone is facilitated to that for which he was created," and Allah — the Glorified — delegates to the embryo inside his mother's belly two angels to inscribe his destiny, sustenance and deed, and whether he is to be miserable or happy;[1] and between the dictations of my reason and conscience, of the justice of Allah, the Glorified and Exalted, and negation of His oppression toward His creatures, as how can it be imagined that He forces them to do certain acts, and then calls them to account for them, or to chastise them for a sin He determined upon them and compelled them to do.

So, I, like many of all other Muslim youths, was experiencing those thought contrarieties, in my belief that Allah, the Glorified, being the Omnipotent and the Compeller,

"Who will not be questioned as to that which He doeth, but they will be questioned (21:23),

and

He is the Doer of what He will (85:16).

And

He created the creatures, making the fate of some to be in heavens, and some others in fire, and then He is so beneficent and merciful toward His bondmen, "doing not injustice even to the weight of an ant" (4:40),

"And thy Lord is not at all a tyrant to His slaves (41:46),

---

[1] *Sahih Muslim*, vol. VIII, p. 44.

and

"Verily, God doeth not any injustice to people, but men to their (own) selves do injustice." (10:44)

Beside all that, He is more compassionate to them than the mother to her child, as stated in the Prophetic *hadith*.[2]

I, most often, encounter such contradiction in comprehending the Qur'ānic verses, as I once understand that man against his own self shall be a witness, and he being alone to be answerable about his acts:

"Then he who hath done an atom-weight of good shall see it. And he who hath done an atom-weight of evil shall see it." (99: 7-8)

And another time I conceive that man is compelled with no might or power, having no power to benefit nor power to hurt, nor sustenance for himself:

"And ye desire not save what God desireth." (76:30),

and

"Verily God leaveth to stray whomsoever He willeth and guideth He Whomsoever He willeth" (35:8).

Certainly, it is not only me but most of the Muslims are experiencing such thought paradoxes. Therefore, when inquiring any shaykh or scholar about the issue of fate and destiny, they can never give a reply that be reasonable and acceptable to themselves before the others. So they say: It is a subject into which we should never indulge. Some of them may even forbid from indulging in it, saying: It is incumbent upon every Muslim to believe in the fate and destiny, its good and evil, and be confident of its being willed by Allah.

When being questioned by any obstinate: How can Allah compel His bondman to perpetrate a sin or crime, throwing him thereafter into the hell-fire? They will accuse him with infidelity and blasphemy and

---

[2] *Sahih al-Bukhāri*, vol. VII, p. 75.

apostasy ... beside other futile charges. Consequently, minds turned inactive and petrified, with prevalence of the belief that everything is destined (by Allah): marriage and divorce, and even adultery is destined when some say: Upon every vulva destined is the name of its male copulater (*nākih*), and so also wine-drinking and self-murder, and even eating and drinking, that you should not eat or drink but only that which is destined by Allah for you!!

After introducing all these issues, I said to some of our '*ulamā*': The Qur'ān refutes all such allegations, and the (Prophetic) *hadith* can never contradict the Quran! Concerning marriage, the Almighty Allah said:

"... then marry those who seem good to you," (4:3),

that indicating the freedom to choose. And regarding divorce he said:

"Divorce (shall be lawful) only twice then (you should) either keep her in fairness or send her away with kindness," (2:229)

which being also through free will. About adultery He said:

"And approach ye not adultery, verily, it is a shameful act and an evil way (opening to many other evils)." (17:32),

which is also an evidence for free will (*ikhtiyār*). And regarding wine He said:

"The Satan only desireth to cause enmity and hatred in your midst through intoxicants and gambling and keep you away from remembering God and from prayer; will you then abstain (from them)?" (5:91)

And in respect of murder, Allah, the Exalted, said:

"... and kill ye not the soul which God hath forbidden save for justice..." (6:152),

and also said:

"And whosoever killeth a believer intentionally, his recompense shall be Hell, he shall abide therein and God's wrath shall be on him and His curse and (there) is prepared for him a great torment." (4:93)

which all indicate free will in killing.

And even in relation to eating and drinking, He has designated for us certain limits when saying:

"... and eat ye and drink ye and commit ye not excesses; Verily He (God) loveth not the extravagants." (7:31),

that indicates free will too.

After all these explicit Qur'ānic evidences, how do you, my master, claim that everything is destined by Allah, and man is compelled in all of his acts??

He replied: Allah, the Glorified, is administering the universe alone. He mentioned as an evidence, the verse:

"Say (O Apostle Muhammad!) "O' God! Master of the kingdom, Thou givest the kingdom unto whomsoever Thou likest and takest away the Kingdom from whomsoever Thou likest! Thou exaltest whomsoever Thou likest and abasest whomsoever Thou likest; in Thine hands is all good, Verily Thou art over all things Mighty." (3:25)

I said: No disagreement between us concerning the Will of Allah, the Glorified, and if Allah wills to do something, neither humans nor jinn, nor all other creatures can oppose or contradict His Will! But our disagreement relates to the deeds of the human beings, are they produced by them or determined by Allah??

He replied: "Unto you be your religion and unto me my religion," closing thus the door of controversy. This, most often, being the argument (*hujjah*) of our *'ulamā'*. I recall that after two days, I returned to him saying: If you believe that it is Allah Who does everything, and the bondmen have no free will to do anything, so why don't you hold the same belief concerning caliphate, and that Allah, the Glorified, creates whatever He will and chooses the best (of His bondmen)?

He said: Yes, I hold this view, as Allah, the Glorified, Himself has elected Abu Bakr, and after him 'Umar, then 'Uthmān, and then 'Ali (as caliphs), and if He willed that 'Ali be the first caliph, neither jinn nor mankind could be able to prevent this.

I said: Now you are trapped.

He said: How is that I am trapped?

I said: Either you believe that Allah has elected the Four Rightly-guided Caliphs, leaving to people then free to choose whomever they like. Or you should believe that Allah has never given free will to choose to people, but He Himself elects all the caliphs after the demise of the Messenger till the Doomsday?

He replied: I hold the second opinion, according to the verse: "Say (O Apostle Muhammad!) "O' God! Master of the Kingdom, Thou givest the kingdom unto whomsoever Thou likest and takest away the kingdom from whomsoever Thou likest..."

I said: So (according to your belief), every deviation, corruption, and crime that occurred in Islam at the hands of the kings and emirs, all being from Allah (destined by Allah), as it is Him Who has made these people as rulers over the Muslims? He replied: "Yes, it is as you say, and so also concerning the righteous men. Then he recited: "And when intend We to destroy a town, (first) send We Our commandment to its people," i.e We made them emirs."

With astonishment I said: Do you mean that slaying of 'Ali at the hand of Ibn Muljam and murdering of al-Husayn ibn 'Ali being intended by Allah??

Triumphantly he said: Yes, of course. Haven't you heard the Messenger's addressing 'Ali, by saying:

"The most wicked of the latters will smite you on this (referring to his head) till this (pointing at his beard) will be wet."

So also in respect of our master al-Husayn, as the Messenger of Allah had pre-knowledge of murdering him in Karbala' apprising Umm Salamah with it. He further was aware that with our master al-Hasan Allah will reclaim two great communities of Muslims, as everything is inscribed and destined in eternity and no escape is there for man. So it is you who are trapped not me.

I kept silent for a while, looking at him feeling so proud at this speech, thinking that he has defeated me through strong evidence. I was meditating how to convince him that God's pre-knowledge of anything never indicating necessarily that He has destined it and compelled His bondmen to do it, as I was pre-aware of the fact that his mind would never comprehend such a theory.

I again asked him: So you hold that all the heads of state and kings, in the past and at present, who fight Islam and Muslims, have been appointed by Allah? He said: Yes, certainly.

I said: Do you mean that even the French colonialism over Tunisia, Algeria and Morocco being destined by Allah?

He said: Yea, and when the destined time was due, France went out from those countries.

I said: Glorified is Allah! But how were you previously defending the Ahl al-Sunnah's belief that the Messenger of Allah (may God's peace and benediction be upon him and his Progeny), died away and left the matter (successorship) to be determined through consultation (*shurā*) among Muslims, so as to elect whom they like?

He replied: Yes it is true, and I still hold the same belief, and will maintain this God-willing!

I said: How do you make concurrence then between the two beliefs: Allah's election and people's election by *shurā*?

Fate and Destiny

He said: When the Muslims elected Abu Bakr, it necessarily means that Allah elected him!

I said: Has God revealed to them in the Saqifah to choose the caliph?

He said: I seek God's forgiveness, no revelation (*wahy*) is there after Muhammad (his demise), as held by the Shi'ah! (The Shi'ah, as is known, never hold such a belief, but it is merely a charge ascribed to them by their foes).

I said: Let the Shi'ah and their superstitions alone, and convince us with what you have (of your own)! How came you to know that Allah has chosen Abu Bakr?

He said: If Allah intended other than this, neither the Muslims, nor all the worlds could ever contradict the will of Allah, the Exalted.

Only then I realized that such people never meditate nor ponder upon the Qur'ān, and according to their opinion no philosophical or scientific theory will be established with evidence.

This recalls to my mind another story, when I was wandering with a friend in a palmy garden, and as I was telling him about fate and destiny (*al-qadā' wa al-qadar*), a ripe fruit fell on my head. I picked it from over the grass in order to eat it, so I put it in my mouth.

My friend wondered saying: You can never eat but only that which Allah has prescribed for you! This fruit fell down in your name. I said: Since you believe that it is destined for me, I shall never eat it ... and I threw it away.

He said: Glorified is Allah! If anything being not prescribed for you, Allah shall verily take it out, even after reaching your belly. I said: I shall eat it then. So I picked it up to prove to him that I have free will to eat or leave it. My friend kept on watching me till I chewed and swallowed it. Thereat he exclaimed: By God it is prescribed for you (meaning that Allah prescribed it for me). In this way, he defeated me, since it was impossible for me to take the fruit out of my abdomen.

Yes, this being the belief of Ahl al-Sunnah regarding the fate and destiny, or say my belief when I was Sunni.

It is natural to be, when holding such a belief perplexed in the midst of opposites, and it is natural too for us to remain in the state of inertia all the time, awaiting that Allah changes what is inside our hearts without trying to change what is in our hearts so as to deserve being changed by Allah. Besides we may try to evade the responsibility we shouldered, seeking to hold Allah responsible for everything. For instance, when you ask the adulterer, or the burglar, or even the wicked man who raped a minor girl, killing her after accomplishing his lust, about the reason that pushed him to do so, he will reply: Allah is conqueror .... my Lord has destined so! Glorified is such Lord Who commands man to bury his daughter (alive) questioning him afer that: For what sin she was slain? Glorified are You, this is verily but a tremendous slander!

Naturally we should be then subject of derision on the part of the Western '*ulamā*', who may ridicule our weak-mindedness, or rather nickname us with some titles, like labelling our doctrine with the name "maktub al-'Arab" (i.e. the Arabs' prescription, making it the factor for our ignorance and backwardness).

It is natural too for the researchers to know that the source of this belief being the Umayyad State runners who used to circulate that Allah, the Glorified, has granted them the Kingdom and made them rulers over people. So obeying and never rebelling against them being incumbent upon all people, since that who obeys them is obeying Allah, and that renegading them is rebellious against Allah who should be slain. The Islamic history contains many evidences, of which we refer to the following:

When 'Uthmān ibn 'Affān was asked to resign (from caliphate), he refused by saying: I never take off a shirt Allah clothed me with.[3] So caliphate, in his opinion, being a garment Allah garbed him with, so no one is entitled to take it off of him but Allah the Glorified, i.e. by death.

Also Mu'āwiyah has once said: I have never fought you in order to fast and pay the *zakāt* (poor-due), but I actually fought you to be a ruler over you, and this being given me while you are averse to it. Thus he goes even farther than 'Uthmān, since he accuses the Almighty Allah with helping him to slay the Muslims so as to be their commander, and Mu'āwiyah's sermon in this regard is commonly known.[4]

Moreover, even in choosing his son Yazid, and appointing him as a governor over people against their will, Mu'āwiyah claimed that Allah made his son Yazid his successor, as a caliph over people. It was reported so by the historians, that he sent letters everywhere demanding swear of allegiance to Yazid, when Marwān ibn al-Hakam was his ruler over al-Madinah. So he wrote him a letter mentioning that allegiance to Yazid was decreed by Allah.[5]

Such was done also by the debauchee Ibn Ziyād, when Zayn al-'Abidin was brought to him fettered in chains, he inquired: Who is that? They replied: He is 'Ali ibn al-Husayn! He said: Hasn't Allah killed 'Ali ibn al-Husayn? Zaynab ('a) answered: Nevertheless, the enemies of Allah and His Messenger killed him.

Ibn Ziyād said to her: How did you view Allah's making regarding your household?

---

[3] *Tarikh al-Tabari,* "bāb hisār 'Uthmān"; *Tarikh Ibn al-'Athir.*

[4] *Maqātil al-Tālibiyyin,* p. 70; *Tafsir Ibn Kathir,* vol. VIII, p. 131; Ibn Abi al-Hadid in *Sharh Nahj al-balāghah,* vol. III, p. 16.

[5] *Al-'Imāmah wa al-Siyāsah,* vol. I, p. 151, "bāb bay'at Mu'āwiyah li-Yazid bi al-Shām".

She said: I never saw but good. These are people upon whom murder was prescribed, so they came forth toward their (destined) beds. And Allah will gather you with them, and you will be argued and disputed. At that day, you shall verily find out who is victorious, May your mother be bereaved of you, O Ibn Marjānah.[6]

In this way, this belief was spread abroad through the Umayyads and their stooges, coming into force among the Islamic *Ummah*, except the followers of Ahl al-Bayt (the Shi'ah).

Shi'ah's Belief in Fate and Destiny

As soon as I became acquainted with the Shi'ah '*ulamā*',[7] reading their books, I became aware of a new science called fate and destiny.

Al-Imām 'Ali (peace be upon him) has elucidated this, through the most express statement, when giving a reply to someone who asked him about fate and destiny (*al-Qadā' wa al-Qadar*), saying:

"Woe to you. You take it as a final and unavoidable destiny (according to which we are bound to act). If it were so, there would have been no question of reward or chastisement and there would have been no sense in Allah's promises or warnings. (On the other hand) Allah, the Glorified, has ordered His people to act by free will and has cautioned them and refrained them (from evil). He has placed easy obligations on them and has not put heavy obligations. He gives them much (reward) in return for little (action). He is disobeyed, not because He is overpowered. He is obeyed but not under force. He did not send down prophets just for fun. He did not send down the Book for the people without purpose. He did not create the skies, the earth and all that is in between them in vain.

---

[6] *Maqātil al-Tālibiyyin*, "Maqtal al-Husayn".

[7] Like the Martyr Muhammad Bāqir al-Sadr (may God sanctify his soul), from whom I benefitted a great deal regarding this issue. Beside al-Sayyid al-Khu'i, al-'Allāmah al-Tabātabā'i, and al-Sayyid al-Hākim, and others.

That is the imagination of those who disbelieve; then woe unto those who disbelieve — because of the fire." (38:27).[8]

What an express statement it is! I have never read a speech more rhetorical than this one, nor a proof better pointing to truth than it. Any Muslim is assured that his acts are (done) according to his free will and choice, as Allah, the Glorified, has given us His command but left for us the free will to choose (the acts), as said by the Imām (Amir al-Mu'minin): "Allah has ordered His people to act by free will."

Besides, He — the Glorified — has prohibited and warned us against contradicting and disobeying Him. So his speech indicated that man being free to do whatever he wills, and can disobey Allah's commandments, deserving in this case the chastisement (*'iqāb*), according to al-Imām's saying: "and has cautioned them and refrained them (from evil)."

The point was more elucidated by al-Imām 'Ali ('a) when he stated that: "He is disobeyed, not because He is overpowered", meaning that if Allah intends to coerce and compel His people to do something, all of them will be unable to overpower Him (or contradict Him). That means that He has granted free will in cases of obedience and disobedience, as indicated clearly in the Holy verse:

"And say thou: "The truth is from your Lord; so let him who pleaseth believer"; and let him who pleaseth disbelieve ..." (18:29)

Then al-Imām 'Ali addresses the conscience of man, to reach the depth of his inner consciousness, giving the decisive proof that if man being compelled in all of his acts as believed by some, so sending down the prophets and scriptures would be but a sort of play and sport, from which Allah is far above. That is due to the fact that the role of the prophets (peace be upon them all) and sending down of scriptures being for the aim of reclaiming people, taking them out from darkness into light, giving them the cure that is beneficial for their psychological

---

[8] *Sharh Nahj al-balāghah* of al-Shaykh Muhammad 'Abduh, vol. IV, p. 673.

illnesses, and clarifying the ideal way of living in felicity. The Almighty Allah said:

"Lo! This Qur'ān guideth unto that which is straightest ..." (17:9)

Al-Imām 'Ali concludes his statement with saying that to believe in good, being the same as believing that "He createth the skies and earth and all that is between them in vain," which being a disbelief whose holders are promised by Allah to be thrown in fire.

When examining the Shi'ah's belief in fate and destiny, we find it quitely an opposite belief and a right opinion. As while a sect went to extremes by believing in determinism (jabr), another one extravagated through holding the belief in free will (tafwid). But Ahl al-Bayt Imāms (peace be upon them) undertook the task of correcting and rectifying the concepts and beliefs held by these and those ones, through calling to believe in the dictum: "Neither determinism nor free will, but a state in between the two."[9]

For this belief, al-Imām Ja'far al-Sādiq cited a simplified example, easy to understand by all people in accordance to their thinking, when he replied to a questioner asking him: "What do you mean by saying: Neither determinism nor free will but a state in between the two"? He ('a) answered him thus: "Your walking on earth is not like your falling down on it", meaning that we walk on earth by our free will, but when we fall down on it, it is out of our will. Is there anyone among us like falling down that may cause fracture of some organs of our body, rendering us disabled?

Hence fate and destiny will be a state in the midst of two states, i.e a part being on our part and by our choice, and we do it according to our free will. And the second part being out of our will, and we submit to it, without being able to repel it. So we shall be called to account for the first one, while we shall not be called to account for the second part. Thus man, in this case and that will be authorized (mukhayyar) and compelled (*musayyar*) at the same time.

---

[9] *'Aqā'id al-Shi'ah fi al-Qadā' wa al-Qadar.*

A. Free in the acts produced by him out of contemplation and meditation, as he goes through the stage of option and struggle between risk-taking or abstaining, concluding at either doing (the act) or abandoning (it). To this Allah, the Glorified referred when saying:

"By the soul as it is perfected. And inspired unto it (against) its vices and (about) its piety! Indeed succeedeth he who purifieth it! And indeed faileth he who polluted it!" (91:7-10)

So purifying and polluting the soul being the result of testing the conscience of every man, as success and failure being the inevitable and fair consequence for that test.

B. Being compelled (*musayyar*) in respect of the surrounding rules and movements of the universe, which all being subdued to Allah's Will with all its parts, components, planets and particles. Man has no option to select his sex, of maleness or femaleness, or to choose his skin colour or his parents, to be brought up, for instance, by well-off parents not poor ones. Moreover he can never choose the length of his stature nor the shape of his body.

Man is verily subject to several compulsory factors, like inherited diseases for instance, beside numerous natural rules made for his advantage, with no need for any toil on his part. As man sleeps when feeling tired, gets up when being restful, eats when feeling hungry, drinks when feeling thirsty, laughs and be delighted when feeling happy, and weeps and frowns when feeling sad, while having inside his body factories that manufacture hormones, vivid cells, and transformative semens, building at the same time his body in a wonderful well-arranged equilibrium. Despite all these manifestations, man being ignorant not knowing that the Divine grace is encompassing him at every moment of his life, and rather even after his death! Allah, the Mighty and Glorious, says in this regard:

"What! Thinkest man that he will be left uncontrolled? Was he not a (mere) drop of sperm emitted? Then was he a clot of blood, then He created (him), and (He) made (him) proportioned. Then made He of

him of two kinds, the male and the female. What! Is not He potent enough to give life (again) unto the dead?" (75:36-40)

True, glorified and praised Your Name, O our Lord, the Most High! You are the One Who created then fashioned (all things), planned and guided, and caused (creatures) to die and to live. Blessed and Exalted are You, and may wretchedness and separation inflict those who contradicted and turned away from You, never esteeming You with the estimation that that befits You.)

We conclude this discussion by a saying for Al-Imām 'Ali ibn Musā al-Ridā, the Eighth of Ahl al-Bayt Imāms, who was known of having abundant knowledge during the reign of al-Ma'mun, though not reaching the age of fourteen, to the extent of being the most knowledgeable of his contemporaries.[10]

A man asked him about the explanation of the *hadith* of his grandfather al-Imām al-Sādiq: "Neither determinism nor free will but a state in between the two (extremes)."

Al-Imām al-Ridā replied:

"Whoever claims that Allah does our acts (determines them), and then chastises us for them, has in fact believed in determinism (*jabr*). And whoever claims that Allah has left the affairs of creation and sustenance completely to (be undertaken by) His trustees (*hujjaj*) — i.e. the Imāms —, has in fact believed in tafwid (authorization). Whoever believes in jabr is a disbeliever, and whoever believes in *tafwid* is a polytheist (*mushrik*). And concerning the phrase "a state in between the two", it shows the way toward doing and undertaking whatever commanded by Allah, and abandoning what He forbade. That is, Allah the Glorified has given him power to do the evil act and abandon it, in the same way as He made him able to do the good and to abandon it, and as He ordered him to do this (act) and forbade him of doing that one."

---

[10] Ibn 'Abd Rabbih, *al-'Iqd al-Farid*, vol. III, p. 42.

By my life, it is verily a sufficient and convincing statement that to be conceived by all minds, and can be comprehended by all people: the educated and uneducated.

The Messenger of Allah (s) disclosed the truth when saying in their regard:

"Do not outstrip them, for then you shall perish, and do not fall short of them, for then you shall perish. Do not teach them for they are more knowledgeable than you."[11]

A Commentary on Caliphate within Fate and Destiny

The uncommon point in this topic lies in the fact that Ahl al-Sunnah, despite their belief in the inevitable fate and destiny, and that Allah — the Glorified — compels His bondmen to act according to His Will without giving them choice in anything, but when it comes to caliphate they hold that the Messenger of Allah (s) passed away leaving the matter (of caliphate) to be determined through consultation (*shurā*) among people, to elect someone for them.

Whereas the Shi'ah hold exactly the opposite opinion, as though believing that man has option in his acts, and that Allah's bondmen can do whatever they like (within the framework of the *hadith*:)

Neither determinism nor free will but a state in between the two, but when it comes to caliphate they hold that no one has any right of option!

All this seems to be a contradiction from both sides: the Sunnah and Shi'ah at first blush, but this being untrue. As when the Sunnah hold that Allah, the Glorified, compels His bondmen in all of their acts, they

---

[11] Ibn Hajar in *al-Sawā'iq al-Muhriqah*, p. 148; *Majma' al-Zawā'id*, vol. IX, p. 163; *Yanābi' al-mawaddah*, p. 41; al-Suyuti in *al-Durr al-Manthur*, vol. II, p. 60; *Kanz al-'Ummāl*, vol. I, p. 168; *Usd al-ghābah*, vol. III, p. 137; *'Abaqāt al-Anwār*, vol. I, p. 184.

in fact contradict the matter of fact, as they believe in Allah's being the real owner of free will, but what He leaves for them being only imaginary option. Since Abu Bakr was elected, on the day of Saqifah, by 'Umar and then by some of the Companions, who being in fact executors of the order of Allah, Who has made them only a medium, according to this allegation.

Whereas the Shi'ah, when holding that Allah, the Glorified, made His bondmen free in their acts, they never contradict their opinion that caliphate being determined according to the Will of Allah alone, as stated in the verse: "Thy Lord bringeth to pass what He willeth and chooseth. They have never any choice..." That is due to the fact that caliphate, exactly like prophethood, is not among the acts done by people, and can never be determined by them or their choice. As Allah selects His apostle from among people, and delegates him (with a mission). The same is true regarding the successor of the Messenger, and people are free then either to obey the command of Allah or to disobey it, as actually happened during the lifetimes of the prophets throughout the course of ages. So (Allah's) bondmen shall be free in accepting Allah's choice, since the upright believer submits to what Allah has chosen and determined for him, while that who being ungrateful to the bounty of his Lord, rejects what Allah chose for him, rebelling against it. The Almighty Allah said:

"... then whoever followeth My guidance, he shall go not astray nor put to grief. And whoever turneth away from My monition, verily his shall be a life straitened, and We shall raise him up on the Day of Judgment, blind. He shall say: "O' my Lord! Why hast Thou raised me blind, whereas indeed I was seeing (before)?" (God) will say: "Thus (is the recompense) for did come unto thee Our signs but thou didst ignore them; And even so art thou forsaken this day." (20:123-126)

After that, when considering the opinion of Ahl al-Sunnah in respect of this issue in particular, you won't blame anyone, as whatever occurred and occurring because of the caliphate, and all the blood that was shed and honours that were violated, altogether were from Allah

Fate and Destiny

(by His Will), as commented some of knowledge-claimants among them by Allah's saying:

"... and had thy Lord pleased they would not have done it..." (6:112)

Whereas the belief of the Shi'ah being to hold responsible whoever caused the deviation and whoever disobeyed the command of Allah, each one according to the extent of his sin and that of everyone followed his heresy up to the Day of Resurrection, in accordance to the *hadith*: "Everyone of you being a guardian, and every one is responsible for his subjects.")

Allah the Exalted said:

And stop them, for verily they must be questioned." (37:24)

AL-KHUMS (ONE-FIFTH)

It is also one of controversial topics between the Shi'ah and Sunnah. Before giving judgement to their benefit or against them, we have to give a brief exposition about the issue of *khums*, and we start it with the Holy Qur'ān; Allah, the Exalted said:

"And know ye (O' believers) that whatever of a thing ye acquire a fifth of it is for God, and for the Apostle and for the (Apostle's) near relatives and the orphans and the needy and the wayfarer ... " (8:41)

The Messenger of Allah (s) said:

"I order you to do four things: To have faith in Allah, to establish prayers, to pay *zakāt*, and to fast the month of Ramadān, and to pay for Allah the fifth of whatever you acquire." [1]

The Shi'ah — complying to the command of the Messenger of Allah (s) — usually take out fifth of whatever they earn of money throughout the whole year, explaining the word "spoil" (*ghanimah*) to mean whatever man earns of profits in general.

Whereas Ahl al-Sunnah concur on specifying *khums* on the spoils of war solely, explaining God's saying: (And know ye that whatever of a thing ye acquire) to mean whatever you acquire during war.

This being the abstract of what the two sects hold regarding *khums*, and their '*ulamā*' have written many articles about this issue.

I know not how can I convince myself or others to accept the opinions of Ahl al-Sunnah, that were based — as I think — on the sayings of the Umayyad rulers, headed by Mu'āwiyah ibn Abi Sufyān who seized the whole estates of Muslims, looting with his retinue all the gold and silver there.

So, no wonder seeing them interpreting the *khums* verse to be specifically related to the spoils of war, since the course of the verse

---

[1] *Sahih al-Bukhāri*, vol. IV, p. 44.

happened to be within the verses of war and fighting. Not only this verse, but they have interpreted many verses in accordance to the course of the preceding verse or the one coming after. For instance, they interpret the verse of removing the uncleanness and purification (*tathir*), to be specifically referring to the Prophet's wives, as whatever preceding and succeeding it being about the wives of the Prophet (s).

They also interpret the Almighty's saying: "...They who hoard up gold and silver and spend it not in the way of Allah, unto them give tidings (O Muhammad) of a painful doom," to be specifically related to the People of Scripture (*Ahl al-Kitāb*).

Also the story of Abu Dharr al-Ghifāri (may God be pleased with him) with Muʻāwiyah and ʻUthmān ibn ʻAffān, and exiling him to al-Rabadhah, is so common, when he vilified them for hoarding up gold and silver, arguing them with the aforementioned verse. But ʻUthmān consulted Kaʻb al-'Ahbar about it, and he answered him that it was specified for Ahl al-Kitāb. Thereat Abu Dharr reviled him saying: May your mother be bereaved of you, O the son of the Jewish woman! Do you teach us our religion? These words angered ʻUthmān, who ordered to exile him to al-Rabadhah, after his displeasure toward him became greater. Then Abu Dharr died there, alone and driven away, with his daughter finding no one to undertake the ceremonies of washing and shrouding him.

Ahl al-Sunnah have a well-known technique and *fiqh* (jurisprudence) in relation to interpretation of the Qur'ānic verses and Prophetic Traditions, following in this respect what the earlier caliphs and famous Companions interpolated against the express texts from the Book and Sunnah.[2]

---

[2] In his book *al-Nass wa al-Ijtihād*, al-Imām Sharaf al-Din cited more than a hundred instances where ta'wil (interpretation) occurred against the express texts. The researchers are required to refer to this book, since in it he has collected only those traditions reported by the Sunni 'ulamā', admitting its veracity.

Intending to investigate respecting this matter, a separate book will be needed to cover it, but it is sufficient for every truth-seeker to refer to the book *al-Nass wa al-Ijtihād*, where he can find out how the interpreters play with Allah's decrees and precepts.

For me, as a researcher, I have no right to interpret the Qur'ānic verses and Prophetic traditions according to my likings, or in accordance with what the school (*madhhab*) I follow dictates upon me. But what to do while noticing Ahl al-Sunnah themselves reporting in their *Sihāh* that *khums* being imposed on the earnings in other than war, contradicting thus their interpretation and school of thought.

It is reported in *Sahih al-Bukhāri*, under the bāb "Fi al-Rikāz al-Khums", that Mālik and Ibn Idris said: *Al-Rikāz* (buried treasure) is the burial (*dafn*) of Jahiliyyah, upon its little and much *khums* is imposed and minerals cannot be considered *rikāz*. The Messenger of Allah (s) said: "On minerals repairment is imposed and on *rikāz* the *khums*."[3] Under the "bāb mā yustakhraj min al-bahr" (what is retrieved from the sea), Ibn 'Abbās is reported to have said: Ambergris is not regarded *rikāz*, but a thing driven forward by the sea. Whereas al-Hasan said: *Khums* is imposed (*wājib*) on ambergris and pearls, and verily the Prophet (s) made *rikāz* liable to *khums*, not that which is retrieved from the sea.[4]

From all these traditions any researcher may conclude that the scope of the term *ghanimah*, on which *khums* made *wājib* by Allah is not confined to the spoils of war, since *rikāz* is a treasure extracted from the earth, and it becomes the property of that who extracted it.But he is obliged to pay its *khums* because it is a *ghanimah*. Moreover anyone extracting ambergris and pearls from the sea is liable to take out the *khums* since it is a *ghanimah*.

According to what is reported by al-Bukhāri in his *Sahih* it becomes clear that *khums* is not confined to the spoils of war.

---

[3] *Sahih al-Bukhāri*, vol. II, p. 137, "bāb fi al-rikāz al-khums."

[4] *Ibid.*, vol. II, p. 136, "bāb mā yustakhraj min al-bahr".

While the Shi'ah's opinion remains always to represent the truth that being devoid of any contradiction and difference, since they refer in all the rules and beliefs to the Imāms of guidance, far from whom Allah removed uncleanliness and purified a thorough purification. The Imāms who are verily equals to the Book (Qur'ān), to whom everyone holds on will never go astray, and feels safe whoever seeking their shelter.

However, we can never depend on wars to establish the State of Islam, since this never goes with the liberality of Islam and its invitation toward peace. Islam is not a colonialist State that is established on exploiting the nations and looting their fortunes and resources, the charge that the Westerners trying to accuse us with when referring to the Prophet of Islam with disgrace, claiming that he (s) extended his dominion through force, compulsion and sword to exploit the peoples.

And as money being the sinew of life, especially when the theory of the Islamic economics necessitates origination of what is called nowadays: the social insurance, for the sake of guaranteeing for the needy and disabled their livelihood with consideration and dignity.

The Islamic State can never be sustained through depending upon the *zakāt* taken out by Ahl al-Sunnah, which never exceeds at the best 2.5 percent. It is a very low percentage that can never meet the needs of the State including: making ready of force, building the schools and hospitals and paving the roads, beside guaranteeing for every individual an income that can be sufficient for his livelihood and insuring his life. Further the Islamic State can never be dependant on bloody wars and fighting people to safeguard its existence, and develop its foundations at the cost of the slain people who were averse to Islam.

The Ahl al-Bayt Imāms (peace be upon them) were the most knowledgeable people in the denotations of the Qur'ān. Why not, while they being its true interpreters, undertaking the task of laying down for the Islamic State the guidelines of economy, and sociology, had they an obeyed opinion.

But, unfortunately and regretfully, power and leadership were in the hands of other than them, those who seized and usurped caliphate by force and subjugation, and assassinating the righteous among the Companions, as practised by Mu'āwiyah. Moreover they altered the rules of Allah according to the dictates of their political and worldly interests and lusts, going astray thus and misleading the others, leaving the *Ummah* to reach the lowest point, with no consideration or power till the present time.

Thus the precepts and teachings of Ahl al-Bayt became mere thoughts and theories, believed only by the Shi'ah with no way to apply them, since they were persecuted and chased out eastwards and westwards of the earth, being pursued by the Umayyads and 'Abbāsids throughout ages.

After the disintegration of these two dynasties, the Shi'ah managed to bring about a society committed to pay the *khums* to the Imāms (peace be upon them) secretly. And nowadays, they pay it to the high religious authority (*marji'*) whom they imitate (in Islamic rules) as a deputy to al-Imām al-Mahdi (peace be upon him), who in turn expends it within its legitimate purposes and uses, such as founding theological schools, charity centres, public libraries, and orphanages, beside other noble works such as paying monthly salaries and stipends to the knowledge-seekers, and alike.

From all this we can conclude that the Shi'ah *'ulamā'* act independently from the ruling authorities, since the *khums* meets all their needs, and out of it they give everyone his due.

Whereas Ahl al-Sunnah being a burden provided by the rulers, and agents working for the ruling authority, with the ruler being free to bring near, or exclude whoever he wills from among them, in accordance with their treatment and behaviour toward him and sacrifice for serving his benefit. In this way the scholar turns to be merely an agent close to the ruler rather than just a scholar ('ālim)!

which being one of the bad consequences that resulted from forsaking and ignoring performing the obligation of *khums*, in its meaning conceived by Ahl al-Bayt (peace be upon them).

IMITATION (TAQLID)

The Shi'ah hold: Regarding branches of religion (*furu'al-Din*), which represent the rules of Shari'ah (Islamic Law) related to worship acts like: *salāt*, *sawm* (fasting), *zakāt* and *hajj*, for whose rules the following conditions are obligatory:

a. Man should exert himself and strive to deduce rules from its valid sources, if being competent for this.

b. Or either he can take precaution in all of his acts if it be in his capacity.

c. Or otherwise he should imitate a mujtahid possessing full qualifications, on condition that he (*mujtahid*) be: alive, sane, just, knowledgeable, and who safeguards his soul, takes care of his *Din*, opposes his desires, and obeys the commands of his Lord.

Ijtihād in the sub-laws being a *kifā'i* obligation on all the Muslims, when any full-qualified one performs it, other Muslims will be exempted from it, and it is permissible for them to imitate him and refer to him regarding branches of religion. Because the position of *ijtihād* can never be attained so easily, or be accessible for all people, but rather requires abundance of time, sciences, knowledge and capability, the characteristics that can never be possessed but only by whoever toiling and striving hard, spending his life in investigation and seeking knowledge.

Ijtihād can never be acquired and attained but only by that who is lord of rare good fortune.

The Prophet (s) said:

"*When Allah intends good for anyone, He shall make him learned in religion.*"

There is no difference between this opinion of the Shi'ah and that of the Sunnah, except in respect of the condition of the *mujtahid*'s being alive.

But the manifest disagreement between them lies in applying taqlid. The Shi'ah believe that the qualified *mujtahid* being the viceroy of the (12th) Imām ('a) during his occultation, and he shall be the ruler and absolute chief, entitled to whatever be in the capacity of the Imām, in settling the disputes regarding all issues and judging among people, and that who contradicts him is contradicting the Imām.

The qualified *mujtahid*, in the perspective of the Shi'ah, is not only a reference (*marji'*) to be referred to in cases of giving verdicts, but also he enjoys all-inclusive *wilāyah* (guardianship) over his imitators, who refer to him in respect of rules (*ahkām*), settling all the disputes and differences among them in judicial matters, handing him the zakāt and khums of their properties and funds, to dispose of them as ordained in the Shari'ah, on behalf of the Imām of Time (peace be upon him).

While, the *mujtahid* does not enjoy this position in the perspective of Ahl al-Sunnah, who refer in the jurisprudential questions to one of the four imāms, leaders of the schools of thought (*madhāhib*): Abu Hanifah, Mālik, al-Shāfi'i and Ahmad ibn Hanbal. The contemporary Sunnis may not abide by imitating anyone of these four in particular, as they may take the rules for some of their questions from one of them and some others from another one, according to what their needs necessitate, as practised by Sayyid Sābiq who composed a *fiqh* derived from the four leaders.

And since the Sunnis believe that blessing lies in their disagreement, so the Māliki is entitled, for instance, to refer to Abu Hanifah when finding near him the solution for the problem he has, that may not be found near Mālik.

I will cite an example to demonstrate for the reader so as to be able to conceive the meaning.

In Tunisia (during the epoch of judicial courts) there was a mature girl who fell in love with some man and intended to get married to him. But her father refused to marry her to that youth, for a reason God knows alone. Then the girl fled her father's house and got married to

Imitation (Taqlid)

that young man, without taking the permission of her father. The father lodged a suit against that marriage.

When the girl and her husband were summoned and brought before the judge, he asked her about the cause behind her escaping from her father's house, and getting married without the permission of her guardian (*wali*). She replied: Sir, I am twenty-five years old, and I desired to marry this man according to the Sunnah of Allah and His Messenger; and since my father intends to marry me to someone I dislike, so I married in accordance with the opinion of Abu Hanifah, who gives me the right to marry the one I love, as I am full-grown (adult).

The judge (who himself narrated this story to me) — may God's mercy be upon him — says: "When we considered and investigated the case, we found her claim to be right, and I think that one of the well-aware *'ulamā'* has taught her what to say". The judge says: Then I rebutted the father's complaint and endorsed the marriage (judged it to be correct). So the father departed the court being at loss, reiterating these words: "The she-dog became Hanafi", i.e his daughter has abandoned Mālik and followed Abu Hanifah, and the word "she-dog" (*kalbah*) implies an insult to his daughter, from whom he has disowned later on.

The issue stems from the difference in the *ijtihād* of the schools. As Mālik is of the opinion that the marriage of the maiden girl (*bikr*) can never be valid but only with the permission of her guardian (*wali*), and even when she be a *thayyib* (that is, a girl who has had sexual intercourse), he will be her partner in marriage, and she is not allowed to decide to marry anyone without his consent. Whereas Abu Hanifah holds that the sane, grown-up female is competent to choose her husband and to contract marriage, irrrespective of being a maiden or a *thayyib*.

So this *fiqhi* issue has caused to separate between the father and his daughter, to the extent that he declared his disavowal of her. Very often fathers used to disown of their daughters for several reasons, one of which being to flee home with the man with whom she likes to get married. This sort of disowning entails inconvenient consequences, as the father most often may resort to deprive his daughter from her right to inherit him, so as the girl remaining to be an enemy to her brothers who, in turn, would disown their sister who brought them shame.

Hence the truth is not as claimed by Ahl al-Sunnah that blessing (*rahmah*) lies in their disagreement, or at the least, blessing can never be implied in all the controversial matters.

Moreover, there is another point of dispute between them, which is imitation of the dead *mujtahid* (*taqlid al-mayyit*). The Sunnis imitate *imāms* who died several centuries ago, closing the door of *ijtihād* since that era, and all the *'ulamā'* succeeding them would be content with the expositions (*shuruh*), and whatever written in poetry and prose from the *fiqh* of the four schools of thought. Then some of the contemporary *'ulamā'* began to call for opening the doors and restoration the practice of *ijtihād*, due to what the time requirements necessitating, and to find solutions for new questions and issues that were unknown during the lifetime of the four *imāms* (leaders of Sunni schools).

Whereas the Shi'ah never permit (anyone) to imitate the dead *mujtahid* (for the first time), referring in all their rules to the alive *mujtahid* possessing all the necessary qualifications we mentioned previously, during the occultation of the Infallible Imām, who charged them to refer to the equitable *'ulamā'* in the time of his occultation (*ghaybah*) till his reappearance.

The Sunni Māliki, for instance, may declare: This thing is lawful (*halāl*) and that thing is forbidden (*harām*) according to the belief of al-Imām Mālik, who is dead more than twelve centuries ago. The same claim is uttered by the followers of the Hanafi, Shāfi'i and Hanbali schools, since these four leaders lived contem prory, with each one of them learning under the hand of the other. Besides, the follower of any of the Sunni schools never believes in the infallibility of these four leaders (*imāms*), who never claimed this trait for themselves, but

Imitation (Taqlid)

believing in the possibility to err and to be correct. Besides, they claim that they are worth rewarding in all their exertions of opinion (*ijtihādāt*), deserving two rewards in case of being right, and one reward in case of being wrong.

While the *Imāmi* Shi'i, for instance, has two stages in *taqlid* (imitation):

First Stage: Which being during the lifetime of the Twelve Imāms that extended for almost three and a half centuries. During that epoch, every follower of the Shi'i school was imitating the Infallible Imām, who never speaks out of his opinion or *ijtihād*, but through knowledge and narrations he inherited from his grandfather (s), saying regarding any issue: My father has reported from my grandfather, from Gabriel, from Allah, the Glorified and Mighty.

Second Stage: Which represents the time of occultation that extended up to the present time. Every Shi'i says: This thing is *halāl* and that one is *harām* according to the opinion held by al-Sayyid al-Khu'i or al-Sayyid al-Khumayni, for instance, who both being alive, and their opinion never exceeds striving (*ijtihād*) in deducing the laws from the texts of the Qur'ān and Prophetic Sunnah, depending on the traditions of Ahl al-Bayt Imāms at first, and after them the trustees among the Companions. The reason behind their discussing the traditions of Ahl al-Bayt Imāms at first, lies in the fact that these Imāms refuse the use of opinion in respect of Shari'ah (Islamic Law), observing: There is nothing but a judgement was revealed regarding it by Allah. When we lack the law (*hukm*) on any issue, this never means that it is neglected by Allah, the Glorified, but our inadequacy and ignorance prevented us from being able to recognize the *hukm* (law) of the issue. Ignorance of anything and inability to realize it can never be an evidence indicating its non-existence, as stated by Allah, the Glorified in the Holy Qur'ān:

"We have not neglected in the Book (the Qur'ān) anything ...."
(6:38)

DOCTRINES WITH WHICH AHL AL-SUNNAH REVILE THE SHI'AH

Among the creeds and beliefs with which Ahl al-Sunnah defame the Shi'ah, there are some that have merely resulted from the abominable partisanship, created by the Umayyads and 'Abbāsids in the early epoch of Islam, out of their grudge and hatred against al-Imām 'Ali, to the extent that they kept on cursing him on the tribunes for forty years.

So no wonder to see them slandering and extremely disgracing everyone following him, to the extent that anyone of them preferred to be called a Jew than to be called a Shi'i. And their followers kept on this practice in every age and region, with the Shi'i being subject to be reviled all the time by Ahl al-Sunnah, since he contradicts them in their beliefs and is regarded a renegade against their company. They used to calumniate him with all sorts of slanders, charging him with all accusations, calling him with numerous (bad) nicknames, and contradicting him in all his sayings and acts.

Some of the well-known Sunni *'ulamā'* say: "Putting on the finger-ring in the right hand being a Prophetic *sunnah* (habit), but it should be abandoned since the Shi'ah made out of it a motto for them.[1]

Further, Hujjatul Islam Abu Hāmid al-Ghazāli says: Flattening the graves is legitimately prescribed by Islam, but when the Rufiddah (Shi'ah) made it a motto for them we substituted it with *tasnim* (making large humps).

Also Ibn Taymiyyah, who is labelled by some of them with the epithet al-Muslih al-Mujaddid (the Reviving Reformer), says: Hence, several *fuqahā'* embarked on abandoning some of the recommended acts (*mustahabbāt*), when noticing that they were turned to a motto for the Shi'ah. Though abandoning these acts is not obligatory, but demonstrating these acts would mean resembling them (the Shi'ah), so

---

[1] *Musannaf al-Hidāyah;* also al-Zamakhshari, in his book *Rabi' al-Abrār*, reported that the first who used the finger-ring in the left, contrary to the Prophetic Sunnah, was Mu'āwiyah ibn Abi Sufyān.

as no one would distinguish between the Sunni and the Rāfidi, and the convenience in being distinguished from them for the sake of forsaking and contradicting them is greater than the convenience implied in the recommended act.[2]

When asked about the way of lowering the turban, al-Hāfiz al-'Iraqi said: I have never come across any evidence indicating the specification of the right side, but only in an unauthentic (*da'if*) *hadith* reported by al-Tabarrāni. And as estimated through his prophecy, it might be that he used to let it down on the right side turning it then to the left as practised by some. But since this practice turned to be a distinguishing motto for the Imāmiyyah, so it should be abandoned and left in order to evade being resembled to them.[3]

Glorified is Allah! And there is neither might nor power but in God! Everyone can observe clearly how the bigotry allows these so-called '*ulamā*' to contradict the Prophet's Sunnah, while the Shi'ah have adhered to those *sunan* (precepts) till becoming a motto for them. Furthermore they see no interdiction in confessing this practice frankly. Praise belongs to Allah Who manifested the truth to everyone having foresight and sincerely seeking for truth. Praise be Allah's Who demonstrated to us that the true followers of the Sunnah of the Messenger of Allah being thet Shi'ah as you yourselves testified! As you gave witness against yourselves that you neglected the Messenger's Sunnah in purpose, so as to contradict the Imāms of Ahl al-Bayt and their devoted Shi'ah, and followed the *sunnah* of Mu'āwiyah ibn Abi Sufyān, as testified by al-Imām al-Zamakhshari when proving that the first to put on a ring in the left hand, contrary to the Prophetic Sunnah, was Mu'āwiyah ibn Abi Sufyān.[4]

You also followed the *sunnah* of 'Umar in his innovation of *al-tarawih* prayers, contrary to the Prophetic Sunnah that commanded the

---

[2] *Minhāj al-Sunnah* of Ibn Taymiyyah, vol. II, p. 143, "bāb al-tashabbuh bi al-rawāfid".

[3] Al-Zarqāni, *Sharh al-Mawāhib*, vol. V, p. 13.

[4] Al-Zamakhshari in his book *Rabi' al-'abrār*.

Muslims to perform the supererogatory prayers (*nāfilah*) by ones (*furādā*) at home, not congregationally, as by al-Bukhāri in his *Sahih*,[5] and as confessed by 'Umar himself of its being a *bid'ah* (heresy)[6] innovated by him, without being performed by him since he never believed in it. It is reported by al-Bukhāri, from 'Abd al-Rahmān ibn 'Abd al-Qāri, that he said: I went out with 'Umar ibn al-Khattāb, during one of the nights of the Month of Ramadān the mosque, when we noticed people separated into groups, with some man praying alone once and also praying as a leader (*imām*) being followed by a multitude of people. Thereat 'Umar said: I opine that gathering all these people under one reciter (*qāri'*), will be more proper and better. Then he ('Umar) gathered them to follow Ubayy ibn Ka'b (in performing supererogatory prayers). 'Abd al-Rahmān added: The next night I went out with him ('Umar), and we found people perform their prayers through following their reciter (leader), when 'Umar said: What a good *bid'ah* (heresy) is this! ....[7]

What arouses our wonder in this respect is considering it a bounty (*ni'mah*) after it was forbidden by the Messenger? That was when they exclaimed loudly, after gathering in front of the door of his house (the Prophet's) asking him to lead them in performing the *nāfilah* prayer of the Month of Ramadān. He (s) went out, furious and angry, saying to them:

"The making of your hands is still pushing you till I thought it to be prescribed on you. You have to abide by performing prayers (*nāfilah*) in your houses, as the best prayer of man being in his house, except the prescribed (obligatory) prayers."[8]

Further, you followed the *sunnah* of 'Uthmān ibn 'Affān, which calls for completing the prayers during travel (*four-rak'ah prayers*),

---

[5] *Sahih al-Bukhāri*, vol. VII, p. 99, "bāb mā yajuz min al-ghadab wa al-shiddah li-amr Allāh".

[6] *Ibid.*, vol. II, p. 252, "kitāb salāt al-tarāwih".

[7] *Ibid.*, vol. II, p. 252, "kitāb salāt al-tarāwih".

[8] *Ibid.*, vol. VII, p. 99, op. cit.

contrary to the Sunnah of the Messenger (s) who used to perform it (travel prayer) in two rak'ahs (*qasr*).⁹

Had I intended to enumerate all the rules in which you contradicted the Messenger's Sunnah, it would need a separate book, but we suffice with your witness through what you confessed against yourselves. Sufficient is also your testimony through your confession that the Rafidite Shi'ah have taken the Prophet's Sunnah as a motto for them.

After all these evidences, will there remain any reason to admit the ignorants claiming that the Shi'ah have followed 'Ali ibn Abi Tālib, while Ahl al-Sunnah have followed the Messenger of Allah? Do these people want to prove that 'Ali contradicted the Messenger of Allah, and invented a new religion? What a greatly slandering word coming out from their mouths! 'Ali is verily the very incarnation, interpreter and guardian of the Prophetic Sunnah, and in his regard the Messenger of Allah (s) said:

"The position 'Ali has to me is the same that I have to my Lord."¹⁰

That is, in the same way as Muhammad (s) being the only one propagating on behalf of his Lord, so also is 'Ali, being alone in propagating on behalf of the Messenger of Allah. But the fault of 'Ali lies in the fact that he never acknowledged the caliphate of those predecessors, and the fault of his followers (Shi'ah) being in their following his guide in refusing to submit and be under the caliphate of Abu Bakr, 'Umar and 'Uthmān, the reason why they were called Rawafid.

If these people (Ahl al-Sunnah) deny the (Prophetic) Sunnah's being followed by the Shi'ah's beliefs and sayings, it stems from two reasons: The first being the animosity flared up by the Umayyad rulers

---

⁹ *Ibid.*, vol. II, p. 35, (... and thus interpreted by 'A'ishah too who performed four rak'ahs) — p. 36.

¹⁰ Ibn Hajar in *al-Sawā'iq al-muhriqah*, p. 106; *Dhakhā'ir al-'uqbā*, p. 64, *al-Riyād al-nādirah*, vol. II, p. 215; *Ihqāq al-haqq*, vol. VII, p. 217.

through spreading falsities and publicities, and composing fabricated narrations.

The second reason being that the Shi'ah's doctrines contradict their (Sunnah's) opinions in supporting the caliphs and confirming their blunders and *ijtihādat* (exertions of opinion) against the texts (*nusus*), particularly the Umayyad rulers, at the head of whom being Mu'āwiyah ibn AbiSufyān.

Hence, every truth-seeker, following up the matter, will find out that the dispute between the Shi'ah and Ahl al-Sunnah originated, in fact, since the Saqifah Day, and exacerbated afterwards, and every dispute erupted after it is verily dependent on and stemmed from it. The best evidence for this being that the beliefs and creeds with which Ahl al-Sunnah vilify their brethren the Shi'ah, are firmly relevant with and ramifying from the issue of caliphate, like the number of the Imāms, the text in determining the Imām, infallibility, the Imāms' knoweldge, the *badā'*, *taqiyyah* (dissimulation), and the Promised al-Mahdi, beside other beliefs.

Investigating the claims of the two parties in an unprejudiced way, we will never see any long distance between their beliefs, finding no justification for this exaggeration and vilification. As when you read the books of the Sunnah in which they revile the Shi'ah, you will imagine that the Shi'ah have contradicted Islam, and violated its principles and legislations, inventing another religion.

While any equitable researcher will find in the Shi'ah's doctrines, a firm origin in the Qur'ān and Sunnah, and even in the books of those contracting them in these doctrines and vilifying them with. Moreover, those doctrines never contain or imply anything contrary to reason (*'aql*), or narration (*naql*) or morals. For proving to you, dear reader, the veracity of my claims, I will review with you those doctrines (*'aqā'id*).

(Belief in) Infallibility

The Shi'ah observe: The Imām — like the Prophet — should be infallible against (perpetrating) all kinds of indecencies and vices, whether the apparent or hidden ones, deliberately or out of forgetfulness, from childhood till death.

Further, he should be immune against any lapse, erring and oblivion, since the Imāms are the guardians of the Islamic Law, and responsible for bringing it into effect, exactly as the Prophet is. The evidence that made us believe in the infallibility of the prophets being the same one obligating us to believe in the infallibility of the Imāms, with no slight difference.

This is clearly the Shi'ah's opinion regarding the issue of infallibility ('*ismah*). Does it contain anything contradicting the Qur'ān and Sunnah? Or what can't be imagined by reason? Or that which disgraces and be detrimental to Islam, or belittling the status of the Prophet or the Imām?

Far it be from it and verily it is not so; we never see in this saying but a confirmation to the Book of Allah and His Prophet's Sunnah, and that which goes on with the sound reason, without contradicting it, but rather that which elevates and honours the Prophet and the Imām. We initiate our discussion with following up the Holy Qur'ān. Allah, the Exalted, said:

"Verily, verily God intendeth but to keep off from you (every kind of) uncleanness O' ye the people of the House, and purify you (with) a thorough purification)...." (33:33)

If removing the uncleanness that includes all kinds of mischiefs, and purifying from all sins, do not denote '*ismah*, but what does it mean then??

The Almighty Allah says:

"Verily those who guard (themselves against evil) when an evil thought from the Satan afflicteth them, they become mindful (of God and get awakened) then lo! They see (aright)." (7:201)

So if the pious believer bring protected by Allah against the stratagems of the Satan, when trying to provoking and misleading him, so as to become mindful and see the truth and follow it, what to say then regarding those whom were chosen by Allah the Glorious, removing uncleanness from and purifying them a thorough purification??

Allah says in another verse:

"Then made We the inheritors of the Book (Qur'ān) those whom chose We from among Our servants ..." (35:32).

And undoubtedly that who is chosen by Allah, the Glorified, should be immaculate from errors. By this verse, in particular, al-Imām al-Ridā ('a) argued against the *'ulamā'* gathered by the 'Abbāsid Caliph al-Ma'mun ibn Hārun al-Rashid, proving to them that they (Ahl al-Bayt Imāms) being verily the ones meant by the afore-mentioned verse, and whom Allah has chosen and made inheritors of the knowledge of the Book, whereat they (*'ulamā'*) admitted and acknowledged that fact.[11,12]

These were some examples from the Holy Qur'ān, and other verses are there indicating infallibility for the Imāms, like His saying, "....leaders guiding (the people) by Our command", beside other verses, but we suffice with these ones due to brevity."

After the Holy Qur'ān, we cite some proofs from the Prophetic Sunnah:

The Messenger of Allah (s) said:

---

[11] *'Aqa' id al-Imamiyyah*, p.67, *'aqidah* No. 24.

[12] Ibn 'Abd Rabbih, *al-'Iqd al-farid*, vol. III, p. 42.

"O people, I am leaving among you that which if you hold on to, you shall never go astray: the Book of Allah and my kindred, my household."[13]

It is expressly indicating the Ahl al-Bayt Imāms' being infallible, since: First, the Book of Allah is verily unassailable, that falsehood cannot come at it from before it or from behind it, and is verily the word of Allah, that whoever doubts it has in fact denied God. Second: Due to the fact that the one holding on to them both (the Book and '*Itrah*) will be safe against astrayal and misguidance. So this *hadith* indicated clearly that lapse can never be found in the Book and '*Itrah*.

The Messenger of Allah (s) has also said:

"Verily, the parable of my ahl al-bayt is that of the boat of Noah; Whoever gets aboard it is saved, and whoever stays away from it is drowned."[14]

As clearly seen, this *hadith* expressly stating that Ahl al-Bayt Imāms ('a) being infallible against (committing) sins, so anyone getting aboard their ark shall be saved, while that staying away from it shall be drowned in misguidance (*dalālah*).

Further, the Messenger of Allah said:

"Whoever desires to live my life and dies my death, and enters the heavens with which my Lord has promised me, which is the Land of the Leal (jannat al-khuld), he should follow the guide of 'Ali and his offspring after him. They shall verily never take you out of the door of

---

[13] *Sahih al-Tirmidhi*, vol. V, p. 328; *Mustadrak al-Hākim*, vol. III, p. 148; al-'Imām Ahmad in his *Musnad*, vol. V, p. 189.

[14] *Mustadrak al-Hākim*, vol. II, p. 343; *Kanz al-'ummāl*, vol. V, p. 95; *al-Sawā'iq al-muhriqah*, of Ibn Hajar, p. 184.

guidance and never bring you into the door of dalālah (misguidance)."¹⁵

It is also expressly stating that the Imāms of Ahl al-Bayt, who are 'Ali and his progeny, being infallible against any lapse, since they never bring their followers into misguidance. And it is intuitive that anyone liable to commit a lapse, can never guide other people.

The Messenger of Allah (s) said:

"I am the warner, and 'Ali is the guide. And the rightly guided will be guided by you O 'Ali after me."¹⁶

Again this *hadith* explicitly shows the Imām's being infallible, as it is unhidden for those who have understanding.

Al-Imām 'Ali himself has proved infallibility to be enjoyed by him and the Imāms among his sons when he said:

"So wither are you going to, and how are you then turned away? Ensigns (of guidance) are standing, indications (of virtue) are clear, and the miracles (of light) have been fixed. Where are you being taken astray and how are you groping while you have among you the descendants of the Prophet? They are the reins of Right, ensigns of Faith and tongues of truth. Accord to them the same good position as you accord to the Qur'ān, and come to them (for quenching the thirst of guidance) as the thirsty camels approach the water spring.

---

15 *Kanz al-'ummāl*, vol. VI, p. 155; al-Haythami in *Majma' al-zawā'id*, vol. IX, p. 108; Ibn Hajar al-'Asqalāni in *al-'Isābah*; al-Tabarāni in *al-Jāmi' al-Kabir*; Tarikh Ibn 'Asākir, vol. II, p. 99; *Mustadrak al-Hākim*, vol. III, p. 128; *Hilyat al-'awliyā'*, vol. IV, p. 349; *Ihqāq al-haqq*, vol. V, p. 108.

16 *Tafsir al-Tabari*, Vol.XIII, p. 108; *Tafsir al-Razi*, vol. V, p. 271; *Tafsir Ibn Kathir*, vol. II, p. 502, *Tafsir al-Shawkani*, vol. III, p. 70; *al-Suyuti in al-Durr al-manthur*, vol. IV, p. 45, *Nur al-absar*, p. 71; *Mustadrak al-Hakim*, vol. III, p. 129; *Tafsir Ibn al-Jawzi*, vol. IV, p. 307; *Shawahid al-tanzil*, vol. I, p. 293; *al-Fusul al-muhimmah*; *Yanabi 'al-mawaddah*.

O' people, take this saying of the last of the prophets that he who dies from among us is not dead, and he who decays (after dying) from among us does not really decay. Do not say what you do not understand, because most of the Right is in what you deny. Accept the argument of one against whom you have no argument. It is I. Did I not act before you on the greater *thaql* (i.e. the Qur'ān) and did I not retain among you the smaller thaql (*al-thaql al-'asghar*, i.e. the descendants of the Prophet). I fixed among you the standard of faith..."[17]

After all these statements and excerptions from the Holy Qur'ān, and the Prophetic Sunnah, and sayings of al-Imām 'Ali all indicating the infallibility of all Imāms (peace be upon them), can the intellect reject the *'ismah* of that who is chosen by Allah to guide (people)? The reply is definitely. No it can't refuse this. On the contrary, reason (*'aql*) believes in the obligation of that *'ismah*, due to the fact that the one who is entrusted the task of leadership and guiding the mankind, can never be an ordinary human being subject to laspe and oblivion, burdened with sins and heavy guilts, so as to be vulnerable to vilification and criticism of people.

Rather, the reason necessitates that he (the Imām) should be the most knowledgeable, equitable, courageous and righteous of his time, the characteristics elevating the position of the leader, and glorifying him in the view of people. They too make all people to venerating and appreciating, and consequently obeying them without any reservation or adulation.

If so be the case, what causes all this vilification and exaggeration against whoever believing in this?

When listening to and reading the Ahl al-Sunnah's critisim regarding the issue of infallibility, one will imagine that it is the Shi'ah who are girding the badge of *'ismah* to whomever they wish, or that

---

[17] *Nahj al-Balāghah*, Sermon No. 87. In his exposition of this sermon, Muhammad 'Abduh made this commentary: Any of Ahl al-Bayt Imams may die, but in fact he is not dead, since his spirit remains effulging light and brighness over the world of being.

the one believing in *'ismah* is claiming an abomination and blasphemy. Whereas the truth is neither this nor that, but *'ismah* in the perspective of the Shi'ah, is in fact the state in which the infallible should be favoured with a Divine care and Lordly patronage, so that neither Satan can seduce him, nor the soul enjoining unto evil can ever overcome his mind, leading him toward (perpetrating) sins. And Allah has never denied His pious bondmen this favour, as referred to in the verse:

"Verily those who guard (themselves against evil) when an evil thought from the Satan afflicteth them, they become mindful (of God and get awakened) then lo! they see (aright)." (7:201)

This provisional infallibility that is imparted upon Allah's bondmen in a certain case, might vanish with the loss of the cause originating it, that is the *taqwā* (piety). As when the bondman being distant from piety of Allah, he shall never be protected by Allah, while the Imām, who is chosen by Allah the Glorified, never deviates or turns aside from *taqwā* and God-fearing.

In the Holy Qur'ān a story is cited about our master Yusuf (peace be upon him):

"And indeed she longed for him, and he (also) would have longed for her, had he not seen the evidence of his Lord; Thus it was that We turn away from him evil and shameful deeds; Verily he was (one) of Our freed servants." (12:24)

And since our Lord Yusuf hasn't longed for adultery (*zinā*) as interpreted by some exegetes, far be the prophets of Allah from such abominable act, but he in fact intended to drive her back and, if necessary, beat her. So Allah the Glorified prevented him from (perpetrating) such a sin, since had he perpetrated it, it would have been exploited as a plea to accusing him of corruption, so as to be a strong proof against him, afflicting him with evil on the part of them.

Number of Imāms (Ithnā 'Ashar)

The Shi'ah hold that the number of the Infallible Imāms, who succeeded the Prophet (s), being twelve Imāms, no more no less. They were mentioned by the Messenger of Allah (s) by name and number,[18] as follows:

1. Al-Imām 'Ali ibn Abi Tālib.
2. Al-Imām al-Hasan ibn 'Ali.
3. Al-Imām al-Husayn ibn 'Ali.
4. Al-Imām 'Ali ibn al-Husayn (Zayn al-'Abidin).
5. Al-Imām Muhammad ibn 'Ali (al-Bāqir).
6. Al-Imām Ja'far ibn Muhammad (al-Sādiq).
7. Al-Imām Musā ibn Ja'far (al-Kāzim).
8. Al-Imām 'Ali ibn Musā (al-Ridā).
9. Al-Imām Muhammad ibn 'Ali (al-Jawād).
10. Al-Imām 'Ali ibn Muhammad (al-Hādi).
11. Al-Imām al-Hasan ibn 'Ali (al-'Askari).
12. Al-Imām Muhammad ibn al-Hasan (al-Mahdi al-MuntaZar).

These are the Twelve Imāms believed to be infallible by the Shi'ah, so as Muslims not to be beguiled and deceived. The Shi'ah, long ago and recently, never acknowledge anyone to be infallible except these Imāms, who were determined by the Messenger of Allah before being born.

Their names, as mentioned before, were reported by Ahl al-Sunnah *'ulamā'*, and al-Bukhāri and Muslim reported in their *Sahihs*, the

---

[18] *Yanābi' al-mawaddah*, of al-Qunduzi al-Hanafi, vol. III, p. 99.

hadith of the Imāms in number, who being twelve ones all from Quraysh.

These traditions never be true and proper but only when taking it to mean Ahl al-Bayt Imāms, as believed by the Imāmiyyah Shi'ah. And the Sunnis are required to solve this enigma, since the number of the Twelve Imāms which they reported in their *Sihāh* remained yet an unsolvable riddle.

The Imāms' Knowledge

The point which is exploited by Ahl al-Sunnah to revile the Shi'ah being their (Shi'ah's) saying: "That the Ahl al-Bayt Imāms (peace be upon them) have been distinguished by Allah the Glorified with a knowledge that no one shared them with. And that the Imām being the most knowledgeable of his time, with no possibility that he being questioned by someone and fails to give a reply!

Is there any evidence for this claim?

Let's begin our discussion, as usual, by the Holy Qur'ān. Allah, the Glorified and Most High, says in His Book:

"Then made We the inheritors of the Book (Quran) those whom chose We from among Our servants..." (35:32),

the verse clealry indicating that Allah, the Glorified, has chosen some servants from among people making them inheritors of the knowledge of the Book. Have we to recognize these upright people?

Previously we stated that the Eighth Imām of Ahl al-Bayt, 'Ali ibn Musā al-Ridā, has proved that the aforementioned verse was revealed in their (Imāms) regard. That was (when the Caliph) al-Ma'mun gathered for him forty famous judges, with every one of them preparing forty questions to put forth to him, for all of which he gave convincing answers that dumbfounded them, making them to admit his knowledgeability.[19] [20]

If this Imām being only fourteen years during this conversation with the *fuqahā'*, who admitted his knowledgeability, so how would it be strange then the Shi'ah's belief in their knowledgeability, while Ahl al-Sunnah *'ulamā'* and leaders acknowledge the same for them.

But when intending to interpret the Qur'ān by the Qur'ān, we shall see many verses indicating one meaning, stating that Allah, for an extreme wisdom, distinguished the Imāms of the Prophet's Household with a given knowledge of His own, so as to be leaders of guidance and lights for darkness.

The Almighty Allah said:

"He granteth wisdom to whomsoever He willeth, and he who hath been granted wisdom hath been given abundant good; and none shall mind it save those endowed with wisdom." (2:269)

He also said:

"But nay! I swear by the setting of the stars. And verily it is a great oath if ye only knew it. Verily it is Qur'ān honourable. In a book hidden. Toucheth it not save the purified ones." (56:75-79)

In this verse Allah the Glorified swore with a great oath, that the Holy Qur'ān contains secrets and inner concealed meanings that can never be comprehended with their real intentions but only by the purified ones, who are the people of the House from whom Allah has removed uncleanness and purified a thorough purification. This verse indicates too the Qur'ān's having an innermost with which Allah, Subhanah, distinguished the Ahl al-Bayt Imāms that can never be recognized but only through them.

---

[19] *Sahih Al Bukhari* vol. VIII, p. 127; *Sahih Muslim*, vol. VI, p. 3.
[20] Ibn 'Abd Rabbih, *al-'Iqd al-farid*, vol. III, p. 42.

Doctrines with which Ahl Al-Sunnah Revile the Shi'Ah   193

To this reality the Messenger of Allah has referred by saying: "Do not outstrip them, for then you shall perish, and do not fall short of them for then you shall perish. Do not teach them for they are verily more knowledgeable than you." [21]

Al-Imām 'Ali himself also said: "Where are those who falsely and unjustly claimed that they are deeply versed in knowledge, as against us, although Allah raised us in position and kept them down, bestowed upon us knowledge but deprived them, and entered us (in the fortress of knowledge) but kept them out. With us guidance is to be sought and blindness (of misguidance) is to be changed into brightness. Surely Imāms (divine leaders) will be from the Quraysh. They have been planted in this line through Hāshim. It would not suit others nor would others be suitable as heads of affairs."[22]

Allah, the Exalted, said:

"Ask the followers of the Remembrance if ye know not." (16:43).

This verse also was revealed in the regard of Ahl al-Bayt (peace be upon them).[23] It indicates that the *Ummah*, after the demise of its Prophet, should refer to the Imāms of the Household, in order to realize the realities. The Companions, as reported, referred to Al-Imām 'Ali ibn Abi Tālib to explain for them the questions they could not solve, and throughout long years, people resorted to the Imāms for recognizing the *halāl* (lawful) and *harām* (unlawful), and to acquire from their knowledge and virtues.

And when Abu Hanifah says: Had not been the two years, al-Nu'mān would have perished (meaning the two years he spent on

---

[21] Ibn Hajar al-Shāfi'i, *al-Sawā'iq al-muhriqah*, p. 148; al-Suyuti, *al-Durr al-manthur*, vol. II, p. 60; *Kanz al-'ummāl*, vol. I, p. 168; *Usd al-ghābah fi ma'rifat al-Sahābah*, vol. III, p. 137.

[22] *Nahj al-balāghah*, Muhammad 'Abduh, Khutbah No. 144.

[23] *Tafsir al-Tabari*, vol. XIV, p. 134; *Tafsir Ibn Kathir*, vol. II, p. 570; *Tafsir al-Qurtubi*, vol. XI, p. 272; *Shawāhid al-tanzil*, of al-Hasakāni, vol. I, p. 334; *Yanabi' al-mawaddah; Ihqāq al-haqq* of al-Tustari, p. 482.

learning under al-Imām Ja'far al-Ṣādiq). And when al-Imām Mālik ibn Anas says: No eye has ever seen, no ear has ever heard, and no heart has ever thought of a human better than Ja'far al-Ṣādiq, in respect of virtue, knowledge, worship and godliness.[24] When this be the case as admitted by Ahl al-Sunnah Imāms, so why all this vilification and disapproval be made against Ahl al-Bayt, after citing all these proofs, and after Muslims history proved that Ahl al-Bayt Imāms were the most knowledgeable men of their time. And why to be wondering when noticing Allah the Glorified distinguish His friends (*awliyā'*) "whom He chose" with wisdom and knowledge of His own, making them an ideal example for the believers and leaders for all Muslims.

Had the Muslims followed up each other's evidences, they would have been convinced of acknowledging Allah and His Messenger, and would be one community some supporting the others, and neither disagreement nor various schools of thought (*madhāhib*) would have been there.

But all this is inevitable, so that Allah might conclude a thing that must be done,

"that he who perished (on that day) might perish by a clear proof (of His Sovereignty) and he who survived might survive by a clear proof (of His Sovereignty). Lo! Allah in truth is Hearer, Knower." (8:42)

Principle of al-Badā'

It means that some idea seems to Him regarding a thing. He intends to do, but then He changes His opinion concerning that thing, doing other than what He determined to do previously.

Concerning what the Shi'ah observe in respect of the *badā'* with ascribing it to Allah, the Exalted, and vilifying them on the basis that it entails ascribing ignorance and incompleteness to Allah, the Glorious and Exalted, as the Sunnites conceive it. Verily this interpretation is false and never claimed by the Shi'ah, and whoever ascribes it to them

---

[24] *Manāqib Al Abi Ṭālib*, "bāb fi ahwāl al-'Imām al-Ṣādiq".

has in fact slandered them. There are many evidences proving their belief, that can be derived from their sayings, in the past and recently.

In his book '*Aqa'id al-Imāmiyyah*, al-Shaykh Muhammad Ridā al-Muzaffar says: "*Al-Badā'* in this meaning is quite impossible to be ascribed to Allah, as it denotes ignorance and incompetence, which can enver be possible for the Most High God, and never believed by the Imāmiyyah."

It is reported that Al-Imām al-Sādiq ('a) said: "Whoever claims that something seemed to be done by Allah in a repentful way (i.e. repented for not doing it before), we consider him as disbelieving in Allah the Great." He also said: "Whoever alleges that something appeared newly for Allah, without being aware of it before, I proclaim freedom from him" (i.e. I never regard him a Muslim).

So the *badā'* believed by the Shi'ah, never transgresses the limits of the Qur'ān, as prescribed by Allah, the Glorified and the Most High, in the verse:

"*(Of it) Effaceth out God whatever He pleaseth and confirmeth He (similarly); and with Him is the Mother (Basic Source) of the Book.*" (15:39)

This belief is held by the Sunnis in the same way as held by the Shi'ah. So why the Shi'ah are vilified while Ahl al-Sunnah are exempted, whereas they (Sunnis) claim that Allah, the Glorified, alters the decrees and changes the prescribed destinies and sustenances (of mankind).

Ibn Mardawayh and Ibn 'Asākir have reported from 'Ali ('a) that he once inquired the Messenger of Allah (s) about the verse: "Effaceth out God whatever He pleaseth and confirmeth He (similarly), and with Him is the Mother (Basic Source) of the Book." In his reply, the Messenger of Allah (s) said:

"I will verily delight you and also my *Ummah* after me with its interpretation. Charity in its due aspect, and to be kind to the parents, and doing the good (ma'ruf), altogether render wretchedness (shaqa') into bliss and increase in life, and safeguard against evil death."

In the book al-Shu'ab, Ibn al-Mundhir, Ibn Abi Hātam and al-Bayhaqi reported from Qays ibn 'Ubbād that he said: On every tenth night of the inviolable months, there is a certain thing (*amr*) for Allah, but on the tenth of Rajab, Allah effaces what He will, and establishes He (what He will).

'Abd ibn Hamid, Ibn Jarir and Ibn al-Mundhir have reported that 'Umar ibn al-Khattāb, while circumambulating round the House (of Allah), said:

"My God, if You have prescribed upon me a wretchedness (*shaqāwah*) or a sin (I implore you to) efface it, as You efface what You will and establish (what You will), and with You is the Mother (Basic Source) of the Book. (I beg You to) make it bliss and forgiveness."[25]

In his *Sahih*,[26] al-Bukhāri reported an amazing and strange story, about the ascension (to heaven) of the Prophet (may God's peace and benediction be upon him and his Progeny), and his meeting with his Lord, beside what is said by the Messenger (s):

"...Then fifty prayers were prescribed upon me, when I came toward Musā ('a) who said: What have you done? I said: Fifty prayers are prescribed upon me. He said: I am better aware of people than you, as I have worked with and treated the Children of Israel so strictly, but your *Ummah* never endures (these prayers). Go back to your Lord and ask Him (to decrease them). So I returned and implored Him, whereat He made them forty. Then the same conversation was repeated with Moses, and they were made thirty. Then again the same thing was repeated and He made them (prayers) twenty, then the same and He made them ten. Thereat I came near Moses and he reiterated his

---

[25] *Al-Suyuti*, op. cit., vol. IV, p. 661.
[26] *Sahih al-Bukhāri*, vol. IV, p. 78, "Kitāb bad' al-khalq", "bāb dhikr al-malā'ikah".

speech. Then God made it only five (prayers), when I came near Musā who said: What have you done? I replied: (He (God) made it five. He said the same aforementioned words. I said: I saluted (Allah), but I heard a call (from Allah) saying: I have prescribed my obligation, and eased for My servants. I shall reward every good deed (*hasanah*) with ten ones."[27]

In another narration reported also by al-Bukhāri, it is said: After reference of Muhammad (s) many many times to his Lord, and after obligating the five prayers, Musā ('a) asked Muhammad (s) to refer to his Lord to ask Him more easiness, since his *Ummah* would never tolerate even five prayers. But Muhammad (may God's peace and benediction be upon him and his Progeny) answered him saying: I feel ashamed of my Lord.[28]

Everyone reading this be baffled and amazed at these beliefs held by the Ahl al-Sunnah traditionists, who, nevertheless, vilify the Shi'ah, the followers of Ahl al-Bayt Imāms, due to believing in the principle of *badā'*.

Through this tale, they presume that Allah the Glorifed has prescribed fifty prayers upon Muhammad (s), then it seemd for Him, after Muhammad's referring to Him, to make them forty, and then, after another reference by Muhammad, to make them thirty, and so on, making them twenty, and then ten, and lastly five prayers after being asked by Muhammad for the fifth time.

Regardless of our admitting or refusing such a notion, it is to be known that holding the idea of *badā'* being a sound belief, going with and complying to the concepts of Islam and spirit of the Qur'ān: "Verily God changeth not the condition of a people until they change what is in themselves ..." And without our belief — Sunnah and Shi'ah — that Allah changes and substitutes, all our prayers and supplications

---

[27] *Ibid.*, vol. IV, 250, "bāb al-mi'rāj", *Sahih Muslim,* vol. I, p. 101, "bāb al-'isrā' bi Rasul Allāh wa fard al-salawāt".

[28] *Ibid.*, vol. IV, 250, "bāb al-mi'rāj", *Sahih Muslim,* vol. I, p. 101, "bāb al-'isrā' bi Rasul Allāh wa fard al-salawāt".

shall verily be devoid of any use or cause or explanation. We further believe that Allah, the Glorified, changes the judgements, and abrogates the laws from one prophet to another, and even in the Shariah of our Prophet (s) verily exist *nāsikh* (abrogating) and *mansukh* (abrogated). Hence, to believe in the principle of *badā'* is neither blasphemy nor renegading from religion (aspotasy). So the Sunnites are asked not to vilify the Shi'ah due to this belief, and the Shi'ah, on their part, have no reason to vilify Ahl al-Sunnah.

On my part, I view this tale of *mi'rāj* (ascension to heaven) as necessarily attributing ignorance (*jahl*) to Allah, the Mighty and the Glorious, and entailing defamation of the dignity of the greatest man ever known throughout mankind history, i.e. our Prophet Muhammad (upon whom and whose Progeny be God's peace and benediction). That is because the tale says that Musā said to Muhammad (s): I am better aware of people than you, indicating that the decrease of prayers was done by virtue of Musā, i.e. without him Allah would have never eased for the *Ummah* of Muhammad (s).

I can never conceive, how would Musā know that the *Ummah* of Muhammad (s) can never endure even five prayers, while Allah knows not this and charges His bondmen with (duties) beyond their capacity, prescribing upon them fifty prayers?!

Brother reader, you can imagine the case in which fifty prayers are performed through one day, which meaning that no work or business shall be executed by the society, and people will never go out for learning or earning their living or undertaking any responsibility. In this way man will turn to be like angels, charged only with (performing) prayers (*salāt*) and worship. By making a simple arithmetic operation, we shall find out the falsification of this narration. When multiplying ten minutes — the reasonable time for performing one obligatory prayer (*salāt*) congregationally — by fifty, the result that we get will show that the determined time (for these prayers) shall be about ten hours. That means, you either have to tolerate and endure this burden, or you can reject such religion that imposes upon its followers duties beyond their capacity prescribing upon them obligations they can never endure.

Here a question is raised: If Ahl al-Sunnah vilify the Shi'ah for believing in *badā'*, and that Allah, after it seems for Him in a thing, changes His decision as He will, why don't they vilify themselves their belief that it seems for Allah something and He changes the rule or judgement five times regarding one duty (*faridah*), and on one night being the night of *mi'rāj* (ascension to heaven)?

May Allah's damnation be upon such bigotry, and detested obstinacy overshadowing the realities, and turning them upside down, when the fanatic persecutes that who contradicts him in opinion, with negating the clear-cut matters. Beside that, he may vilify him, and disseminate rumours against him, with exaggerating regarding the simplest issues, in more horrible than which he may believe.

This reminds me of what is said by our master Jesus (peace be upon him) when addressing the Jews:

"You look at the straw in the eyes of people, but you never see the wood in your eyes."

Or (reminds of) the proverb saying: "She infected me with her illness and slipped away." Some may object that the term *badā'* was never used by Ahl al-Sunnah, and that this story, though giving the meaning of changing and altering the judgement, but it never confirms decisively that something seemed (*badā*) for Allah in it.

I utter this since most often when I was citing the tale of *mi'rāj*, making it as a proof to show the belief in the *badā'* by the Sunnites, I was encountered with objection of some of them in relation to this opinion. But later on they submitted and admitted it when I showed them another narration from *Sahih al-Bukhāri*, that referring to the *badā'* by a doubtless express term.

It is reported by al-Bukhāri, from Abu Hurayrah, that the Messenger of Allah ('a) said: It was seemed for Allah to test three Israelites, a leprous, a blind and a bald. So He sent them an angel who came to the leprous one and asked him: Which thing you desire more? He replied: A good colour (for the feature) and a well-shaped skin, as I became disgustful for people. Then the angel rubbed him and he recovered from leprosy, with being given a good colour and well-shaped skin. After that the angel said to him: Which kind of property you like more? He said: The camels. So he was given a pregnant she-camel. Then he went to the bald one, and asked him: Which thing you desire more? He replied: A well-formed hair and be recovered from this (baldness). The angel rubbed his head when his baldness disappeared, and he was given fine hair. Then he asked him: Which kind of property you love more? He said: The cows. So he gave him a pregnant cow. Then he (the angel) came unto the blind one, and questioned him: Which thing you desire more? He said: May Allah give me back my sight. Then he wiped him and Allah returned his sight to him. Again he asked him: Which property you love more? He said: The sheep. Thereat he gave him a productive sheep ...

Then the angel returned to them, after multiplication of their camels, cows and sheep, until everyone of them turned to be owning a herd (of animals). He approached the leper and the bald and the blind, each with his same image. He asked each one of them to give him from what he owns. The bald and the leper repelled him (refused to give him), so Allah restored them to the same condition they were in. While the blind man gave him (of what he owned), as a result of which Allah increased in his property, and kept him wont to see. [29]

Therefore I address my brothers with this verse:

"O' ye who believe! Let not a people laught at (another) people (to scorn) who haply may be better than them; nor let women laugh at other women who haply may be better than these and find out not fault with your own selves nor call ye one another by nicknames; evil is a bad name (for any one) after his accepting the faith; and whoso turneth not (repenting against such of his conduct), these are they who are the unjust (ones)." (49:11)

---

[29] *Sahih al-Bukhāri*, vol. II, p. 259.

I also have a heart-felt wish that Muslims come to their senses, forsake bigotry and let alone passion so as to be replaced by reason in every debate, even with their enemies. I hope that they learn from the Holy Qur'ān the proper way of investigation, discussion and argumentation with that which is better (method), as Allah revealed to His Messenger (s) to tell the obstinate:

"...Lo! We or you assuredly are rightly guided or in error manifest." (34:24)

Thus the Messenger of Allah (s) elevates the position of these polytheists, with making concessions on his part, to make them feel equal to him so as to introduce their proofs and reason, had they been truthful. What a sublime morality had he, that can never attained by ordinary people.

Taqiyyah (Dissimulation)

In the same way we referred previously to the belief in the principle of *badā'*, *taqiyyah* (dissimulation) too is among the points disapproved and deplored by Ahl al-Sunnah. They misuse it to vilify their brethren, the Shi'ah, labelling them among the hypocrites, as they claim that they (Shi'ah) show the opposite of what they hide inside their hearts!!

Most often I conferred some of them (Sunnis), endeavouring to convince them that *taqiyyah* is never like hypocrisy (*nifāq*), but all was in vain. Even you may see some of them feel disgusted sometimes, and other times may be amazed and baffled, thinking that such beliefs being innovated (as heresies) into Islam, as if they be among the fabrications and bida'(heresies) of the Shi'ah.

When any truth-seeker fairly investigates the matter in an equitable way without any prejudice, he will verily find out that all these beliefs being (derived) from the kernel and essence of Islam, and a product of the Holy Qur'ān and Prophetic Sunnah. Rather the magnanimous Islamic concepts and sound Shari'ah can never be established and straight but only through these beliefs.

What is amazing about Ahl al-Sunnah, being that they disapprove of creeds (held by the Shi'ah) in which they themselves believe, and with which their books, *Siḥāḥ* and *Musnads* are replete, testifying against them.

We can read together what is said by Ahl al-Sunnah regarding the issue of *taqiyyah*:

— It is reported that Ibn Jarir and Ibn Abi Hātam, with the chain of al-'Awfi, from Ibn 'Abbās that regarding Allah's saying: "... except (when) ye (have to) guard yourselves against (them) for fear from them...", he said: *Taqiyyah* (dissimulation) is verily by the tongue, and whoever intends to talk about a thing implying disobedience to Allah, disclosing it then for fear from people (to avoid their evil) with his heart being still content with the Faith. This will verily be not detrimental for him, since *taqiyyah* is in fact with the tongue."[30]

— It is reported and confirmed by al-Hākim, and by al-Bayhaqi in his *Sunan*, from 'Ata', from Ibn 'Abbās, that regarding Allah's words: "...except (when) ye (have to) guard yourselves against (them) for fear from them ..." he said: *Taqiyyah* is verily uttering something by the tongue with the heart being still content with the Faith.[31]

— 'Abd ibn Hamid reported from al-Hasan ('a) that he said: The *taqiyyah* is permissible till the Day of Resurrection.[32]

— 'Abd ibn Abi Raja' said that he used to read thus: "... except (when) ye (have to) guard yourselves against (them) with *taqiyyah*."[33]

— It is reported by 'Abd al-Razzaq, Ibn Sa'd, Ibn Jarir, Ibn Abi Hātam, and Ibn Mardawayh, and confirmed by al-Hākim in *al-Mustadrak*, and by al-Bayhaqi in *al-Dalā'il*, that he said: The polytheists took away 'Ammār ibn Yāsir, never letting him alone till he

---

[30] *Al-Suyuti,* op.cit.
[31] Sunan al-Bayhaqi, *Mustadrak al-Hākim*.
[32] *Al-Suyuti,* op. cit., vol. II, p. 176.
[33] *Al-Suyuti,* op. cit., vol. II, p. 176.

slandered the Prophet (s) and referred to their idols with good terms, only then they left him. When the Messenger of Allah (s) came, he asked him: What is the matter with you? He replied: I have bad news, I was never forsaken till defaming you and mentioning their idols with good (glorifying them). The Prophet said: How do you feel inwardly (in heart)? He replied: My heart is still content with the faith. He (s) said: If they return and resume you can resume. Thereat the following verse was revealed:

"...save he who is compelled while his heart remaineth steadfast with the faith..." (16:106)

— Ibn Sa'd reported from Ibn Sirin that he said: The Prophet (s) encountered 'Ammār as he was crying. He wiped his eyes (the tears) saying: "Have the disbelievers taken and plunged you into water, and you said so and so (?), (no problem) if they return to it you can tell them the same."[34]

— It is reported by Ibn Jarir, Ibn al-Mundhir, Ibn Abi Hātam, and al-Bayhaqi in his *Sunan*, through the chain of 'Ali, from Ibn 'Abbās, that regarding the verse: "He who disbelieveth in God after his belief in Him, save he who is compelled while his heart remaineth steadfast with the faith ...", he said: Allah the Glorified informs that: Whoever disbelieves in God after having faith in Him, on him is the wrath of God and for him shall be a great torment. Whereas that who is compelled and coerced, saying something (bad) with his tongue while his heart contradicting this through (firm) faith, so as to protect himslef and be safe from his enemy, for him no harm is there and he is not to blame. This due to the fact that Allah calls His bondmen to account for what is deliberately determined insdie their hearts.[35]

— Ibn Abi Shaybah, Ibn Jarir, Ibn al-Mundhir and Ibn Abi Hātam, reported from Mujahid that he said: This verse was revealed in regard to some of the Meccans who believed (in Allah). Then some of

---

[34] Ibn Sa'd, *al-Tabaqāt al-Kubrā*.

[35] *Sunan* al-Bayhaqi.

Sahābah at al-Madinah wrote (a letter) to them telling them: Travel toward us, as we never regard you belonging to us till you migrate toward us. So they went out, starting their travel to al-Madinah. On the way, they were caught by some Qurayshi people who seduced them, compelling them to disbelieve. Then in thier regard this verse was revealed: "... save he who is compelled while his heart remaineth steadfast with the faith..."[36]

— In his *Sahih*, under *bāb al-Mudārāt ma'a al-nās*, al-Bukhāri reported from Abu al-Dardā' that he said: "We grin (the teeth) before some people while our hearts are cursing them."[37]

— Al-Halabi in his Sirah, is reported to have said: "When the Messenger of Allah (s) conquered the Town of Khaybar, Hajjāj ibn 'Allāt said to him: O' Messenger of Allah, I have a property at Makkah, in which I have a household, and I intend to go there. Would you absolve me if I speak ill of you, and utter something (bad) about you? The Messenger of Allah (s) permitted him to say whatever he would like.[38]

— Al-Imām al-Ghazāli, in his book Ihyā' al-'ulum, is reported to have said: "To prevent shedding the blood of the Muslim is obligatory. Whatever be the purpose for shedding the blood of a Muslim hiding (himself) from the oppressor, then to lie about him (not divulging his place) is verily obligatory.[39]

— In his book *al-'Ashbah wa al-naZa'ir*, Jalāl al-Din al-Suyuti is reported to have said: "It is permissible to eat the (meat of) carrion during hunger, and to wash down the morsel into wine, and pronouncing word of infidelity. When *harām* prevails in a country, to the extent that *halāl* (lawful) can rarely be found, thereat using whatever is needed is permissible."

---

[36] *Al-Suyuti,* op. cit., vol. II, p. 178.

[37] *Sahih al-Bukhāri,* vol. VII, p. 102.

[38] *Al-Sirah al-Halabiyyah,* vol. III, p. 61.

[39] *Ihyā' 'ulum al-Din,* of Hujjatul Islām Abu Hāmid al-Ghazāli.

— Abu Bakr al-Rāzi, in his book *Ahkām al-Qur'ān*, is reported to have interpreted Allah's words "... unless (it be) that ye but guard yourselves against them, taking (as it were) security ..." thus: It means that when you fear loss of life or some of body organs, you can guard yourselves against them and show loyalty without believing in it (in the heart). This is the outward meaning of the utterance, on which multitude of men of knowledge are unanimously concurring, as reported by Qatādah about Allah's saying: "Let not the believers take the disbelievers as their friends rather than the believers" that he said: It is not permissible for any believer to take a disbeliever as his friend (*wali*) in his religion. And regarding His saying: "... unless (it be) that ye but guard yourselves against them, taking (as it were) security", he said: It necessitates the permissibility of showing disbelief in case of *taqiyyah* (dissimulation)."[40]

— In *Sahih al-Bukhāri*, it is reported from Qutaybah ibn Sa'id, from Sufyān, from Ibn al-Mukandar, who narrated on the authority of 'Urwah ibn al-Zubayr that 'A'ishah told him that: A man took permission to enter upon the Prophet (s), when he (s) said: Let him in, how bad is the son (or the brother) of the clan! As he entered, the Prophet talked to him so mildly and tenderly. I said: O Messenger of Allah, after you uttered those words, you talked to him so gently (what for)? The Prophet (s) said: "O 'A'ishah, verily the most wicked person in position near Allah, is that whom people forsake or be gentle with for the sake of guarding against his obscenity of language." [41]

After reviewing all these traditions, we have a sufficient proof that the Sunnites believe in permissibility of *taqiyyah*, in the extreme, holding that it is permissible till the Day of Resurrection as previously mentioned. They believe in the obligation of lying, as reported by al-Ghazāli, and in demonstrating disbelief (*kufr*) as unanimously concurred by a multitude of the learned men, and confessed by al-Rāzi, and in permissibility of showing ostensible smile while cursing

---

[40] Al-Rāzi, *Ahkām al-Qur'ān*, vol. II, p. 10.

[41] *Sahih al-Bukhāri*, vol. VII, p. 81, "bāb lam yakun al-Nabi fāhishan wa la mutafahhishan".

inwardly, as confessed by al-Bukhāri. Besides, they hold that man is free in defaming or slandering the Messenger of Allah (s) with any words he likes for protecting his money and properties, as expressed by the author of *al-Sirah al-Halabiyyah*, and to say whatever implying disobedience to Allah or obscenity for fear from people, as reported by al-Suyuti.

So Ahl al-Sunnah need not to vilify and negate the Shi'ah for a doctrine believed by them, and reported in their *Sihāh* and *Musnads* as permissible or rather obligatory (belief). The Shi'ah never went farther than what is held by the Sunnites, except that they became known in practising it more than other sects, due to the oppression and persecution they suffered at the hands of the Umayyads and 'Abbāsids. At those times, just saying: This man is following and taking the part of Ahl al-Bayt, was a reason enough to make him face his end, and being murdered so savagely at the hands of the enemies of Ahl al-Bayt ('a).

Therefore, they (the Shi'ah) had no alternative but to practise and apply *taqiyyah*, following the instructions of Ahl al-Bayt Imāms (peace be upon them). Al-Imām al-Sādiq is reported to have said: Verily *taqiyyah* is of my *Din* (religion) and the *Din* of my fathers, and one who does not keep *taqiyyah* has no din. *Taqiyyah* was verily a motto for the Ahl al-Bayt Imāms themsleves, to safeguard themselves and their followers and lovers against all sorts of danger and damage, and sparing their lives, and reforming the conditions of the Muslims who were afflicted with trial in their *Din*, as occurred to'Ammar ibn Yāsir (may God be pleased with him) or even more.

While the Sunnites were far from such a trial since, most the time, they were on good terms with the rulers, as a result of which they were never subjected to murder, looting and injustice. So it was quite natural for them to negate *taqiyyah*, and vilify those practising it, with the Umayyad and 'Abbāsid rulers playing a great role in defaming the Shi'ah because of the *taqiyyah*.

And since regarding it (*taqiyyah*) Allah revealed a verse to be recited and laws to be executed, and since the Messenger of Allah (s), as reported in *Sahih al-Bukhāri*, practised it himself, permitting 'Ammār ibn Yāsir to revile him and declare his disbelief if the infidels resumed torturing him, and also since the *'ulamā'* of Muslims permitted this practice (*taqiyyah*), following the precepts of the Book of Allah and Sunnah of His Messenger, how is it correct then to vilify and deplore the Shi'ah, and for what reason?!

Taqiyyah was practised by the dignified Companions during the eras of the tyrant rulers, like Mu'āwiyah, who used to kill whoever refusing to curse 'Ali ibn Abi Tālib. The story of Hijr ibn 'Adiyy al-Kindi and his fellowmen is widely known. And the likes of Yazid, Ibn Ziyād, al-Hajjāj, and 'Abd al-Mālik ibn Marwan, and their equals are so many, that intending to gather the examples and evidences indicating the Companions' practice of *taqiyyah*, we shall need a separate book to cover them, we shall need a separate book to cover them, but the reasons of Ahl al-Sunnah that I cited can be sufficient, thanks to God.

I avail myself of this opportunity to cite a nice story I personally experienced with one of the Sunni scholars. It coincided that we met on board of an airplane, while we were among those invited to attend an Islamic conference in Britain. We exchanged our viewpoints about the Shi'ah and Sunnah for nearly two hours. He was one of callers to unity, and I admired him. But I was displeased when he said that: the Shi'ah are asked now to abandon some of the beliefs that create disagreement among the Muslims, and causing them to defame and attack each other. When I asked him: Like what? He immediately replied: Like the *mut'ah* (temporary marriage) and *taqiyyah*. I tried my best to convince him that *mut'ah* being a legitimate and legal kind of marriage, and *taqiyyah* being a permission from Allah, but he insisted on his opinion, never be persuaded by all the evidences I cited for him. He claimed that whatever I cited and mentioned was correct and true, but it should be abandoned for the sake of a higher and more significant convenience, being unity of Muslims.

I found strange his logic which calling to abandon the precepts and rules of Allah for the sake of unity of Muslims. In a courteous way, I said to him: Had the unity of Muslims mainly depended on this thing, I would have been the first to respond and submit.

We disembarked in London airport, and I was walking behind him. As we approached the airport policemen, we were questioned about the reason of travelling to Britain. He answered by claiming that he came for treatment, and I claimed that the reason of my coming being to visit some of my friends. We passed safely and without any delay, toward the hall of bags delivery. Thereat I whispered in his ear: Have you noticed how *taqiyyah* be valid and possible at all times? He said: How? I said: Because we lied to the police, I through claiming to have come to visiting my friends, and you through claiming to have come for treatment, while we actually came for participating in the conference.

He smiled, while recognizing that he told a lie in the hearing of me, saying: Don't the Islamic conferences have a remedy for our souls? I laughed saying: And don't they have a visit to our brethren?!

I resume the topic and say that *taqiyyah* is verily not in the way claimed by the Sunnah — that it be a sort of hypocrisy — but the opposite is right. As hypocrisy means to show out faith (*Imān*) and conceal disbelief (*kufr*), while *taqiyyah* being to demonstrate kufr and conceal faith, and what a great difference is there between the two positions. Regarding the former one, i.e. hypocrisy (*nifāq*), Allah said:

"And when they meet with those who believe, they say, "We believe", but when they go apart to their devils, they say, "Surely we are with you, verily, we did but mock." (2:14)

That means: outward faith + inward kufr = hypocrisy (*nifāq*). While regarding the second situation, i.e. *taqiyyah*, Allah, the Glorified and Most High, said: **"And said a man who was a believer, from among the people of Pharaoh; who used to conceal his faith ..."** which means: outward disbelief (*kufr*) + inward faith (*imān*) = *taqiyyah*.

The believing man of the people of Pharaoh used to conceal his faith inwardly, with no one being aware of it except Allah, pretending before Pharaoh and all people of his being the follower of the *Din* of Pharaoh. (Allah referred to him in His Holy Book as a sign of extolness and glorification for his status).

Dear reader, I invite you to recognize in full what the Shi'ah hold in regard of *taqiyyah*, so as not to be beguiled by what falsely and calumniously claimed about them.

In his book '*Aqa'id al-Imāmiyyah,* al-Shaykh Muhammad Ridā al-Muzaffar is quoted to have said:

"There are certain rules for *taqiyyah*, in respect of its obligation and non-obligation, in accordance with the difference of situations of fear from damage. They are stated classified of fear from damage. They are stated classified under their relevant chapters in the *fiqhi* books sof the *'ulamā'*. It is not obligatory in all cases, but rather it may be or should be contradicted in certain cases, such as when disclosing and proclaiming the truth implies a support to the *Din*, and a service rendered to Islam and *jihād* in its way. Only then it can be disposed of funds and properties, and selves can never be endeared or held on. *Taqiyyah* may be forbidden in respect of the acts obligating the killing of honourable persons, or spreading abroad of falsehood (*bātil*), or corruption in *Din*, or an extreme loss for the Muslims, through misleading them, or making injustice and despotism to prevail among them."

"However, *taqiyyah*, in the perspective of the Imāmiyyah, never makes them an underground society working for destruction and sabotage, as intended to be portrayed by their enemies who never endeavour to realize the matters in their true sense, bothering not themselves to comprehend the correct opinion held by us."

"Also its purpose is not to render *Din* and its rules a secret that it is impermissible to be divulged to those denying it. How can it be so while the Imāmiyyah books and works, in the fields of *fiqh*, laws and themes of *kalām* and doctrines, have covered the East and West and gone beyond the limits expected from every community believing in them." (End of his speech).

Everyone can clealry observe that there neither be any *nifāq* (hypocrisy), nor deceit, nor foist, nor cheating, as claimed by their enemies.

Al-Mut'ah (or Temporary Marriage)

It means the *mut'ah* marirage (*nikāh*), or unpermanent marriage, or temporary marriage to a determined term. It is like the perpetual marriage, as can never be valid but only through a marriage contract including a consent and corresponding acceptance, when recited by the bride employing the words: I have married myself to you (*zawwajtuka nafsi*), with so and so dower, and for so and so period. Thereat the man says: *qabiltu* (I have accepted).

For this kind of marriage certain conditions are stated in the *fiqhi* books of the Imāmiyyah, such as determining the dower (*mahr*) and period. It will be valid with any condition agreed by both parties, and like the prohibition of concluding a marriage contract (temporarily) with female relations (*al-muharramāt*), due to consanguinity, as in the case of the permanent marriage.

The temporarily married woman should, after expiry of the term (*ajal*), undergo '*iddah* (waiting without concluding another marriage contract) for two menstrual courses, and in case of the death of her husband for four months and ten days.

There is neither inheritance nor maintenance (*nafaqah*) between the couple married temporarily, that is neither of them can inherit the other side after death. But the child born due to temporary marriage has the same rights granted to the child born due to permanent marriage, in regard of inheritance and maintenance (*nafaqah*), beside all other breeding and material rights, and should be acknowledged as the legal child of his father.

Doctrines with which Ahl Al-Sunnah Revile the Shi'Ah

This is *mut'ah* with all its conditions and limits, which can certainly never be like fornication, as claimed by some people.

The Sunnis, like their brethren the Shi'ah, unanimously concur on that the legitimacy of such a marriage being prescribed by Allah, the Glorified and the Exalted, in the verse 24 of *Surah al-Nisā'*:

"... And as such of them ye had mut'ah with them, give them their dowries as a fixed reward; and it shall not be a sin on you, in whatever ye mutually agree (to vary) after the fixed reward; Verily God is All-Knowing, All-Wise."

They also concur that the Messenger of Allah (s) has permitted this kind of marriage, and the Sahābah exercised it during his lifetime. But they (the Shi'ah and Sunnah) differ regarding its being abrogated or not. Ahl al-Sunnah believe in its being abrogated and forbidden after it was *halāl* (lawful), and that the abrogation was made by the (Prophetic) Sunnah not by the Qur'ān. Whereas the Shi'ah believe in its being not abrogated, and its being lawful till the Day of Resurrection.

Hence, the dispute concerns only whether it was abrogated or not, and to review the beliefs of the two sects so as to elucidate to the dear reader where the truth lies, for being followed without any fanaticism and prejudice.

Regarding the Shi'ah believing in its not being abrogated, and its being *halāl* till the Day of Resurrection, their proof being: It is never confirmed for us that the Messenger of Allah (s) has ever forbidden it (*mut'ah*), and our Imāms from the Pure Kindred (*'itrah*) believe in its being lawful (*halāl*). Had there been any abrogation issued from the Messenger of Allah (s), the first to know it would have been the Ahl al-Bayt Imāms headed by al-Imām 'Ali ('a), as Ahl al-Bayt (household) are better aware of what is there inside it (the house). But that which is established for us being that it is the 2nd Caliph 'Umar ibn al-Khattāb who has forbidden it and considered it unlawful (*harām*), through exerting his own opinion as testified by the Sunni *'ulamā'* themselves. But we can never leave the *ahkām* (rules) of Allah and His Messenger to be ordained by the opinion and *ijtihād* of 'Umar ibn al-Khattāb! This was altogether the belief held by the Shi'ah regarding the lawfulness of *mut'ah,* which is verily an apposite belief and a sober opinion, since all Muslims are required to follow and adhere to the precepts of Allah and His Messenger, refusing everyone other than them whatever high his position be, when his *ijtihād* being contradictory to the Qur'ānic or Prophetic texts.

Whereas Ahl al-Sunnah believe that the *mut'ah* was lawful, a verse was revealed in its regard, and the Messenger of Allah (s) permitted people to prarctise it, and it was exercised by the Companions, but it was abrogated afterwards. But they differ concerning who has abrogated it, some saying that the Messenger of Allah (s) has forbidden it before his death. And some other hold that it was 'Umar ibn al-Khattāb who forbade it, claiming that his words being *hujjah* (authority) in their view, due to the *hadith* of the Messenger of Allah (s):

"Adhere to my *sunnah* and the Sunnah of the rightly-guided successors after me. Hold on to it and cling on it stubbornly."

Concerning those believing in its being unlawful due to its being prohibited by 'Umar ibn al-Khattab, and that his act being a binding *sunnah*, we have nothing to do with them, nor any debate, since their belief is a mere bigotry and affectation. Otherwise, how is it feasible for any Muslim to abandon and contradict the precepts and sayings of Allah and His Messenger, and adhere to the words of a human being exerting his opinion, liable to err and be correct, in case his *ijtihād* being about a matter regarding which no text in the Book (Qur'ān) and Sunnah is found. But how would be the case when a text (*nass*) is revealed (in the Qur'ān):

"And it is not for a believer man or woman to have any choice in their affair when God and His Apostle have decided a matter, and whoever disobeyeth God and His Apostle, indeed he hath strayed off a manifest straying." (33:36)

Whoever disagrees with me regarding this rule (or principle), is asked to reconsider his information in respect of the concepts of the Islamic Law, and study the Holy Qur'ān and the Prophetic Sunnah. Because the Qur'ān itself indicated in the above-mentioned verse, beside many other similar Qur'ānic verses, that whoever not adhering to the Qur'ān and Prophetic Sunnah is verily but a disbeliever and strayed (misled).

Further, many proofs are found in the noble Prophetic Sunnah, of which we suffice with this *hadith* uttered by the Messenger of Allah (s):

"Whatever deemed *halāl* (lawful) by Muhammad is *halāl* (for you) till the Day of Resurrection and his *harām* is *harām* (unlawful) till the Day of Resurrection".

So no one is entitled to deem lawful or unlawful regarding any matter on which a text (*nass*) and rule is revealed and established by Allah or his Messenger (s).

Due to all that is mentioned, we tell those trying to convince us that the acts and exertions (*ijtihādat*) of the Rightly-guided Caliphs are binding, i.e. we should follow them, we tell them this verse:

"Say thou (unto the people of the Book), Dispute ye with us about God; whereas He is our Lord, and your Lord, and for us are our deeds and for you are your deeds; to Him (alone) we are (exclusively) loyal?" (2:139)

But those believing in this proof agree with the Shi'ah in their claim, and will be verily a *hujjah* against their brethren from among Ahl al-Sunnah.

Our debate is limited only with those claiming that it is the Messenger of Allah (God's peace and benediction be upon him and his Progeny) who has prohibited it (*mut'ah*), abrogating the Qur'ān by the *hadith*.

Such people are confused and non-established in their sayings, with their proof being unsubstantial and never established on a firm basis, even though the forbiddance (*nahy*) from it was reported by Muslim in his *Sahih*. Because had there been any *nahy* issued by the Messenger of Allah, it would have never been neglected by the Sahābah who practised mut'ah (temporary marriage) during the era of Abu Bakr and a part of the era of 'Umar himself, as reported by Muslim in his *Sahih*.[42]

'Ata' said: Jābir ibn 'Abd Allāh came back from 'Umrah (short pilgrimage), when we visited him in his house. Then some of us questioned him about several matters, till referring to the mut'ah, where he said: Yes, we practised it during the lifetime of the Messenger of Allah (s) and that of Abu Bakr and 'Umar.

Had the Messenger of Allah (s) forbidden the mut'ah, it would have never been permissible for the Companions to practise it during the reign of Abu Bakr and 'Umar, as mentioned before. The fact is that it was not the Messenger of Allah (s) who forbade or deemed it *harām*, but the forbiddance was issued by 'Umar ibn al-Khattab, as reported in *Sahih al-Bukhāri*.

— Musaddad said: It is reported by Yahya, from 'Imran Abu Bakr, from Abu Raja', from 'Imran ibn Husayn, that he said: The verse of mut'ah is revealed in the Book of Allah, and we exercised it during the lifetime of the Messenger of Allah (s) with no verse being revealed deeming it unlawful or its being forbidden (by anyone) till he (s) died. Then a man exerted his opinion, ascribing it to Muhammad, who is said to be 'Umar.[43]

It is made quite clear that the Messenger of Allah (s) has never forbidden it till the end of his life, as expressed by this Companion who ascribed forbiddance to 'Umar so expressly and with no any obscurity, adding that he exerted his opinion in everything, as he

---

[42] *Sahih Muslim*, vol. IV, p. 158.
[43] *Sahih al-Bukhāri*, vol. V, p. 158.

desired.

Also Jābir ibn 'Abd Allāh al-'Ansari so explicitly says: We used to consummate temporary marriage (*mut'ah*) with (only) a handful of dates and flour during the lifetime of the Messenger of Allah (s), and era of Abu Bakr, until it was forbidden by 'Umar in the case of 'Amr ibn Hurayth.[44]

No wonder to see some of the Sahābah were of the opinion of 'Umar, as previously mentioned during our discussion about the Thursday Misfortune, when they agreed with him in his saying: The Messenger of Allah (s) utters obscene language and we suffice with the Book of Allah! So when they supported him in that critical situation, implying that much of defamation against the Messenger, how wouldn't they agree with him in respect of some of his *ijtihādat*? The evidence can be seen in this utterance of one of them: I was with Jābir ibn 'Abd Allāh, when someone entered upon him saying: Ibn 'Abbās and Ibn al-Zubayr disagreed about the two enjoyments (of *hajj* and marraige). Thereat Jābir said: We did both of them during the lifetime of the Messenger of Allah (s), till the time of 'Umar who forbade us, when we stopped practising them both.[45]

Therefore I personally believe that some Companions ascribed prohibition of mut'ah to the Messenger of Allah (s), for the sake of justifying the position of 'Umar ibn al-Khattab, and approving of his opinion.

Otherwise, how would the Messenger of Allah (s) forbid what is deemed lawful (*halāl*) in the Qur'ān, as it is infeasible for us to find any of the Islamic rules that being deemed *halāl* by Allah, the Glorified, while being forbidden by His Messenger. Such a claim can never be expressed but only by that who being obstinate and fanatic. Even when presuming so for argument's sake that the Messenger (s) has forbidden it, it was not for al-Imām 'Ali ('a), the nearest in kinship

---

[44] *Sahih Muslim*, vol. IV, p. 131.

[45] *Ibid.*, vol. IV, p. 131.

to the Prophet (s) and the most knowledgeable in the (Islamic) rules, to say:

"Mut'ah is verily a blessing showered from Allah upon His bondmen, and had not been 'Umar's forbiddance no one would have committed fornication but the wretched."[46]

It is to be known that 'Umar ibn al-Khattab himself has never ascribed the prohibition to the Prophet (s), but rather he uttered his widely-known proclamation, so outspokenly:

"Two enjoyments were commonly practised during the lifetime of the Messenger of Allah (s), from which both I forbid and on which I punish: *mut't al-hajj* (pilgrimage) and enjoyment (*mut'ah*) with women."[47]

The *Musnad* of al-Imām Ahmad ibn Hanbal is the best evidence proving the presence of great differences among the Sunnis concerning this issue, as some of them deem it lawful, heeding in this regard to the Messenger's precepts, while some others deeming it *harām* (unlawful) following the opinion of 'Umar ibn al-Khattab. Al-Imām Ahmad is reported to have said:

— Ibn 'Abbās said: The Prophet (s) practised the *Mut'ah* (temporary marriage) once, when 'Urwah ibn al-Zubayr said: *Mut'ah* is forbidden by Abu Bakr and 'Umar! Thereat Ibn 'Abbās said: What is that uttered by 'Uryah? (belittlement for 'Urwah)? He said: He says that *mut'ah* was forbidden by Abu Bakr and 'Umar. Then Ibn 'Abbās said: I am sure that they shall verily perish, and I say: The Prophet said, while they say: Abu Bakr and 'Umar forbade."[48]

---

[46] Al-Tha'labi in *al-Tafsir al-kabir*, and al-Tabari in his *al-Tafsir al-Kabir* too, in his interpretation of the verse on mut'ah.

[47] Al-Fakhr al-Rāzi, in *al-Tafsir al-kabir*, in his interpretation of the verse: "And those of whom ye seek content (by marrying them) ..." (4:24).

[48] Al-'Imām Ahmad in his *Musnad*, vol. I, p. 337.

Also in *Sahih al-Tirmidhi*, it is reported that 'Abd Allāh ibn 'Umar was questioned about the *hajj* enjoyment. In reply he said: It is *halāl*. Then the questioner said to him: But your father has forbidden it? He replied: When my father forbids something practised by the Messenger of Allah (s), what do you think me to do better: to follow the order of my father or that of the Messenger of Allah (s)? The man said: Certainly you have to obey the commandment of the Messenger of Allah (s)." [49]

It is known that Ahl al-Sunnah obeyed Umar regarding the *mut'ah* with women, and disobeyed him regarding *mut'ah* of pilgrimage, though forbidding from them both was issued by him, altogether in one position, as previously referred to. The most important point in all this discussion and debate, being that the Ahl al-Bayt Imāms and their followers (the Shi'ah) contradicted and negated his ('Umar's) claim, considering it (*mut'ah*) as *halāl* (lawful) till the Day of Resurrection. This belief (held by the Shi'ah) was pursued also by some Sunni *'ulamā'*, of whom I refer to the eminent Tunisian scholar, the leader of the Zaytunah Mosque al-Shaykh al-Tāhir ibn 'Ashur (may God's mercy be upon him). In his famous *Tafsir* (exegesis) he cited for its (*mut'ah*) lawfulness the verse: "... and as such of them ye had *mut'ah* with them (marrying them), give them their dowries as a fixed reward..." [50]

True, such should be the *'ulamā'*, free in their creed, never being influenced by any prejudice or bigotry, and never fearing on the way of Allah the blame of any blamer.

After this brief discussion, no justification or plea is left for Ahl al-Sunnah's vilification and defamation against the Shi'ah due to their permitting the marriage of *mut'ah*, beside the fact that the decisive proof and evident argument being on the side of the Shi'ah.

---

[49] *Sahih al-Tirmidhi*, vol. I, p. 157.
[50] Al-Tāhir ibn 'Ashur, *al-Tahrir wa al-tanwir*, vol. III, p. 5.

Every Muslim is asked to portray in the mind the words of al-Imām 'Ali ('a) that: "Mut'ah is verily a blessing showered from Allah upon His bondmen. Actually, is there any blessing greater than such one which quenches a refractory lust that might overwhelm man, male or female, renderring him/her like a beast of prey.

All Muslims in general, and the youth in particular, have to know that Allah, the Glorified, has imposed upon the adulterer the punishment of death through pelting stones (*rajm*), when perpetrated against the married, males and females. It is not for Allah to forsake His servants with no mercy, while He being the Creator of them and their instincts, having full knowledge of what can ameliorate them. And when Allah, the Beneficent and the Merciful, has showered His mercy upon His bondmen through permitting them to practise *mut'ah*, so no one would commit adultery thereafter, but only the mischievous, exactly like passing the sentence of amputating the thief's hand. And in the same way, as long as there being a treasury dedicated exclusively for the destitute and needy people, no one will steal but only the mishievous.

Claim of Tahrif of the Qur'ān

This claim in itself being so horrible that no Muslim, Shi'i or Sunni, believing in the message of Muhammad (s), can ever endure or accept. This is due to the fact that the Lord of Glory has undertaken its preservation, when He said:

"Surely We have revealed the Reminder and We will most surely be its preserver." (15:9)

Thus it is immune from any addition and loss even with one letter, being the miracle of our Prophet (s), which will never die or fall into oblivion, and falsehood cannot come at it from before it or from behind it, being a revelation from the Wise, the Owner of Praise.

The Muslims' practical status quo refuses the *tahrif* of the Qur'ān, since many Sahābah were memorizing it by heart, competing in memorizing it and teaching their children to learn it by heart,

Doctrines with which Ahl Al-Sunnah Revile the Shi'Ah 219

throughout the course of time till the present day. It is infeasible for any man, group, community or government to mutilate or alter the Qur'ān, at all.

Traversing all Muslim countries, eastwards and westwards, northwards and southwards, all over the world, we will surely find the same Qur'ān with no addition or loss whatsoever. Though Muslims being separated into schools (*madhāhib*), sects, cults and religions, the Qur'ān remains the sole incentive able to gather them, with no disagreement between even two among them, except regarding exegesis and interpretation (*ta'wil*), as each group rejoicing in its tenets.

So the *tahrif* (corruption) attributed to the Shi'ah is no more than a vilification and exaggeration, having no existence in the Shi'ah's beliefs. When going through the Shi'ah's view regarding the Holy Qur'ān we can notice that they unanimously believe in its being guarded against any mutilation.

Al-Shaykh al-Muzaffar, the author of the book 'Aqā'id al-Imāmiyyah, says in this regard:

"We believe that the Qur'ān being the Divine revelation (*wahy*) sent down from Allah, the Exalted, upon His noble Prophet, containing an exposition of all things. And also it is His everlasting miracle disabling all mankind of keeping pace with it in respect of rhetoric and eloquence, and the realities and sublime knowledge it contains, being guarded against any alteration or changing or mutilation (*tahrif*). The Qur'ān we have nowadays being surely the same one revealed to the Prophet, and anyone claiming other than this is but a violater, or obstinate errant or mistaken, all being misguided and misled, as it is surely Allah's word that falsehood can never come at it from before it or from behind it." (His speech is over).

Besides, all the Shi'ah lands are widely known and their rules in *fiqh* are commonly recognized by all. Had they possessed any Qur'ān other than that we have nowadays, it would have been discovered by people. I remember that when, for the first time, I visited the Shi'ah land, such gossips were filling my mind, that whenever seeing a bulky volume, I would pick it up hoping to put my hand on that alleged Qur'ān. But very soon, such fancy has vanished away, recognizing later on that it was only one of the fabricated vilifications aimed at causing people to have aversion to the Shi'ah. Nonetheless, there is, ever and anon, someone vilifying and arguing the Shi'ah with a book named: *Fasl al khitāb fi ithbāt tahrif Kitāb Rabb al-'Arbāb*, whose author is Muhammad Taqi al-Nuri al-Tabrasi (d. 1320 H.), who was a Shi'i. In this way those transgressors intend to overburden the Shi'ah the responsibility for this book! The act that is far from equity.

So many books were written, that in fact never express but the viewpoints of their writers and authors, containing the lean and strong, truth and falsehood, and implying wrong and correct. This fact includes all the Islamic sects, and is not confined to the Shi'ah alone. Are we permitted to hold Ahl al-Sunnah responsible for what was written by the Egyptian Culture Minister and dean of Arabic literature Dr. Tāhā Husayn regarding the Qur'ān and pre-Islamic (*Jāhili*) poetry? Or what al-Bukhāri reported, which is considered veracious near them, about the presence of loss and addition in the Qur'ān, and so also is *Sahih Muslim,* and other sources? [51]

Let's turn aside from this and return good for evil. What an excellent words uttered in this regard, those said by the Professor Muhammad al-Midyani, Dean of al-Shari'ah College in al-'Azhar University, when writing:

"And as regards the claims that the Imāmiyyah believe in presence of loss in the Qur'ān, I seek God's protection... they are no more than narrations reported in their books, the like of which are reported in our books. The investigators from among both the sects have refuted them, proving their falsehood and fabrication. No one among the *Imāmi*

---

[51] As the book *Fasl al-khitāb* has no consideration among the Shi'ah whatsoever, while the narrations about the loss and addition in the Qur'ān being reported by the *Sihāh* of Ahl al-Sunnah like those of al-Bukhāri and Muslim, with *Musnad Ahmad.*

Shi'ah or Zaydiyyah is ever believing in this, neither is there anyone among the Sunnis.

Anyone desiring to have more information can refer to al-Suyuti's book *al-'Itqān*, in which he can see the likes of such narrations, of which we turned aside.

"In 1498, an Egyptian compiled a book calling it *al-Furqān*, interpolating it with such poor, exotic and rejected narrations, reporting quotations (in their confirmation) from the Sunni books and references. Al-'Azhar then asked the Government to stop publication of (confiscate) the book, after demonstrating with scientific proof and argument the aspects of falsehood and deviation in it.The Government responded to this request and confiscated the book. Its author then filed a case demanding an indemnity, but the Administrative Judiciary in the State Cabinet dismissed the case.

"Should we say then that Ahl al-Sunnah deny the sanctity of the Qur'ān? Or believe in presence of loss in the Qur'ān due to a narration reported by so and so? Or due to a book compiled by so and so?

The same is true concerning the *Imāmi Shi'ah,* that reports can be found in their books similar to those recorded in some of our books (the speech to al-Midyani). Al-Imām al-'Allāmah Abu al-Fadl ibn al-Hasan al-Tabrasi, an eminent Imāmi scholar in the 6th Hijrah Century, in his book *Majma' al-bayān li 'ulum al-Qur'ān,* says in this respect:

"There is consensus and unanimity among the Muslims that there is not any 'excess' in the Holy Qur'ān. But with regard to the deficiency of the text of the Holy Qur'ān, a group of Imāmiyyah and a group of Hashwiyyah who are Sunnis have claimed presence of atterations and deficiencies in the Holy Qur'ān, but the true belief accepted by the Imāmiyyah holds otherwise.

This is supported by al-Sayyid al-Murtada (may God sanctify his soul), giving it its full due in reply to the questions of *al-Tarābulusiyyāt,* saying in some places: Knowledge and certainty of the validity of the narration of the Holy Qur'ān are like the knowledge and certainty on the existence of countries, cities, famous historical events, popular books, and the poems compiled by the Arabs. This is because the specific regard and attention and the strong motive for the narration of the text of the Holy Qur'ān and its upkeeping had been much stronger than the precision and attention given to the above-cited items, since the Qur'ān being the miracle of Prophethood, source of legal sciences and religious rules. And Muslim *'ulamā'* paid so great attention in preserving and safeguarding it, to the extent that they came to recognize all controversial things regading which disagreement was there, including its syntax *(i'rāb)*, readings, letters and verses. So how is it permissible to believe in its being altered, or decreased, with the presence of this sincere attention and strict precision."[52]

To elucidate for you, dear reader, the fact that this accusation (decreasing and increasing the Qur'ān), should verily be attributed to Ahl al-Sunnah rather than being ascribed to the Shi'ah. This was one of the motives urged me to reconsider all of my beliefs, as whenever I tried to criticize the Shi'ah and negate or disapprove them regarding anything, they would prove their acquittal from it, with attributing it to me. Then, with passage of days, and through investigation, I recognized the truth of their claims, of which I was convinced, for which I praise God. Hereunder I shall present the evidences proving my claim in this topic: Al-Tabarrāni and al-Bayhaqi are reported to have said: There are two *surahs* (dropped) in the Qur'ān, one being:

بسم الله الرحمن الرحيم

إنا نستعينك ونستغفرك ونثني عليك الخير كله ولا نكفرك ونخلع ونترك من يفجرك

---

[52] The article written by the Professor Muhammad al-Midyani, the dean of al-Shari'ah College in *al-Jāmi' al-'Azhar*, appeared in the journal *Risālat al-'Islām*, issue No. 4, the 11th year, pp. 382-383.

Doctrines with which Ahl Al-Sunnah Revile the Shi'Ah

meaning: We ask You to help us and seek Your forgiveness, and praise You with all good, never deny You, and disavow from and forsake whoever dissipates You). The second one is thus:

بسم الله الرحمن الرحيم

اللهم إياك نعبد ولك نصلي ونسجد وإليك نسعى نحن نرجو رحمتك ونخشى عذابك بالكافرين ملحق.

(Its translation is: O God, we worship You and for You we pray and prostrate, and toward You we endeavour and haste. We seek Your mercy and fear Your serious torment. Your chastisement will verily afflict the disbelievers).

These two (alleged) *surahs* are called by al-Raghib in *al-Muhādarāt* as suratayn *al-Qunut* (two *surahs* of supplication) that were read by 'Ummar ibn al-Khattab during *qunut* in his prayers, and are found in the *mushafs* of Ibn 'Abbās and of Zayd ibn Thābit.[53]

Al-Imām Ahmad ibn Hanbal in his *Musnad*, is reported to have said:

Ubbay ibn Ka'b asked someone (Zirr ibn Hubaysh) How many verses do you recite in the *Surah al-'Ahzāb*? He replied: Seventy and a few verses. He (Ubayy) said: 'Never, I read it with the Messenger of Allah (s), and it is about the length of the *Surah al-Baqarah* or lengthier, and in it is the *āyat al-rajm* (verse of stoning).'[54]

It is obvious for every witty reader that these two *surahs*, which are called *suratayn al-qunut*, mentioned in the books *al-'Itqān* and *al-Durr al-manthur* of al-Suyuti, and reported by al-Tabarrāni and al-Bayhaqi, can never be found in the Book of Almighty Allah.

---

[53] *Al-Suyuti, op. cit.,* and *al-'Itqān*.
[54] *Musnad Ahmad*, vol. V, p. 132.

This means that the Qur'ān we have today is missing these two *surahs*, that are recorded in the *mushaf* of Ibn 'Abbās and that of Zayd ibn Thābit, indicating also the presence of *masāhif* other than those we have. This also recalls to my mind Ahl al-Sunnah's claim of the Shi'ah's having Fatimah's *mushaf*, so it is to be conceived!

Ahl al-Sunnah used to recite these two *surahs* in the *qunut* supplication of every morning prayers, and I personally learn them by heart and used to read them in the dawn prayer *qunut*.

The second *riwāyah* (narration) reported by al-Imām Ahmad in his *Musnad*, which claims that three quarters of Surah *al-'Ahzāb* have dropped, since *Surah al-Baqarah* contains 286 verses while their number in *al-'Ahzāb* doesn't exceed 73. When consdiering the counting of the parts of Qur'ān through *hizbs*, we conclude that *Surah al-Baqarah* is composed of five *hizbs*, whereas *Surah al-'Ahzāb* never exceeds one *hizb* (the whole Qur'ān is 120 *hizbs*).

Also the utterance expressed by Ubayy ibn Ka'b: "I used to read it during the lifetime of the Messenger of Allah (s), and it was the length of the *Surah al-Baqarah* or lengthier." This man who was the most famous among the reciters who used to learn the Qur'ān by heart, during the lifetime of the Prophet (s), and who was chosen by 'Umar[55] to lead people in *salāt al-tarawih*, by so saying will verily and undoubtedly confuse the readers and create doubts inside their hearts.

Again al-Imām Ahmad ibn Hanbal reported in his *Musnad*, [56] from Ubayy ibn Ka'b that he said: The Messenger of Allah (s) said:

"Allah, the Glorious and Most High, has commanded me to recite for you the Qur'ān: Those who disbelieve among the people of the Scripture could not ..., (Ubayy said:) then he (s) read in it:

---

[55] *Sahih al-Bukhāri*, vol. II, p. 252.
[56] *Musnad Ahmad*, vol. V, p. 131.

لو أن إبن أدم سأل وادياً من مال فاعطيه لسأل ثانياً فلو سأل ثانياً فأعطيه لسأل ثالثاً لا يملاء جوف إبن أدم إلا التُراب ، يتوب الله على من تاب ، وإنَّ ذلك الدين القيّم عند الله الحنيفةً غير المشركةً ولا الهوديةً ولا النصرانيةً من يفعل خيراً فلن يكفره.

(Meaning that: If son of Adam demanded a valley of funds and was given it, he will demand another one, and if given it would demand a third one, and nothing would fill the belly of the son of Adam except the earth (*turāb*). Allah shall verily return in mercy toward that who returns (in penitence). That is the straight religion near Allah, the Hanafi other than the polytheists, Jewish and Christians. Whoever does good it will never be denied).

Al-Hāfiz ibn 'Asākir reported in interpretation of Ubayy ibn Ka'b, that Abu al-Dardā' betook himself toward al-Madinah with a number of people of Damascus. On reaching, he entered upon 'Umar ibn al-Khattab, reciting for him the following (alleged) verse:

إذا جعل الذين كفروا فى قلوبهم الحميّة حميّة الجاهلية ولو حميتم كما حموا لفسد المسجد الحرام.

(meaning): *Hamiyyah* (fervour) of Jahiliyyah was made inside the hearts of disbelievers, and if you become impetuous as they are, corruption would afflict the Sacred Mosque (Ka'bah)."

Thereat 'Umar asked: Who taught you to recite such reading? They replied: Ubayy ibn Ka'b did. He summoned Ubayy, and asked them to read (before him). So they read:

ولو حميتم كما حموا لفسد المسجد الحرام.

Ubayy said to 'Umar: True, I taught them to read thus. Then 'Umar said to Zayd ibn Thābit: O Zayd, read. Zayd read the common one (ordinary). Then 'Umar said: O God, I never know other than this (reading)! Ubayy ibn Ka'b then said:

"O 'Umar, by God you know well that I used to attend (the Prophet's meetings) and they were absent, and I used to come near while they be away. I swear by Allah, if you wish, I will stay home and never talk to anyone or teach anyone to read, till my death." 'Umar said: "I seek God's forgiveness; you know that Allah has gifted you with knowledge, so teach people whatever you know."

He (Ibn 'Asākir) also said: 'Umar passed by a youth reading in a *mushaf*:

النبيّ أولى بالمؤمنين من أنفسهم وأزواجه أمّهاتهم وهو أب لهم.

(meaning: The Prophet has more right over the believers than they over themselves, and his wives are their mothers, and he is their father.) 'Erase it, boy', said 'Umar. 'I will not erase it, for it is so in the *mushaf* of Uhayy ibn Ka'b', said the youth. 'Umar went to Ubayy who told him: 'The Qur'ān has kept me busy, and you have been busy making transactions in the bazaar.'[57]

The same *riwāyah* was reported too by Ibn al-'Athir in *Jāmi' al-'usul*, and Abu Dāwud in his *Sunan*, and also by al-Hākim in his *Mustadrak*.

This time, I leave to you, dear reader, to comment yourself on such reports which are filling the books of Ahl al-Sunnah who are unaware of them, but vilifying the Shi'ah with whom even one-tenth can never be found.

But some of the Sunni obstinates may have aversion to such narrations, rejecting them as usual, disapproving al-Imām Ahmad's reporting such superstitions. They may consequently weaken the

---

[57] Ibn 'Asākir, *Tarikh Dimashq*, vol. II, p. 228.

authenticity of the asānid of such narrations, regarding the *Musnad* of al-Imām Ahmad and *Sunan* of Abu Dāwud as not viewed by Ahl al-Sunnah at the same level of *Sahih al-Bukhāri* and *Sahih Muslim*, whereas such riwāyāt are recorded in both the *Sahihs*.

Al-Bukhāri, in his *Sahih*[58] under *"bāb Manāqib 'Ammār wa Hudhayfah (r)"*, reported from 'Alqamah that he said: I entered the Sham, performed two-rak'ah prayer and said: My God, bring me a virtuous companion. Then I came near a people, sitting with them, when a man entered and sat beside me. I asked: Who is that man? They replied: He is Abu al-Dardā'. I said I invoked Allah to send me a righteous associate, and He sent you. He asked me: Where are you from? I said, from people of Kufah. He said: Don't you have among you the son of Umm 'Abd, the owner of the two sandals and the pillow and purger, and the one whom Allah protected against the Satan, as confirmed by the Prophet (s)? Isn't there among you the trustee of the Prophet (s), other than whom no one has knowledge? Then he said: How do you read "By the night when it spreadeth its evil!"? Then I recited for him:

واللّيل إذا يخشى. والنهار إذا تجلّى. وما خلق الذكر والأنثى.

in 92:3). (Then He asked: Did you hear it from your teacher's mouth?) I said: By God, I heard it from the Prophet's mouth (mouth to mouth)."

In another narration he added: "... and yet they reject my assertion of something I heard from the Messenger of Allah, may God's peace and benediction be upon him and his Progeny.[59]

Again, in another report he said:

واللّيل إذا يخشى. والنهار إذا تجلّى. وما خلق الذكر والأنثى.

---

[58] *Sahih al-Bukhāri*, vol. IV, p. 215.
[59] *Ibid.*, vol. IV, p. 216.

Then he said: "The Prophet (s) has read it to me, from his mouth, and yet those people insist till it was about to reject my assertion."[60] All these narrations indicate that in the Qur'ān we have today the words "وما خلق" are added.

Al-Bukhāri, in his *Sahih*, on the authority of Ibn Abbas reported that 'Umar ibn al-Khattab said: Allah has delegated Muhammad, upon whom be God's peace and benediction, with the truth, and revealed upon him the Book. Among what He revealed was *āyat al-rajm* (verse of stoning), which we read, accepted and comprehended. So the Messenger of Allah (s) stoned and we stoned after him. I fear that when time prolongs, someone may say: By God we can never find *āyat al-rajm* in the Book of Allah, as a result of which people may go astray through ignoring an obligation prescribed by Allah. And stoning is a punishment mentioned in the Book of Allah against any married man or woman when perpetrating fornication, when it is proved by evidence or through the woman's conceiving and confession. We also used to recite in our reading of the Book of Allah:

أن لا ترغبوا عن أبائكم فإنه كفر بكم أو أن كفرا بكم إن ترغبوا عن أبائكم.

(meaning: Don't shun your parents since this will be counted as ingratitude on your part, or: It is ingratitude to shun your parents).[61]

In his *Sahih*,[62] under the "bāb: Law anna libn Adam wādiyayn labtaghā thālithan" (If the son of Adam has two valleys he would ask for a third one), Al-Imām Muslims said:

---

[60] *Ibid.*, vol. IV, p. 218, "bāb manāqib 'Abd Allāh ibn Mas'ud".
[61] *Ibid.*, vol. VIII, p. 26, "bāb rajm al-hublā min al-zinā idhā uhsinat".
[62] *Sahih Muslim*, vol. III, p. 100, "bāb law ann li-ibn Adam wādiyān la-ibtaghā thālithan".

"Abu Musā al-'Ash'ari sent for the *qurrā'* (reciters) of Basrah. Three hundred *qurrā'* of the Qur'ān came to him. He told them: "You are the elect of the people of Basrah'. He asked them to recite, which they did. (He told them): 'Do not remain long without reciting the Qur'ān, lest your hearts, like those who went before you, should harden. Indeed we used to recite a *surah* similar in length and power to the *Surah al-Barā'ah*, which I forgot except for a single verse:

لو كان لإبن أدم واديان من مال لأبتغى وادياً ثالثاً ولا يملاء جوف إبن أدم إلا التراَّب.

We would also read a *surah* like one of the *al-Musabbihit*, which I forgot all except this:

يا أيها الذين أمنوا لما تقولون ما لا تفعلون فتكتب شهادةً فى أعناقكم فتسألون عنها يوم القيامة.

(Meaning: O you who believe! Why say you that which you do not? Then it will be counted a testimony against you and you be answerable about it on the Day of Resurrection).[63]

These two alleged *surahs*, which were forgotten both by Abu Musā al-'Ash'ari, one resembling *Surah al-Barā'ah*, i.e. 129 verses, and the other resembling one of the *Musabbihit*, i.e. twenty verses, have both no existence except in the imagination of Abu Musā. It is really astonishing. I leave the judgement to the equitable reader.

When Ahl al-Sunnah's books and *Musnads* and *Sihāh* be replete with such reports, claiming once that the Qur'ān is incomplete, and increased another time, so what is the reason behind all this vilification

---

[63] *Sahih Muslim*, vol. III, p. 100, "bāb law ann li-ibn Adam wādiyān la-ibtaghā thālithan".

against the Shi'ah who unanimously concurred on the invalidity of such claims.

And when the Shi'i man, the author of *Fasl al-Khitāb fi ithbāt tahrif Kitāb Rabb al-'Arbāb*, who died in 1320 Hijrah, had compiled his book about a hundred years ago, he was preceded by the Egyptian Sunni writer, the author of the book *al-Furqān* with about four centuries, as referred to by al-Shaykh Muhammad al-Midyani, the Dean of al-Shari'ah College in Al-'Azhar University.[64]

The important point to be got from all this discussion, is that the Sunni and Shi'ah investigating *'ulamā'* have annulled such narrations, regarding them as eccentric and unusual, proving through convincing evidences that the Qur'ān we have today being the very Qur'ān that was revealed to our Prophet Muhammad (s) without any addition or omission or substitution or alteration.

How can Ahl al-Sunnah vilify the Shi'ah because of traditions deserving no credence whatsoever near them, acquitting themselves from this charge, while their *Sihāh* confirm the veracity of those traditions?

While referring to such narrations so bitterly and regretfully, how badly are we in need of disposing of them and discarding them away, had not been the outspreading campaign launched by some writers and authors claiming to be committed to the Prophetic Sunnah. They are backed, behind the scenes, by uncovered circles, financing and urging them to defame and charge the Shi'ah with impiety, particularly after the culmination of the Islamic Revolution in Iran.

I address such people and their supporters with these words: Observe your duty toward Allah regarding your brethren, and hold you fast by the cord of God all together, and be not divided (among yourselves) and remember the bounty of God bestowed upon you, when you were enemies (of each other) He united your hearts together with (mutual) love, and thus by His favour you have become brethren.

---

[64] The Journal *Risālat al-'Islām*, issue No. 4, the 11th year, pp. 382, 383

Performing Two Prayers Together

The other point which is exploited to revile the Shi'ah with, being their performing *salāt al-zuhr* (noon prayers) and *salāt al-'asr* (afternoon prayers) together, and so also *salāt al-maghrib* and *al-'ishā'*.

While vilifying the Shi'ah (for the alleged defect), Ahl al-Sunnah, in contrast, assert their being adherent to preserving the *salāt*, complying to Allah's words when saying:

"Verily prayer is (imposed) upon the believers as ('a) timed Ordinance." (4:103)

Before issuing any judgement for or against them, we have to discuss the subject from all dimensions and aspects, reviewing what the two sects hold in its regard.

There is unanimous agreement among Ahl al-Sunnah concerning the permissibility of performing *salāt al-zuhr* and *al-'asr* (noon and afternoon prayers) together at 'Arafāt (Mount), which is called *jam' taqdim* (precedent joining), and also the permissibility of performing maghrib and '*isha*' prayers at the time of '*isha*', the act called *jam' ta'khir* (late joining). This act is unanimously concurred by all Muslims, including the Shi'ah and Sunnis, and rather all the Islamic communities, with no exception.

The disagreement between the Shi'ah and Ahl al-Sunnah lies in the permissibility of performing together the two obligatory prayers of *zuhr* and '*asr*, and also the *maghrib* and '*isha*' prayers, throughout the whole days of the year during settlement, without the presence of excuse of travel.

The Hanafi school believes in its impermissibility even during travel, despite the existence of express texts permitting it (*jam'*) especially during trave, contradicting thus the unanimity of the *Ummah*: Shi'ah and Sunnah.

The Mālikis, Shāfi'is and Hanbalis concur on the permissibility of *jam'* (performing together) between two obligatory *salāts* during travel, but disagree concerning its permissibility in the times of (public) panic (*khawf*), sickness, raining and mud (flood).

The Imāmiyyah Shi'ah unanimously concur on its absolute permissibility, without the excuses of travel or raining or panic, following in this respect the guide of Ahl al-Bayt Imāms among the Pure Kindred (peace be upon them).

In this point, in particular, we should take an accusative and skeptical standpoint toward them, as whenever the Sunnis argue against the Shi'ah with a proof, they would rebut the argument with saying that the Ahl al-Bayt Imāms have taught and explained to them all the unsolvable matters, boasting of following the example of Infallible Imāms having full knowledge of the Qur'ān and (Prophetic) Sunnah!

I remember that the first time I performed *salāt al-zuhr* and *salāt al-'asr*, was led by the Martyr Muhammad Bāqir al-Sadr (may God be pleased with him). I used to perform the noon and afternoon (*'asr*) prayers separately, when being in the Holy City of Najaf, till the coming of that blessed day. In that day, I went out with al-Sayyid Muhammad Bāqir al-Sadr from his house to the mosque where he used to lead the congregational prayers, before his imitators who welcomed me respectfully, leaving me a room just behind him. When the noon prayers expired and *iqāmah* was made for the *'asr prayers*, I had a presentiment to quit and leave them. But I remained for two reasons, the first being the dignity of al-Sayyid al-Sadr and his profound solemnity in his prayer, that I wished to be prolongated. The second reason was my presence in that place, being the nearest worshipper to him, feeling as if a force majeure pulling me toward him. As we finished performing the *'asr prayers*, people accumulated around him putting forth their questions before him, when I stayed behind him listening to the questions and their answers given by him, except for some undisclosed ones. Then he accompanied me home for lunch, where I found myself as honorary guest. I availed myself of the opportunity of that meeting, and asked him about performing two *salāts* together, thus:

— O master! Can the Muslim perform two obligatory prayers together in case of exigency?

He replied: He can do so in all cases with no necessity of presence of exigency.

I said: What is your proof for this?

He said: Since the Messenger of Allah (s) has performed two obligatory prayers in al-Madinah with no travel, fear, raining or exigency, but only for keeping us away from troubles. This fact, thanks to God, is confirmed and established for us through the pure Imāms, and it is also established for you.

I said: I wonder how could it be established for us while I have never heard of it before, nor seen any Sunni applying it. Rather, on the contrary, the Sunnis believe in the invalidity of the *salāt* if performed even one minute before the *adhān* (call for prayer), so what about that performing prayers hours before (its time) with the noon prayers, or performing the *'isha'* prayers together with the *maghrib*, the act we view to be indecent and invalid.

Al-Sayyid Muhammad Bāqir al-Sadr realized my perplexity and wonder. He whispered in the ear of someone of the attendants, who hurriedly went and brought him two books, which I recognized to be *Sahih al-Bukhāri* and *Sahih-Muslim.* Al-Sayyid al-Sadr asked that knowledge-seeker to make me acquainted with the traditions related to performing two prayers together. I myself read in *Sahih al-Bukhāri* (the traditions showing) how the Prophet (s) performed together the *zuhr* and *'asr* prayers and *maghrib* and *'isha'* prayers. In *Sahih Muslim* I came across a full chapter on *al-jam' bayna al-salātayn* (performing two prayers together) at time of presence (*hadar*) other than times of fear or raining or travel.

I could not hide my wonder and astonishment, while being doubtful that al-Bukhāri and Muslim with them might be falsified, deciding privately to review these two books in Tunisia.

After that proof, al-Sayyid al-Sadr sought to know my opinion. I said: You are quite right, and what you say is the very truth. I would like to put forth another question.

He said: Please do.

I said: Is it permissible to perform together the four *salawāt* (prayers), as practised by a lot of people who perform the prayers of *zuhr*, *'asr*, *maghrib* and *'isha'* together out of (due) time (*qadā'*) when returning home at night?

He said: This is impermissible.

I said: You yourself said before that the Messenger of Allah (s) used to perform the prayers separately and altogether, the practice through which we recognized the due times (mawāqit), approved by Allah the Glorified.

He said: There is a common time for the two *faridahs* (obligatory prayers) of *zuhr* and *'asr*, that starts from the meridian till sunset. And also for the prayers of *maghrib* and *'isha'*, that starts from sunset till the midnight. While the morning prayer has one time beginning from breaking of dawn till sunrise. Whoever contradicts these fixed times, has in fact contradicted the Holy verse:

"Verily prayer is (imposed) upon the believers as ('a) timed Ordinance." (4:103).

So we cannot, for instance, perform the morning prayer before dawn-breaking, nor after sunrise. Also it is impermissible to perform the *zuhr* and *'asr* prayers before the meridian or after sunset. And further we are not allowed to perform the *maghrib* and *'isha'* prayers before sunset or after midnight.

I then thanked al-Sayyid Muhammad Bāqir al-Sadr. And though I was content with all his words, but I never performed two ordinances together after departing him, till my return to Tunisia, where I engaged myself deliberately in investigation and research till being enlightened.

This was my story with Martyr al-Sadr (may God's mercy be upon him), concerning the performing together of two obligatory prayers, intending from citing them that my brothers, among the Sunnis may realize, first, the morality of the *'ulamā'* who humbled themselves to deserve the epithet of being the inheritors of the prophets in respect of knowledge and ethics. Second, to show how we be unaware of what our *Sihāh* contain, while reviling the others on some matters in whose veracity we verily believe, and which are stated in our *Sihāh*.

In his *Musnad*,[65] Al-Imām Ahmad ibn Hanbal reported from Ibn 'Abbās that he said: The Messenger of Allah (s) performed seven and eight (*rak'ahs*) altogether (i.e. *maghrib* with *'isha'*, and *zuhr* with *'asr* prayers) at al-Madinah while being resident not traveller.

In *al-Muwatta'*,[66] Al-Imām Mālik reported that Ibn 'Abbās said: The Messenger of Allah (s) performed the *zuhr* with *'asr* prayers, and *maghrib* with *'isha'* prayers together, without presence of fear or travelling. The same tradition is reported also by al-Imām Muslim, in his *Sahih*, under the bāb "al-jam' bayna al-salātayn fi al-hadar".[67]

Muslim also reported from Ibn 'Abbās that he said: The Messenger performed together *zuhr* with *'asr* prayers, and *maghrib* with *'isha'* prayers at al-Madinah, with no fear or travel. He (Muslim) said: I asked Ibn 'Abbās: Why did he do so? He replied: So that he would never cause any problem for his *Ummah*.[68]

The fact indicating that this Prophetic Sunnah was widely known among the Sahābah, and practised by them, can be sought in the

---

[65] Musnad al-'Imām Ahmad, vol. I, p. 221.
[66] *Muwatta' al-'Imām Mālik (Sharh al-Hawālik)*, vol. I, p. 161.
[67] *Sahih Muslim*, vol. II, p. 151, "bāb al-jam' bayna al-salātayn fi al-hadar".
[68] *Ibid.*, vol. II, p. 152.

tradition reported by Muslim too in his *Sahih*, under the same *bāb*, by saying: Ibn 'Abbās addressed us in a sermon after the *'asr* (afternoon), and continued till sunset and appearance of the stars, when people started calling: *al-salāt, al-salāt*. Thereat a man from Banu Tamim, while perpetually exclaiming: *al-salāt, al-salāt.*, came toward him. Ibn 'Abbās said to him: O son of no mother! Do you teach me the Sunnah? Then he said: I have seen the Messenger of Allah (s) performing together the *zuhr* with *'asr* and *maghrib* with *'isha'* prayers. In another narration, Ibn 'Abbās said to the man: O motherless man, do you teach us the prayers, and we used to perform two prayers together during the lifetime of the Messenger of Allah (upon whom be God's peace and benediction).[69]

In his *Sahih*,[70] under the *bāb* "*waqt al-maghrib*", al-Imām al-Bukhāri said: Adam informed us saying, Shu'bah told us and said, 'Amr ibn Dinar said: I heard Jābir ibn Zayd, quoting Ibn 'Abbās who said: The Prophet, upon whom be God's peace and benediction, performed seven (*rak'ahs*) together and eight togetherr (meaning *maghrib* with *'isha'* and *zuhr* with *'asr* prayers).

Also, in his *Sahih*,[71] under the *bāb* '"*waqt al-'asr*", al-Bukhāri is reported to have said: I heard Abu Imāmah saying: We performed with 'Umar ibn 'Abd al-'Aziz the *zuhr* prayer, after which we went out and entered upon Anas ibn Mālik whom we found performing the *'asr* prayer. I said: What is that prayer you performed? He said: It is the *'asr* prayer, and it is the prayer of the Messenger of Allah, upon whom be God's peace and benediction, which we used to perform with him.

Despite the plainness of these traditions, still there are some who exploit this point to revile the Shi'ah with. It has once upon a time occurred in Tunisia, when the prayers leader (*imām*) in the City of Qafsah, stood up for reviling and defaming us in the midst of the worshippers, saying: Have you noticed the religion they brought ...

---

[69] *Ibid.*, vol. II, p. 153, "bāb al-jam' bayna al-salātayn fi al-hadar".

[70] *Sahih al-Bukhāri*, vol. I, p. 140, "bāb waqt al-maghrib".

[71] *Ibid.*, vol. I, p. 138, "bāb waqt al-'asr".

after performing the *zuhr* prayer they rise up and perform the *'asr*. It is a new religion other than the *Din* of Muhammad the Messenger of Allah. These people contradict the Qur'ān which says: *"Verily prayer is (imposed) upon the believers as ('a) timed Ordinance."* He spared nothing but reviled with it those who were enlightened and guided.

One of the enlightened, who was a highly learned youth, came toward me and cited to me so sadly and bitterly what hte leader (of prayer) said. So I handed him both *Sahih al-Bukhāri* and *Sahih Muslim*, asking him to show the imam the (traditions proving the) veracity of *jam'*(performing two prayers together), which being of the Prophet's Sunnah. As I never intended to debate with him; since I did this before by that which is better but he responded with reviling and slander, and baseless charges.However, my friend never stopped praying behind him and when the prayers finished, the imam sat as usual to give the lessons. Then my friend advanced to him and put forth the inquiry about performing two faridahs together. He replied: It is one of the Shi'ah's heresies. My friend said to him: But it is recorded in *Sahih al-Bukhāri* and *Sahih Muslim,* with giving them to him. On reading the bāb al-jam' bayna al-salātayn", he was shocked by the truth, before all the worshippers, attending his classes. So he immediately closed the books, and returned them to me saying: This (*sunnah*) belongs in particular to the Messenger of Allah, and when you become an apostle of Allah you can apply it. After that this friend said to me: I realized then that this man was no more than a bigoted illiterate (*jāhil*), making an oath not to pray behind him any more (being led by him).[72]

---

[72] It is narrated that two men went out for hunting, when they met a black thing at a far distance. The first one thought it to be a crow, while the second opposed him saying it was a she-goat. Each one of them insisted on his claim, persisting in his opinion. But on approaching to it they found it to be a crow, who became disturbed and flew away. Thereat the first man said: Haven't I told you that it was a crow? Are you satified now? But his friend persisted in his opinion saying: Glorified is Allah! (how can) a she-goat fly?!

Thereafter, I asked my friend to go back to him to let him be acquainted with the fact that Ibn 'Abbās used to perform that *salāt* (two prayers together) besides Anas ibn Mālik and many a Companion, so why does he intend to distinguish the Messenger of Allah to perform it alone? Haven't we had a good example in the Messenger of Allah? But my friend begged me to excuse him of this task, saying: No need for this, since I am sure that he will never be convinced even when the Messenger of Allah (s) himself comes to him.

All praise belongs to Allah, that a large number of the youths, after recognizing this reality, (the performing together of two prayers), resumed their (performance of) prayers after discarding it. That was because they were suffering from missing the performing of the prayers in their due times, in a way they used to resort to perform the four prayers altogether at night, the act causing them troubles and their hearts being fed up.But they realized then the wisdom that lies behind performing two prayers together, as all employees, students and common people would, through this *sunnah*, be able to perform the daily prayers in their due times with restful hearts. Only then they realized the true meaning of the Messenger's expression: ".... so that I never create any trouble for my *Ummah*.

Prostration on Clay

All Shi'ah *'ulamā'* unanimously agree on the preferability of prostrating on the earth, in accordance with the tradition they report from the Messenger of Allah (s): "The best prostration is on the earth."

In another narration, he (s) said:

"It is not permissible to prostrate but only on the earth, or any plant coming out from it, provided it be unedible and unwearable."

The author of *Wasā'il al-Shi'ah*, reports from Muhammad ibn 'Ali ibn al-Husayn, with the authority of Hishām ibn al-Hakam, from Abu 'Abd Allāh ('a) that he said: *"Prostration on the earth is preferable since it is more extremely indicative of modesty, and submission to Allah, the Mighty and the Glorious."* In another narration, he reported from Muhammad ibn al-Hasan, through his isnād from Ishaq ibn al-Fadl, that he questioned Abu 'Abd Allāh (al-Imām al-Sādiq) [A] about prostration on mats (hasir) woven from reed (qasab). He ('a) replied: *"There is no objection to it, but to prostrate on earth is more preferable to me, and the Messenger of Allah, may God's peace and benediction be upon him and his Progeny, liked this, that to make the forehead touch the earth. I like for you whatever was liked by the Messenger of Allah (s)."*

Whereas the Sunni *'ulamā'* see no objection to prostrate on pens (*zaribah*) and carpets, though they prefer it to be (reedy) mats.

There are some narrations reported by al-Bukhāri and Muslim in their *Sahihs*, confirming the Messenger's having a mat made of palm leaves, using it for prostration. Muslim reported in his *Sahih* under *kitāb al-hayd*, on the aurhotiy of Yahya ibn Yahya and Abu Bakr ibn Abi Shaybah, from Abu Mu'āwiyah, from al-'A'mash, from Thabit ibn 'Ubayd, from al-Qasim ibn Muhammad, from 'A'ishah who said: The Messenger of Allah (s) said to me, hand me the khumrah from the mosque. She says: I said: I am menstruant. He said: Your menstruation is not from your hands.[73] (Muslim says: *Al-Khumrah* is a small rug-like, with the size enough for prostration).

The evidence indicating that the Messenger of Allah was much preferring prostration on earth, can be sought in the tradition reported by al-Bukhāri in his *Sahih*, on the authority of Abu Sa'id al-Khudri (may God be pleased with him), who said that the Messenger of Allah, may God's peace and benedictions be upon him and his Progeny, used to seclude himself during the second ten days of the Month of Ramadān. He kept on this habit for one year, till the coming of the twenty-first night, the morning of which he was supposed to end his seclusion, when he said: Whoever secluded himself with me, should do so in the last ten days. I saw this night, and was made to forget it; I saw myself (in dream) wading in water and mud, in its morning. So seek it

---

[73] *Sahih Muslim*, vol. I, p. 168, "bāb jawāz ghasl al-hā'id ra's zawjihā"; *Sunan Abu Dāwud*, vol. I, p. 68, "bāb al-hā'id tunāwil min al-masjid".

(the night) in the last ten days, and in every odd night. At that very night, it rained, and the mosque which was supported by a trellis, started to leak, when my eyes felt on the Messenger of Allah, may God's peace and benediction be upon him and his Progeny, seeing the trace of water and mud on his forehead, in the morning of the twenty-first day.[74]

The other evidence demonstrating the Companions' preferring prostration on earth, in the presence of the Prophet (s), being the *hadith* reported by al-Imām al-Nasā'i in his *Sunan*, under "bāb tabrid al-hasā Lis-sijud 'alayh" (cooling the stones for prostrating on them), who said: Qutaybah informed us and said, 'Abbād reported, from Muhammad ibn 'Amr, from Sa'id ibn al-Harth, from Jābir ibn 'Abd Allāh, who said: When we were performing the *zuhr* prayers with the Messenger of Allah (s), I picked up a handful of stones in the palm of my hand, cooling them and shifting them to the other palm, and when prostrating I would place them to put my forehead on.[75]

Added to this, the *hadith* uttered by the Prophet (s):

"The earth is made for me a place for prostration (masjid) and a purifier."[76]

He also said:

"The earth as a whole is made to us a place for prostration and its soil made a purifier."[77]

Why are Muslims then be fanatic against the Shi'ah because of their prostration on earth instead of *zarābi* (moquette)?

---

[74] *Sahih al-Bukhāri*, vol. II, p. 256, "bāb al-'i'tikāf fi al-`ashr al-'awākhir".

[75] *Sunan al-'Imām al-Nasā'i*, vol. II, p. 204, "bāb tabrid al-hasa li al-sujud 'alāyh".

[76] *Sahih al-Bukhāri*, vol. I, p. 86, "kitāb al-tayammum".

[77] *Sahih Muslim*, vol. II, p. 64, "kitāb al-masājid wa mawādi' al-salāt".

Doctrines with which Ahl Al-Sunnah Revile the Shi'Ah

And how dare they to charge them with impiety, reviling and defaming them, falsely and calumniously with the charge of being idolaters?

Further how do the Saudis beat them (the Shi'ah) merely for keeping the *turbah* (piece of clay on which foreheads are put) in their pockets or bags?

Is this truly the Islam that commands us to respect each other, and never insult any monotheist Muslim witnessing that there is no god but Allah and Muhammad is the Messenger of Allah, establishing prayers, pyaing the poor-due, fasting the Month of Ramadān and making pilgrimage to the House of Allah (Makkah)? And can it stand to reason that the Shi'i undergoes all those troubles, sustaining all those losses to make pilgrimage to the House (Ka'bah), and visit the Prophet's tomb, while being worshippers of stones, as some people desire to portray?

Can't the Sunnis be convinced with the statement of the Martyr Muhammad Bāqir al-Sadr, which I quoted in my first book *Thumma Ihtadayt* (Then I was guided), when I asked him about the piece of clay (on which they put their foreheads during their prayers, calling it *al-turbah*, and he answered thus: We all prostrate on the dust for Allah, but not for the dust, as some people claim that the Shi'ah do. And there is difference between prostration on the dust and prostration for the dust! For the prostration is only for Allah, praise be to Him the Highest.

And when the Shi'i takes care so as the place of his prostration be pure and accepted by Allah, responding to the commands of the Messenger of Allah and the Pure Imāms of Ahl al-Bayt. Especially nowadays where all mosques being carpeted with soft moquette, which are made of unknown material to all the Muslims, and never be made in Islamic countries, besides some of them being made of materials on which prostration is forbidden... are we to discard and renounce the Shi'i who is concerned about the validity of his *salāt*, and accuse him of being infidel and polytheist just for a fictitious suspicion?

The Shi'i who cares about the affairs of his *Din* (religion), particularly his *salāt* which is the backbone of religion (*'amud al-Din*), taking off his belt and watch whose band is made of leather of unknown origin; and sometimes his foreign trousers so as to pray in a loose and waving trousers, for the only reason to take precaution and attaching much importance to that magnificent halting before Allah, so as not to meet his Lord with any undeirable thing ... does all this deserve to be met with all this scorning and aversion, or it should be met with respect and exaltation? Since he has magnified the offerings consecrated to Allah, as said in the Qur'ān:

"And whoever respecteth the signs of God verily it is (the reflection) of the piety of the hearts." (22:32)

O bondmen of Allah, fear the wrath of Allah and speak words straight to the point. Allah says:

"And had it not been God's grace upon you and His mercy in this world and the hereafter, indeed had seized you for the slander ye entered into, a grievous chastisement." (24:14, 15)

Al-Raj'ah (Restoration to Life)

This is exclusively held by the Shi'ah. I investigated and searched in all the Sunni books but failed to find any trace of it.

In this regard, the Shi'ah depend upon akhbār (reports) and narrations they quoted from the pure Imāms (peace be upon them), which indicate that Allah, the Glorious and the Exalted, will resurrect some of the believers and some corrupt culprits so as the believers revenge against their and Allah's enemies in this worldly life before the hereafter.

These reports, through being *sahih* (correct) and *mutawātir* (narrated through authentic chains), but are not necessarily binding upon Ahl al-Sunnah if they trust not their veracity, and consequently it is not incumbent upon them to believe in them, just because Ahl al-Bayt Imāms reported them from their grandfather the Messenger of Allah (s)! Nay, as we have committed ourselves to be equitable in research, and discard bigotry, so we never task them but only with that they bind themselves to, and report in their *Sihāh*, since the traditions on *raj'ah* have never been cited in their books or transmitted by them. Therefore, they are quite free to disbelieve in these reports, and reject them, in case anyone of the Shi'ah intends to let them be acquainted with such narrations.

Due to the fact that the Shi'ah have never imposed on or coerced anyone to believe in the *raj'ah*, nor they charge with impiety anyone denying it, so no need is there for all that vilification and exaggeration against the Shi'ah, specially when taking into consideration their interpreting some Qur'ānic verses in a way denoting this meaning and confirming it, such:

"And on the Day when We will collect from every people a party from those who belied our signs, then will they be formed into groups" (27:83).

In *Tafsir al-Qummi*, it is reported from Ibn Abi 'Umayr, from Hammād, from Abu 'Abd Allāh (al-Imām) Ja'far al-Sādiq (peace be upon him), that he said: What do people say about this āyah "And on the Day when We will collect from every people a party"? (Hammād says:) I replied: They believe this to be on the Day of Resurrection. He ('a) said: It is not that which they claim, but it is verily about the *raj'ah* (restoration to life) ... is it proper for Allah to resurrect a party of every *Ummah* (community) and leave the rest? (No) but the āyah on Resurrection (Day) be this one:

"We will gather them (and) then leave not behind, of them any one." (18:47)

It is also reported in the book *'Aqā'id al-Imāmiyyah* of al-Shaykh Muhammad Ridā al-Muzaffar, that he said: The belief held by the Imāmiyah in accordance with what is reported from Al al-Bayt (the Prophet's Household), peace be upon them, that Allah, the Most High, will resurrect a group of the dead and return them to the world (*dunyā*), with the same shapes they were before, dignifying some and humiliating some others, distinguishing between the rightful from falsifiers and the oppressed from the oppressors. This shall occur during the reappearance and rise of al-Mahdi of Al Muhammad, upon him and them be the best benediction and peace.

And no one will be resurrected but whoever attained the extremest degree of faith (*imān*) or the extremest degree of corruption, who all shall be caused to die afterwards, and then to nushur (gathering for reckoning) and to get the thawāb (reward) and 'iqāb (punishment) according to what they deserve. It is exactly as stated by the Almighty Allah in His Noble Book, about those resurrected ones, who were never reclaimed through restoration to life, deserving consequently Allah's wrath, desiring then to be resurrected for the third time with the hope of being reclaimed: They shall say: "O' our Lord! Twice dist Thou cause us to die, and twice didst Thou give us life, and (now) we do confess our sins: Is there then a way to get out (of this)?"[78]

My view is that if Ahl al-Sunnah never believe in the doctrine of *raj'ah*, they are quite rightful in this respect, but they have no right whatsoever to revile and defame whoever believing in it, due to the establishment of the texts regarding it for him.As that who knows not has no authority over that who knows, and also the ignorant has no authority over the learned, and disbelieving in something can never be an evidence on its non-existence or falsehood, as there are many irrefutable proofs being approved by the Muslims while being disapproved by the people of scripture (Ahl al-Kitāb) including the Jews and Christians.

And there are numerous beliefs and narrations held by the Sunnis concerning God's friends (*Awliyā'*) and the pious, and followers of the Sufi creeds, that seem impossible and abominable, but not calling for vilification and exaggeration against the Sunnis' faith.

---

[78] *'Aqā'id al-'Imāmiyyah of al-Muîaffar*, p. 80, doctrine No. 32.

On the other hand, the doctrine of *raj'ah* has a support in the Qur'ān and the Prophetic Sunnah, besides its being not imposible for Allah, Who cited for us examples about it in the Qur'ān, like His saying:

"Or (didst thou not see) like him who passed by a town and it had fallen on its roofs, he exlaimed, (Oh) How can God (ever) bring it to life (again), after (this) its death," Where-upon God caused him to die a hundred years and thereafter raised him (again to life)." (2:259)

Or the Almighty's saying:

"Didst thou not see those who went forth from their homes, and they were in thosuands, for fear of death; then God said unto them, 'Die ye!' (and they died) and thereafter He restored them to life ..." (2:243)

Allah caused some people from among the Children of Israel, and thereafter restored them to life, in accordance with the following verse:

"And (remember ye!) when ye said, "O' Moses! Never will we believe in thee until we see God manifestly," the Thunder seized you while ye looked on. Then We raised you after your death that haply ye might be thankful." (2:55, 56)

Further, about the fellows of the Cave who stayed dead in their cave for more than three hundred years, God says:

"Then We raised them up that We might know which of the two parties reckoneth best the duration of their stay." (18:12)

Thus we noticed how the Book of Allah indicates that the *raj'ah* happened for the previous nations, so its occurrence for the *Ummah* of Muhammad is not impossible, especially when it is to be reported and confirmed by Ahl al-Bayt Imāms, peace be upon them, who are the truthful and knowledgeable.

But there are some intruders who claim that to believe in *raj'ah* is the same as believing in the *tanāsukh* (transmigration), which is held by some of the atheists. This claim is manifesty devious and false, the purpose of which being no more than vilification and *tahwil* (exaggeration) against the Shi'ah. Since those believing in the principle of *tanāsukh*, never hold that man is restored to life with his own body, soul, shape and nature, but say that the soul is transmitted from the body of a man died to that of another man born anew, or even to an animal.

This, as known by all, is absolutely far off from the creed and beliefs of Muslims who say that Allah will raise up the dead from their graves with their bodies and souls. While the *raj'ah* in fact has nothing to do with the *tanāsukh*, which is held only by the ignorant and illiterate people who have no knowledge, or the impious who have evil intentions.

Extravagance (*Ghuluww*) (In Loving the Imāms)

We never mean by *ghuluww* here to deviate from the path of truth and follow the hawā (desire), till the beloved turning to be the worshipped god, which is verily a blasphemy and polytheism that can never believed by any Muslim having faith in the Islamic message and prophethood of Muhammad (s).

The Messenger of Allah (s) determined fixed limits for such love, when he said to al-Imām 'Ali ('a):

"Two categories of people will face ruin on account of you: he who loves you with exaggeration, and he who hates you intensely."

He (s) also said:

"O 'Ali, in you there is a parable of Jesus, the son of Mary, who was detested by the Jews to the extent astonishing his mother, and loved by the Christians till imparting upon him the position that he was unfit for it."[79]

---

[79] *Mustadrak* al-Hākim, vol. III, p. 123; Ibn 'Asākir in *Tarikh Dimashq*, vol. II, p. 234; al-Bukhāri's *al-Tarikh al-Kabir*, vol. II, p. 281, al-Suyuti in *Tarikh al-Khulafā'*,

Doctrines with which Ahl Al-Sunnah Revile the Shi'Ah

This being the negative meaning for *ghuluww*, when love exceeds the bounds till rendering the beloved as a god, giving him a rank higher than his own, or when hatred exceeds the bounds reaching the extent of calumny and false accusation.

While the Shi'ah have never gone to the extremes in loving 'Ali and the Imāms among his sons, but imparted upon them the reasonable position determined by the Messenger of Allah (s), as his executors (*awsyā'*) and successors, with no one claiming their attaining the degree of prophethood let not the divinity. We should never care or give heed to the allegations of some troublesome persons claiming that the Shi'ah have made a god of 'Ali and believed in his deity. Such people, if what is reported be correct, could neither represent a sect, nor a school of thought (*madhhab*), nor Shi'ah, nor Kharijites (*khawārij*).

And what is the fault of the Shi'ah if the Lord of Power and Glory says in His Book: "Say (O Muhammad, unto mankind): I demand not of you any recompense for it (the toils of the apostleship) save the love of (my) kinsfolk." And the *mawaddah* (loving kindness), as is known, is greater than mere love (*hubb*). Also the Messenger of Allah (s) says:

"None of you will be a (true) believer till loving for his brother (in *Din*) what he loves for himself, and *mawaddah* enjoins on you to deprive you of something so as to love with it another one."

And what fault the Shi'ah have when the Messenger of Allah (s) says:

"O 'Ali, you are a master in this world and a master in the Hereafter. Whoever loves you has loved me and whoever hates you is hating me.

---

p. 173; *Khasā'is al-Nasā'i,* p. 27; *Dhakhā'ir al-'uqbā,* p. 92; Ibn Hajar's *al-Sawā'iq al-muhriqah,* p. 74.

Your lover is the lover of Allah and your hater is the hater of Allah, and woe be unto that who detests you."[80]

He further says: "To love 'Ali is faith, and to hate him is hypocrisy."[81]

He also says:

"Whoever dies with the love of Al Muhammad be in his heart, his death is that of a martyr. Verily that who dies upon the love of Al Muhammad shall die forgiven, and whoever dies upon love of Al Muhammad shall die penitent. Whoever dies upon love of Al Muhammad shall die a believer of perfect faith, and that who dies upon love of Al Muhammad the angel of death will augur him with heavens..."[82]

And why to blame or reproach the Shi'ah if they love a man about whom the Messenger of Allah (s) said: "Tomorrow I will give my standard to a man loves God and His Messenger, and God and His Messenger love him..."[83]

As the lover of 'Ali is the lover of Allah and His Messenger, with being a *mu'min* (true believer), while the hater of 'Ali is in fact the hater of Allah and His Messenger, and being a *munāfiq* (hypocrite).

It will not be out of context here to cite al-Imām al-Shāfi'i's famous quartrain on their love:

---

[80] Al-Hākim in his *Mustadrak*, vol. III, p. 128, says that it is a correct *hadith* on the condition it be accepted by al-Shaykhayn; *Nur al-'absār of al-Shablanji*, p. 23; *Yanābi' al-mawaddah*, p. 205; *al-Riyād al-nādirah*, vol. II, p. 165.

[81] *Sahih Muslim*, vol. I, p. 48; *al-Sawā'iq al-muhriqah*, p. 73; *Kanz al-'Ummāl*, vol. XV, p. 105.

[82] Al-Tha'labi in *al-Tafsir al-kabir*, about *āyāt al-mawaddah* (42:23); al-Zamakhshari in his *Tafsir al-Kashshāf*; *Tafsir al-Rāzi*, vol. VII, p. 405; al-Tustari in *Ihqāq al-haqq*, vol. IX, p. 486.

[83] *Sahih al-Bukhāri*, vol. IV, p. 20 and vol. V, p. 76; *Sahih Muslim*, vol. VII, p. 120, "bāb fadā'il 'Ali ibn Abi Tālib".

O Household of the Messenger of Allah, love for you.

Is an obligation from Allah, revealed in the Qur'ān.

It suffices as the greatest honour bestowed on you,

That his prayer is as nothing who does not salute you.

In regard of them and their love, al-Farazdaq disclosed his famous poem:

From a folk whose love is *Din*, and hatred is.

Kufr and their nearness is deliverance and refuge.

When counting pious people, they be their leaders,

Or said who the best on earth, none be except them.

The Shi'ah loved Allah and His Messenger, and through this love they were made to love Ahl al-Bayt: Fātimah and 'Ali and al-Hasan and al-Husayn, the fact on which countless traditions are there, reported by the Sunni *'ulamā'* in their *Sihāh*, some of which I have cited for the sake of brevity.

And when the love for 'Ali and Ahl al-Bayt represents in general the love for the Messenger of Allah (s), we have to know the extent of love required from the Muslims so as to learn if there be *ghuluww* (excess) as alleged by some.

The Messenger of Allah (s) said:

"None of you will be a (true) believer till I become for him more beloved than his children, and father and all people."[84]

On this basis, every Muslim should love 'Ali and the Pure Imāms among his sons more than people as a whole including his family and

---

[84] *Ibid.*, vol. I, p. 9, "bāb hubb al-Rasul min al-'imān"; *Sahih Muslim*, vol. I, p. 49, "bāb wujub mahabbat Rasul Allāh akthar min al-'ahl wa al-walad wa al-wālid wa al-nās ajma'in; *Sahih al-Tirmidhi*.

children, as only through this the faith (*imān*) can be established, as confirmed by the Prophet (s) in the aforementioned *hadith*.

Thus the Shi'ah never overstate, but give each right owner his due, and they were commanded by the Messenger of Allah to hold 'Ali in a position parable to that of the head to the body, and the same position of the two eyes to the head. Is tere anyone ready to relinquish of his eyes or his head?

On the other side, an excessive extravagance is found with Ahl al-Sunnah in their love for the Sahābah and undue consecration.But it seems as merely a reaction against the Shi'ah, who never believed in the '*adālah* (justice, straightforwardness) of the Sahābah as a whole.Whereas the Umayyads used to elevate the status of the Sahābah, belittling and degrading on the other hand the Prophet's Household, to the extent that when sending benedictions upon Muhammad and his Progeny, they would add: "and upon his Companions all." All this is due to the fact that sending benedictions upon Ahl al-Bayt has a virtue to which there was no precedent, nor can be reached by anyone.So they (the Umayyads) intended to elevate the Sahābah to that sublime degree, being unaware of the fact that Allah the Glorified has commanded the Muslims on top of whom be all the Sahābah, to send benedictions upon Muhammad and 'Ali and Fātimah with al-Hasanayn. And the prayer of that who does not send blessings upon them is rejected and can never be accepted by Allah if it be confined upon Muhammad alone, as is confirmed and recorded in *Sahih al-Bukhāri* and *Sahih Muslim*.

The reason why we call it *ghuluww* on the part of the Sahābah lies in the fact that Ahl al-Sunnah exceed the logic limits when ascribing justice to all of the Sahābah while Allah and His Messenger bear witness that among them are debauchees, renegades, deviators and hypocrites.

Their *ghuluww* is quite manifest when claiming that the Messenger of Allah (s) may err and be corrected by a Companion, or that the Satan plays and sports in the presence of the Prophet, but escapes when seeing 'Umar. And also the *ghuluww* is explicit when they say that if Allah inflicts the Muslims, including the Messenger of Allah, with a tribulation, no one would be in safe of it except Ibn al-Khattāb. The extravagance is even more explicit when they annul the Prophet's Sunnah and follow the *sunnah* of the Sahābah particularly al-Khulafā' al-Rāshidun. Till now I have revealed instances of some of these practices, and anyone desires to get more information, has to search and meditate in order to put his hand on more of such misconceptions.

Al-Mahdi, the Awaited

He also became one of the topics misused by Ahl al-Sunnah to revile the Shi'ah. Some of them transgressed the limits by making of it a point of mockery and derision, as they negate, or say, believe it impossible for a human being to be alive and unseen for twelve centuries. Some of the contemporary writers even dare to say: "The Shi'ah have fabricated and forged the idea of the occulted Imām who will verily deliver them, because of the much oppression and persecution they experienced from time immemorial to the present day. So they consoled themselves by the wish of the Awaited al-Mahdi, who will fill the earth with justice and equity and take their revenge from their enemies."

The topic of the Promised al-Mahdi has become the town-talk in the recent years after the culmination of the Islamic Revolution in Iran, with the Muslims, especially the educated youth starting everywhere, to inquire about the truth and authenticity of al-Mahdi.... whether is he factually there and has existence in the Islamic doctrines or just one of the compositions or forgeries of the Shi'ah?

Despite the books and researches compiled and written by the Shi'ah *'ulamā'*, long ago and recently[85] and despite the communications between many Sunnis and their brethren the Shi'ah

---

[85] Like the Martyr Muhammad Bāqir al-Sadr in his book *Bahth hawl al-Mahdi*. Translated to English *"The Awaited Saviour"* and available at: https://www.al-islam.org/the-awaited-saviour-muhammad-baqir-sadr-murtadha-mutahhari

through numerous conferences and discussions on miscellaneous doctrinal subjects, this topic remains so ambiguous to many of them, since they never used to hear the like of these episodes.

What is then the reality of the Promised al-Mahdi in the Islamic creeds?

The discussion about the topic is divided into two parts: the first relates to make a research on al-Mahdi through the Book (Qur'ān) and (Prophetic) Sunnah. The second focuses on his life (biography), occultation and reappearance.

Concerning the first research, it can be said that there is agreement between the Shi'ah and Sunnah on the fact that the Messenger of Allah (s) has foretold about him, informing his Companions that Allah, the Glorious and Exalted, shall verily make him to reappear at the end of Time (world, *zamān*). It is to be noticed that both the Shi'ah and Sunni *'ulamā'* have reported many traditions about al-Mahdi ('a) in their authentic books (*Sihāh*) and *Musnads*.

I, in my turn, and as usual, to fulfil the commitment I undertook on myself in all the subjects discussed in this book, that not to infer (as a proof) but only through what is confirmed and *sahih* (correct, authentic) for Ahl al-Sunnah and the Shi'ah.

In *Sunan Abi Dāwud*,[86] it is reported that the Messenger of Allah (s) said:

"If there remained but a single day of the (end of) Time, Allah would prolong that day till He sends a man of my progeny, whose name is like mine, and whose father's name is my father's, who will fill the earth with justice and equity as it had been filled with oppression and tyranny."

In *Sunan Ibn Mājah*,[87] the following tradition is reported. The Messenger of Allah (s) said:

---

[86] *Sunan Abi Dāwud*, vol. II, p. 422.

"We are the Ahl al-Bayt for whom Allah has chosen the hereafter to this world. My Ahl al-Bayt will face after me difficulties, hardships and persecution in the lands, until a people will come from the east (*mashriq*) bearers of black banners. They will demand the right but it will be denied. So, they will fight and will emerge victorious. They will be given what they demanded, but will not accept it till they give it (the right to rule) to a man from my Ahl al-Bayt, who would fill it (the earth) with justice as it was filled with oppression."

In his *Sunan*, Ibn Mājah said: The Messenger of Allah (may God's peace and benediction be upon him and his Progeny) said:

"Al-Mahdi is from us, the Ahl al-Bayt. Al-Mahdi is among the children of Fātimah."

He said:

"Al-Mahdi will verily rule my *Ummah*, for seven years if it (his rule) be short, or otherwise it be nine years. During this period my *Ummah* will live in an unprecedented bounty, giving its fruit, saying nothing of it. Fortunes will be, in that period, accumulated. A man would rise and say: O Mahdi, give me. He will say: Take."[88]

In *Sahih al-Tirmidhi*,[89] it is reported that the Messenger of Allah (s) said:

"A man of my Ahl al-Bayt whose name is like mine, will verily rule (the world). And if there remained but a single day of the (end of) time, Allah would prolong that day till he assumes the rule. Further the Messenger of Allah (s) is reported to have said:

"The world shall never end till the Arabs will verily be ruled by a man of my Ahl al-Bayt, whose name is like mine."

---

[87] *Sunan Ibn Mājah*, vol. II, *hadiths* no. 4082 & 4087.
[88] *Ibid.*, vol. II, *hadith* No. 4086.
[89] Al-Tirmidhi in *al-Jāmi' al-Sahih*, vol. IX, pp. 74-754.

In his *Sahih*[90] al-Imām al-Bukhāri is reported to have said: Ibn Bukayr, told us saying we are told by al-Layth, from Ibn Shahab, from Nafi' the mawlā of Abu Qatādah al-'Ansari, that Abu Hurayrah said: The Messenger of Allah (upon whom be God's peace and benediction) said: "What would be your condition when the son of Mary (Jesus) is raised down among you, and your leader (Imām) be of you."

The author of *Ghāyat al-ma'mul* says: It is commonly known among the old and contemporary *'ulamā'*, that at the end of Time, a man of Ahl al-Bayt called al-Mahdi should appear. The *ahādith* (traditions) about al-Mahdi reached us through a group of pious Sahābah and chains of reliable traditionists like: Abu Dāwud, al-Tirmidhi, Ibn Mājah, al-Tabarani, Abu Ya'lā, al-Bazzaz, al-Imām Ahmad ibn Hanbal, and al-Hākim (may God be pleased with them all). And mistaken is whoever has weakened all the traditions about al-Mahdi.

Al-Hāfiz, in *Fath al-Bāri*, says: There are many authentic traditions (*mutawātir*) confirming that al-Mahdi is of this *Ummah*, and that Jesus the son of Mary will reappear and perform his prayers behind him.[91]

In *al-Sawā'iq al-Muhriqah*, Ibn Hajar al-Haythami said: The *ahādith* containing references to the reappearance of al-Mahdi are so many and *mutawātir* (authentic)."[92]

Al-Shawkāni, in his risālah (treatise) called: *al-Tawdih fi tawātur mā jā'a fi al-muntazar wa al-dajjāl wa al-Messiah,* after citing the traditions about al-Mahdi, says: "Whatever we cited, that reaching the extent of tawātur, as is not covered or unknown for that who has honour of cognizance."

In *al-Lumu'āt*, al-Shaykh 'Abd al-Haqq says: "The *ahādith* reaching the extent of *tawātur* (authentic chains) unanimously confirm that al-Mahdi is of Ahl al-Bayt and son of Fātimah."[93]

---

[90] *Sahih al-Bukhāri*, vol. IV, p. 143, "bāb nuzul 'Isā ibn Maryam".

[91] *Fath al-Bāri*, vol. V, p. 362.

[92] Ibn Hajar, *al-Sawā'iq al-Muhriqah*, vol. II, p. 211.

Also al-Sabbān, in his book *Is'āf al-Rāghibīn*, says: "Many authentic (*mutawātir*) akhbār reported from the Messenger of Allah (may God's peace and benedictions be upon him and his Progeny) confirming his (al-Mahdi's) reappearance, and his being of Ahl al-Bayt, and that he will fill the earth with equity and justice."[94]

In his book *Sabā'ik al-dhahab*, al-Suwaydi is reported to have said:

"That upon which all the *'ulamā'* have concurred is al-Mahdi's being the one who is to rise (*al-qā'im*) at the end of the Time (*al-zamān*), and that he will fill the earth with justice. The *ahādith* that confirm his reappearance are so many."[95]

Ibn Khaldun, in his *Muqaddimah*, also says: "Know that what is widely known among Ahl al-Islām (*'ulamā'* and people) throughout course of time, is that at the end of the Time a man of Ahl al-Bayt should appear, who would support the Din, and establish justice. He is called al-Mahdi."[96]

Moreover, many traditions about al-Mahdi are reported by contemporary *'ulamā'*, such as the Mufti of al-'Ikhwān al-Muslimun al-Sayyid Sābiq in his book *al-'Aqā'id al-'Islāmiyyah*, deeming the idea of al-Mahdi to be among the Islamic doctrines (*'aqā'id*) in which all should believe.

With their multiplicity, the *ahādith* about al-Mahdi are reported and cited in the Shi'ah books, to the extent it is said that the *ahādith* reported from the Messenger of Allah (s) about al-Mahdi exceed in number all his *ahādith* about other subjects.

Further, the researcher Lutf Allāh al-Sāfi, in his encyclopedia *Muntakhab al-'athar*, reported many traditions about al-Mahdi from more than sixty sources of Ahl al-Sunnah books, including *al-Sihāh al-*

---

[93] *Hāshiyat Sahih al-Tirmidhi*, vol. II, p. 46.
[94] *Is'āf al-Rāghibīn*, vol. II, p. 140.
[95] *Sabā'ik al-dhahab*, p. 78.
[96] *Muqaddimat Ibn Khaldun*, p. 367.

Sittah (the Six *Sahihs*), and more than ninety references of the Shi'ah books, including *al-Kutub al-'Arba'ah*.

In regard of the second subject, which deals with the birth, life, occultation of al-Mahdi and his being alive. This part also was never negated by some of the reliable Sunni *'ulamā'*, who believe al-Mahdi to be Muhammad ibn al-Hasan al-'Askari, the Twelfth Imām of Ahl al-Bayt. And that he was born, and is still alive, and will reappear at the end of the Time to fill the earth with equity and justice, and through him Allah will surely make His *Din* victorious. In this respect they agree with the beliefs held by the Imāmiyyah Shi'i. Hereunder some of those *'ulamā'*:

1. Muhyi al-Din ibn al-'Arabi, in *al-Futuhāt al-Makkiyyah*.

2. Sibt ibn al-Jawzi, in his book *Tadhkirat al-Khawāss*.

3. 'Abd al-Wahhāb al-Shirāni, in *'Aqā'id al-Akābir*.

4. Ibn al-Khashshāb in *Tawarikh Mawalid al-'A'immah wa Wafayātihim*.

5. Muhammad al-Bukhāri al-Hanafi, in *Fasl al-Khitāb*.

6. Ahmad ibn Ibrāhim al-Balādhuri, in *al-Hadith al-Mutasalsil*.

7. Ibn al-Sabbāgh al-Māliki, in *al-Fusul al-Muhimmah*.

8. Al-'Arif 'Abd al-Rahmān, in *Mir'āt al-'asrār*.

9. Kamāl al-Din ibn Talhah, in *Matālib al-sa'ul fi manāqib Al al-Rasul*.

10. Al-Qunduzi al-Hanafi, in *Yanābi'al-Mawaddah*.

If any researcher pursues the matter, he will verily come across among Ahl al-Sunnah *'ulamā'*, in greater number than those we referred to, who believe in the birth of al-Mahdi and that he is still alive till Allah the Most High makes him to reappear.

Then we are left with only those among Ahl al-Sunnah who deny his birth and his being alive, though admitting the veracity of the *ahādith* about him (al-Mahdi). But they can never be considered hujjah (authority) over the others believing in such issue.

Such assumption is not denied by the Holy Qur'ān, in which Allah coined many a similitude about this for those having inactive minds, so as to be liberated from the fetters and to give the reins to their thoughts and intellects to be certain and submit that Allah, Subhanah, is Able to do all things.

So the Muslim, whose heart is filled with faith, can never be astonished when hearing that Allah has caused 'Uzayr (Ezra) to die for a hundred years, then brought him back to life. Thereat he would look at his food and drink which have not rotted, and to his ass how would Allah assemble its bones and then clothe them with flesh, rendering it to its former condition after its bones have rotted away. And when the matter became clear unto him, he said: I know now that Allah is Able to do all things. Glorified is Allah! How soon he changes his mind. As before the event, he wondered and thought it to be impossible when passing by a township, which had fallen into utter ruin, exclaiming: How shall Allah (ever) bring this (township) to life (again), after its death?

The Muslim believing in the Qur'ān never finds strange the story of our master Abraham, when he made the bird into parts, placing each of them on the hills, calling them then, when they would come to him in haste.

And any Muslim would never find strange the fire's being cool, and never burning or harming our lord Abraham, as when he be thrown into it, Allah said to it: O fire, be coolness and peace (for Abraham).

The (true) Muslim also would never find strange that our doyen Jesus was born without the male's sperm-drop (*nutfah*), i.e. with no father, and that he is still alive, not dead, and will be restored to the earth.

Moreover, every Muslim would never find strange to see our master Jesus Christ raising the dead, healing that who was born blind, and the leper; and that the sea be split for our master Moses and the Children of Israel, so as they would walk through it without being moistened, and his staff be turned into a serpent, with his transforming the Nile water into blood.

The Muslim would also never find strange when knowing that our lord Solomon used to talk to the birds, and the jinn, and the ants, with his throne be carried and flown in the skies place to place, and the throne of Balqis be straightened within moments.

Even the Muslim would never find strange that Allah caused the fellows of the Cave to die for three hundred years, and more other nine (years), raising them again to life, when the grandson of the grandson became older than the grandfather's grandfather.

Further he would never find strange being told that our master al-Khidr (peace be upon him) is still alive, and never died, and that he met our lord Moses ('a).

He would never find strange too the fact that Iblis (upon whom be God's damnation) is not dead and still alive, and that he was created before Adam (peace be upon him). And also he is still joining the procession of mankind from the first day of his creation till the day of his perishness. However he is hidden with no one being ever able to see him, despite his hideous deeds and abominable acts, while he can see all the people.

Every Muslim has faith in all these things, never wondering or finding their occurrence to be strange, so why should he consider the existence of al-Mahdi unseen for some time — for a wisdom ordained by Allah the Glorious — to be strange or incredible.

It is to be noted that whatever is stated in the Qur'ān, which is extensively more than the instances we referred to, cannot be regarded ordinary or common things among people, besides being impossible to be done by them even if they combine together for the purpose.

Doctrines with which Ahl Al-Sunnah Revile the Shi'Ah

But it is altogether the making of Allah, Whom nothing in the earth or heavens can escape or strive against. And it also should be trusted by all Muslims, as they have believed in whatever revealed in the Holy Qur'ān, without any exceptio or reservation.

And due to the fact that al-Mahdi is the Imām of the Shi'ah, who lived among them beside his forefathers, so they should be better aware of whatever is related to him and said about him, and the people of Mecca are better aware of its (mountain) passes.

Further, the Shi'ah revere and glorify their leaders, making for Ahl al-Bayt Imāms special tombs, which they constructed and kept abide to make pilgrimage to, seeking blessings through them. Based on this, had the Twelfth Imām — al-Mahdi ('a) — deceased, there would have been a tomb (or shrine) known for all. Besides, it would have been feasible for them to claim the permissibility of raising him (to life) after death, the thing possible to come true, as is referred to by the Qur'ān, when taking into consideration their belief in the doctrine of *raj'ah* (restoration of life). Moreover, they even insist on the belief that al-Mahdi ('a) is alive and having provision, and his being unseen for a wisdom willed by Allah, the Glorious and the Exalted, that is only known by those who are firmly rooted in knowledge and their *awliyā'* (followers).

Anyhow it should be known that the disagreement between the Sunnah and Shi'ah regarding the case of al-Mahdi ('a) is not of essential nature, as they both believe in his reappearance at the end of the Time, and that Jesus ('a) will perform his prayers behind him.Further they both believe that he will fill the earth with equity and justice as it had been filled with oppression and tyranny, and the Muslims taking possession of the whole earth during his reign, with prevalence of welfare and prosperity that no poor shall be there.

The only point of controversy between them being that the Shi'ah believe that he is born, while the Sunnah hold that he is to be born (in future), with concurring both on his reappearance at the end of the Time.

So let the Sunnah and Shi'ah unite and be in agreement on truth word, and on bringing together the disintegrated *Ummah* with striving to eliminate any difference, and gathering it again. Further, all of them should sincerely invoke Allah, with good intentions during their prayers, to hasten his reappearance in which lies the deliverance, and which entails victory for the *Ummah* of Muhammad (may Allah's peace and benediction be upon him and his Progeny).

Our last prayer is that all praise belongs to Allah, the Lord of the Worlds, and benediction and peace be upon the most honourable of the prophets and apostles, our master and lord Muhammad and his good and pure Progeny.

Muhammad al-Tijāni al-Samāwi

BIBLIOGRAPHY-EXEGESIS BOOKS

1. *The Holy Qur'ān*
2. *Tafir al-Tabari*, by Muhammad ibn Jarir al-Tabari
3. *Tafsir Ibn Kathir*, by Ismail ibn Kathir
4. *Tafsir al-Qurtubi*, by Abu 'Abdullah Al-Qurtubi
5. *Tafsir al-Jalālayn*, by Jalal ad-Din al-Maḥalli and al-Suyuti
6. *Al-Tafsir al-Kabir*, of al-Fakhr al-Rāzi
7. *Tafsir al-Manār*, of Muhammad 'Abduh
8. *Tafsir al-Nasafi*, by Ahmad bin Mahmud al-Nasafi
9. *Tafsir al-Khāzin*, by al-Baghawi
10. *Tafsir al-Kashshāf*, of al-Zamakhshari
11. *Tafsir al-Hākim*, of al-Hākim al-Hasakāni
12. *Tafsir al-Nayshāburi*, by Hākim Nayshāburi
13. *Al-Durr al-Manthur fi al-tafsir bi al-Ma'thur*, of al-Suyuti
14. *Zād al-masir fi 'ilm al-tafsir*, of Ibn al-Jawzi
15. *Shawāhid al-Tanzil*, of al-Hākim al-Hasakāni
16. *Tafsir al-Fath al-Qadir*, of al-Shawkāni
17. *Al-Tashil li-'ulum al-tanzil*, of al-Kalbi
18. *Asbāb al-nuzul*, of al-Imām al-Wāhidi
19. *Ahkām al-Qur'ān*, of al-Jassās
20. *Al-Tafsir al-Kabir*, of al-Tha'labi
21. *Nuzul al-Qur'ān*, of al-Hafiz Abu Nu'aym

22. *Mā Nazala min al-Qur'ān fī 'Ali,* of Abu Nu'aym al-Isfahāni
23. *Muqaddimat Usul al-Tafsir,* of Ibn Taymiyyah
24. *Tafsir al-Mizān,* of al-'Allāmah al-Tabātabā'i

HADITH BOOKS

1. *Sahih al-Bukhāri,* by Imam Muhammad al-Bukhari
2. *Sahih Muslim,* by Imam Muslim ibn al-Hajjaj
3. *Sahih al-Tirmidhi,* by Muhammad ibn 'Isa al-Tirmidhi
4. *Sunan Ibn Mājah,* by Muhammad Ibn Mājah al-Qazwini
5. *Sunan Abi Dāwud,* by Sulaymān ibn al-Ash'ath al-Sijistānī
6. *Sunan al-Nasā'i,* by Alī ibn Sīnān al-Nasā'ī
7. *Musnad al-Imām Ahmad,* by Imam Ahmad ibn Hanbal
8. *Muwatta' al-Imām Mālik,* by Imam Malik ibn Anas
9. *Mustadrak al-Hākim,* by Hakim al-Nishapuri
10. *Kanz al-'Ummāl,* by 'Ali al-Muttaqi al-Hindi
11. *Sunan al-Dārimi,* by 'Abd al-Rahman al-Darimi
12. *Sunan al-Bayhaqi,* by 'Alī ibn Mūsa al-Bayhaqi
13. *Sunan al-Dāraqutni,* by Imam Abul Hasan al-Dāraqutni
14. *Jam' al-Jawāmi',* of al-Suyuti
15. *Minhāj al-Sunnah,* of Ibn Taymiyyah
16. *Majma' al-zawā'id,* of al-Haythami
17. *Kunz al-haqā'iq,* of al-Manāwi
18. *Jāmi' al-'Usul,* of Ibn al-'Athir
19. *Fath al-Bāri fi Sharh al-Bukhāri,* by Ibn Hajar al-'Asqalani

HISTORY BOOKS

1. *Tarikh al-'umam wa al-muluk*, of al-Tabari
2. *Tarikh al-khulafā'*, of al-Suyuti
3. *Tarikh al-Kāmil*, of Ibn al-Athir
4. *Tarikh Dimashq*, of Ibn 'Asākir
5. *Tarikh al-Mas'udi (Muruj al-Dhahab)*, by Mas'udi
6. *Tarikh al-Ya'qubi*, by Ja'far ibn Wahb ibn Wadīh al-Ya'qūbī
7. *Tarikh Baghdād*, of al-Khatib al-Baghdādi
8. *Tarikh Abi al-Fidā'*, by Abu al-Fida Ismā'īl al-Ayyubi
9. *Tarikh Ibn al-Shahnah*, by Ahmad bin Abi Talib
10. *Tarikh Ibn Kathir*, by Ismail ibn Kathir
11. *Al-Tarikh al-Kabir*, of Imam Muhammad al-Bukhāri
12. *Al-Imāmh wa al-Siyāsah*, of Ibn Qutaybah
13. *Al-'Iqd al-Farid*, of Ibn 'Abd Rabbih
14. *Al-Tabaqāt al-Kubrā*, of Ibn Sa'd
15. *Muqaddimah (Tarikh)*, by Ibn Khaldun
16. *Sharh Nahj al-Balāghah*, of Ibn Abi al-Hadid

SIRAH (BIOGRAPHY) BOOKS

1. *Sirat Ibn Hisham,* by 'Abd al-Malik bin Hisham
2. *Al-'Isābah fī tamyiz al-Sahābah,* by Ibn Hajar al-'Asqalānī
3. *Al-Sirah al-Halabiyyah,* by 'Alī b. Burhān al din al-Halabi
4. *Usd al-Ghābah fī ma`rifat al-Sahābah,* by Muhammad ibn `Abd al-Karim al-Jazri
5. *Al-Riyād al-Nādirah,* of al-Tabari
6. *Al-'Isti'āb,* by Ibn 'Abd al-Barr
7. *Hayat Muhammad,* of Muhammad Hasanayn Haykal
8. *Al-Ma'ārif,* of Ibn Qutaybah
9. *Ansāb al-Ashrāf,* of al-Balādhuri
10. *Hilyat al-Awliyā',* of Abu Nu'aym
11. *Al-Fitnah al-Kubrā,* of Tāhā Husayn

OTHER REFERENCES

1. *Al-Sawā'iq al-Muhriqah*, of Ibn Hajar Makki
2. *Al-Futuhāt al-Makkiyyah*, of Ibn 'Arabi
3. *Al-Silah bayn al-Tasawwuf wa al-Tashayyu'*, of al-Shibibi
4. *'Aqā'id al-Akābir*, of al-Sha'wāni
5. *Khasā'is Amir al-Mu'minin*, of al-Nasā'i
6. *Tawārikh mawālid al-A'immah*, of Ibn al-Khashshāb
7. *Al-Milal wa al-Nihal*, of al-Shahristāni
8. *Fasl al-Khitāb*, of Muhammad al-Bukhāri
9. *Dalā'il al-Imāmah*, of al-Tabari
10. *Al-Hadith al-Mutasalsil*, of al-Balādhuri
11. *Balāghāt al-Nisā'*, of Ibn Tayfur
12. *Mir'āt al-Asrār*, of al-'Arif 'Abd al-Rahmān
13. *A'lām al-Nisā'*, of 'Umar Ridā Kahhālah
14. *Ihqāq al-Naqq*, of Qādī Nūr Allāh Tustarī (Shūshtarī)
15. *Kifāyat al-Tālib*, of al-Kanji al-Shāfi'i
16. *Sharh al-Mawāhib*, of al-Zarqāni
17. *Al-'Izdihār fimā 'aqadahu al-shu'arā' min al-'ash'ār*, of al-Suyuti
18. *Siyar a'lām al-Nubalā'*, of al-Dhahabi
19. *Al-Wilāyah*, of Ibn Jarir al-Tabari
20. *Sirr al-'Alāmin*, of Abu Hāmid al-Ghazāli
21. *Tadhkirat al-Khawāss*, of Ibn al-Jawzi

22. *Ihyā' 'ulum al-Din,* of al-Ghazāli

23. *Tadhkirat al-Sibt,* of Ibn al-Jawzi

24. *Matālib al-Sa'ul,* of Ibn Talhah al-Shāfi'i

25. *Irshād al-Sāri,* of al-Qastalāni

26. *Yanābi' al-Mawaddah,* of al-Qunduzi al-Hanafi

27. *Nur al-Absār,* of al-Shablanji

28. *Fadā'il al-Khamsah min al-Sihāh al-Sittah,* by Syed Murtadha Firouzabadi

29. *Rabi' al-Abrār,* of al-Zamakhshari

30. *Al-Fusul al-Muhimmah,* of Ibn al-Sabbāgh

31. *Sharh Nahj al-balāghah,* of al-Shaykh Muhammad 'Abduh

32. *Al-Talkhis,* of al-Dhahabi

33. *Al-Mu'jam al-Kabir & al-Mu'jam al-Saghir,* of al-Tabarāni

34. *Al-Jāmi'al-Kabir & al-Jāmi' al-Saghir,* of al-Suyuti

35. *Al-Bidāyah wal-Nihāyah,* of Ibn Kathir

36. *Is'āf al-Rāghibin,* by al-Sabbān

37. *Manāqib 'Ali ibn Abi Tālib,* by Muhammad Ibn Shahr Ashoub

38. *Bahth hawl al-Mahdi* by Syed Muhammad Baqir al-Sadr

www.ingramcontent.com/pod-product-compliance
Lightning Source LLC
LaVergne TN
LVHW041908070526
838199LV00051BA/2545